AQUINAS AND THE INFUSED MORAL VIRTUES

AQUINAS
and the Infused Moral Virtues

ANGELA McKAY KNOBEL

UNIVERSITY OF NOTRE DAME PRESS
NOTRE DAME, INDIANA

Copyright © 2021 by the University of Notre Dame
Notre Dame, Indiana 46556
undpress.nd.edu

All Rights Reserved

Published in the United States of America

Paperback edition published in 2024

Library of Congress Control Number: 2021943084

ISBN: 978-0-268-20109-8 (Hardback)
ISBN: 978-0-268-20110-4 (Paperback)
ISBN: 978-0-268-20111-1 (WebPDF)
ISBN: 978-0-268-20108-1 (Epub)

IN MEMORY OF RODERICK H. MCKAY

*A good man leaves an inheritance
to his children's children.*

—Proverbs 13:22

Contents

Acknowledgments		ix
Abbreviations		xi
	Introduction	1
ONE	The Structure of Natural Virtue	11
TWO	Habits of Being: The Structure of Supernatural Virtue	47
THREE	Relating the Virtues: Aquinas's Texts	81
FOUR	Interpretive Options, Part I: Coexistence	107
FIVE	Interpretive Options, Part II: Unification	127
SIX	A Proposal for a Way Forward	149
Notes		181
Bibliography		199
Index		205

ACKNOWLEDGMENTS

The thoughts that culminated in this book originated in a dissertation I wrote under the direction of Fred Freddoso at the University of Notre Dame. In Fred, I had the luxury of having a dissertation director who left me to my own devices, who was glad to serve as a sounding board, but who never imposed his own vision of the outcome. I am grateful to him as to so many others who have made this book possible: to my husband, without whose support I would not have been able to finish this book; to my colleagues in the School of Philosophy at the Catholic University of America, particularly Michael Gorman, who so generously served as a sounding board for much of the content here; to Bill Mattison, who has discussed and debated these topics with me for many years; and to many others. Last but not least, I would like to thank my research assistant, Benjamin Erikson, for his tireless help in formatting this manuscript.

ABBREVIATIONS

WORKS OF THOMAS AQUINAS

DV *Quaestiones disputatae de veritate*

DQVG *Disputed Questions on the Virtues in General (Quaestiones disputatae de virtutibus)*

DQVC *Disputed Questions on the Cardinal Virtues (Quaestiones disputatae de virtutibus cardinalibus)*

CS *Scriptum super libros Sententiarum*

ST *Summa theologiae*

INTRODUCTION

In 2007, an acquisitions editor at the University of Notre Dame Press asked me if I had any interest in publishing my 2004 dissertation on Thomas Aquinas's theory of infused virtue. I revised my dissertation and submitted a manuscript, but it (providentially, I now think) never saw the light of day. In the intervening years, I made half-hearted attempts to return to it, but I never made any real progress. Any number of reasons can be given, but one important one lay beneath them all. I simply wasn't sure what I wanted to say. The interpretation of Aquinas that I so enthusiastically defended in my dissertation had begun to seem increasingly inadequate. Interpretations I had once written off as old-fashioned or simply dead wrong had begun to seem considerably more substantial. Perhaps most importantly of all, I became increasingly unsure that there was even a single comprehensive "theory of virtue" to be found in Aquinas. In the midst of all this, however, I also realized that I do have a very specific view about the account of natural and supernatural virtue that makes the most sense of both Aquinas's Aristotelian foundation and his Christian commitments. This book is an attempt to offer that account.

I defend four claims. First, Aquinas offers a very clear and detailed account of what I call the "structure" of both the natural and the supernatural virtues. Second, in spite of his clarity about the structure of natural and supernatural virtue, Aquinas is altogether unclear regarding the relationship between the virtues that perfect nature (natural virtues) and the virtues that perfect graced nature (supernatural virtues).

Third, the most commonly advanced theories of the relationship between the virtues—including the one that Aquinas himself hints at—do not do a good job of accommodating Aquinas's most fundamental insights into the structure of the natural and supernatural virtues. Fourth, I propose a different account of the relationship between natural and supernatural virtue, one that can and does make sense of Aquinas's most fundamental claims about the virtues.

I argue that the sole coherent goal of the Christian moral life is the practice and cultivation of the infused moral virtues. However, the transformation effected by grace is imperfect and incomplete, so much so that even those transformed by grace frequently fall short of the goal of the Christian moral life. It is plausible to think that all one's previously cultivated habits persist as dispositions in the person transformed by grace, and that those dispositions are what we end up cultivating when we fall short of the goal of the Christian moral life.

TERMINOLOGY

The broad distinction that Aquinas makes between kinds of virtue is typically referred to as the distinction between "infused" virtue and "acquired" virtue. This labeling has centuries of precedent behind it and is used by Aquinas himself, but it is also imprecise and misleading. The labels "acquired" and "infused" refer to how virtue *comes to be*—whether it arises from one's own repeated good acts or whether it comes directly from an external source, namely, God. However, the real distinction that Aquinas (along with countless other Christian writers) is interested in concerns what the virtues are *ordered to*, that is, whether they are ordered to the fulfillment of our created human nature or to the fulfillment of human nature that has been perfected by the gift of God's saving grace. The former are "natural" virtues; the latter "supernatural" virtues. The natural virtues are often referred to as "acquired" virtues because Aquinas, like Aristotle, thinks that we can acquire natural virtues with our own resources and by our own repeated good acts. The supernatural virtues are often called "infused" virtues because Aquinas insists that the virtues that order us to our supernatural fulfillment cannot be acquired by our own efforts but must be infused by God. But distinguishing virtues as "infused" or "acquired" does not get at the real difference. Natural virtues *can be* and typically are acquired through our own power via our own repeated good acts, but Aquinas thinks that God could "infuse" the natural virtues if He so desired. Therefore, the important difference is not how the virtue came to be but what kind of fulfillment—natural or supernatural—the virtue is ordered to. I will use the terms "infused" virtue and "acquired" virtue because most of the scholarly literature, and even Aquinas himself, uses them. Yet, it is worth keeping in mind that the real distinction in question is the distinction between natural and supernatural, not merely acquired and infused.

ASSUMPTIONS AND APPROACH

Writing a book about Aquinas's theory of virtue can seem overwhelming. It is not merely the sheer quantity of ink that has already been spilled on the topic, but the many and vast disagreements surrounding Aquinas's account of virtue. There are questions of textual interpretation. Is there really "one" Aquinas to interpret? Is the early Aquinas the same as the late Aquinas? Does his theory of virtue change substantially over the course of his career, or does it remain more or less the same? How should certain pivotal texts be interpreted? Then there are the more general questions, the answers to which—at least according to some—have ramifications for how one must interpret Aquinas's theory of virtue. Does Aquinas envision a single, supernatural end for man, or does he recognize both a natural and a supernatural end? If Aquinas does recognize that man has a natural fulfillment, what does this fulfillment consist in? Is Aquinas really the Aristotelian he is so often made out to be, or is he more accurately characterized as an Augustinian? Is he perhaps both an Augustinian and an Aristotelian? Is that even possible?

Then there are the vexed questions about his account of virtue itself. What does it mean to say that God "infuses" virtues in the

Christian? What portions of his detailed accounts of virtue are intended as descriptions of "infused" virtue and which are intended to be descriptions of Aristotelian acquired virtue? How are the two types of virtue related? How does he understand the difference between the virtues the Christian possesses and those the pagan possesses? Does he even think that "pagans" can cultivate virtues at all? When these debates are taken together, they can seem so wide and so deep that there is no navigating them.

Over the course of this book I will necessarily address many of these questions, but I will not address most of them head-on, for the following reasons. First, an excessive focus on specific interpretive debates (about the "right" interpretation of a few ambiguous sentences or over which "theory" captures the authentic Aquinas) can lead scholars to talk past each other in unproductive ways. Second, too much focus on these types of questions risks missing the forest for the trees. This is not to say, of course, that I don't have views about these questions. I have views in abundance, and most of them will become clear in the course of this book. However, I think the most productive way to understand Aquinas's account of virtue is to begin with what is most clear and least controversial. I contend that Aquinas's account of nature and its capacities provides the bedrock not just for his account of natural virtue, but also for his account of supernatural virtue. I argue that his accounts of nature and supernature, understood as building on and interwoven with each other, make a certain account of Christian virtue plausible. The account of Christian virtue I ultimately wish to defend in this book is the one Aquinas's own framework renders most plausible, and in that regard it is certainly "Thomistic." I am not interested in claiming, however, that it is explicitly defended by Aquinas, or even that it is Aquinas's view. I am not at all convinced that Aquinas actually has what could be called a "view" or a "theory" of the relationship between the natural and supernatural virtues. Instead, there are views implied in Aquinas's texts, some of Aquinas's views change over time, and the view most "consistently" (if a view implied by two or three scattered sentences can merit such a description) implied by his texts is clearly problematic. But it is unproductive to spend too much time worrying about the "right" interpretation of Aquinas. It is much better to simply worry about what the right view is.

I wish to avoid addressing specific interpretive debates head-on. However, two preliminary clarifications are necessary. The first concerns certain historical interpretations of Aquinas's view of the relationship between the infused and acquired virtues. The second has to do with the centuries-old debate over whether Aquinas envisions a "twofold end" for human life.

The Thomist Commentatorial Tradition

In one sense, it is correct to say that Thomists have only "recently" become interested in the infused moral virtues. Interest in the infused moral virtues is "recent" in the following sense: as recently as 1997, scholars had to be reminded that Aquinas ever even posited them. Books and papers on Aquinas's moral theory, if they mentioned supernatural virtues at all, typically mentioned only the theological virtues of faith, hope, and love. It took articles such as Jean Porter's "The Subversion of Virtue" and Thomas O'Meara's "Virtues in the Theology of Thomas Aquinas" to remind scholars of what they ought to have known already.[1] Porter's article, in particular, served as an important reminder that the natural sits at best uneasily with the supernatural, that the fit is by no means as seamless as so many overviews of Aquinas's thought imply. In another sense, of course, in the sense in which nothing in Thomist scholarship is really "new" at all, interest in the infused moral virtues is as old as Thomist scholarship itself.

Robert Coerver's 1948 dissertation-turned-book, *The Quality of Facility in the Moral Virtues*, details well the centuries-old commetatorial discussion over the relationship between the infused and acquired moral virtues.[2] Several other books and articles, particularly those published in the early to mid-1900s, refer to or assume this commentatorial tradition.[3] Although I will sometimes refer to the views of some historical commentators, I will not be concerned with rehashing or evaluating that tradition of commentary in its own right. That

The Debate over the "Twofold End"

I have said that my goal in this book is to approach Aquinas's theory of virtue by focusing on the broad structure of the account found in his own texts, and that I wish to abstract as far as possible from historical disputes about the proper interpretation of Aquinas, and especially from the detailed historical theories of the relationship between the infused and acquired virtues. There is one interpretive question, however, that has proven so divisive and created so much confusion that I feel I must say something about it right now: the debate over Aquinas's view of the "twofold" end of man.

A few years ago, I attended a paper presented by a young graduate student at the annual conference of the American Catholic Philosophical Association. During the course of his presentation on Aquinas's account of virtue, the student made a reference to man's "natural end," something for which he was roundly scolded in the question session by an eminent scholar. Everyone knows, the poor young man was told, that Aquinas thinks we only have a single, supernatural end, and only very bad interpreters of Aquinas think otherwise. In different company, the young man's reference to the "natural end" would have received the opposite response. A great many books over the course of a great many years have been written on this question, and anything I say here will necessarily be incomplete. However, it is necessary to say something about this debate, not only because it has proven so divisive, but also because some participants in this debate have insisted that one's position on it will affect even the kind of interpretation that can be offered of Aquinas's theory of virtue.

The debate over Aquinas's view of the "twofold" end of man concerns Aquinas's claim that man has a "natural desire" for God. Does Aquinas mean that man by his very nature has a desire for something *supernatural*, namely, the union with God and participation in the divine life that Christ promises? Or does Aquinas merely mean that man by his very nature desires to know and love God in the manner appropriate to his created, human nature? Both answers can seem deeply problematic. On the one hand, Aquinas is committed, or at least seems to be committed, to the Aristotelian position that there is no natural desire without a corresponding capacity. In other words, to possess a natural desire for some kind of fulfillment is to possess the resources to satisfy that desire. If this is true, and if Aquinas also holds that man possesses a natural desire for supernatural union with God, then Pelagianism follows: we would be attributing to Aquinas a view he clearly did not hold, namely, that heaven is ours for the taking, that we can achieve supernatural beatitude through our own efforts. On the other hand, if man does *not* naturally desire supernatural beatitude but only some variation of the kind of natural flourishing that Aristotle envisions, then it is not clear why man would ever desire supernatural union with God in the first place: nature seems self-sufficient and excessively cut off from grace, so that there are disconnected "tiers" in the moral life.[4]

Both sides of this debate often exaggerate and distort the claims of the other. For instance, "single-end" theorists do not actually hold that man's natural desire for supernatural beatitude is of the same kind as those natural desires that man can actualize through his own efforts, and they do acknowledge that man has a natural fulfillment. They simply resist the notion that this natural fulfillment can accurately be characterized as a distinct *end* in its own right. Similarly, "two-end" theorists need not (and most do not) hold that human nature has *no* inherent ordering whatsoever to the divine, that the human has no more natural receptivity for the divine than Balaam's ass had for speech, or even that an individual who realized his natural fulfillment would have nothing more to desire. It is my own view that when the claims of the best representatives of both sides are sufficiently clarified, the distance between them becomes vanishingly small. However, a full discussion of the merits of the respective views is outside the scope of the present examination. For now I merely wish to clarify the language I use in this book as it relates to or touches on this debate.

I assume that Aquinas believes that (1) there is a fulfillment proportionate to our created human nature and that (2) our created human nature provides us with the resources (albeit resources impeded by original sin) to pursue that fulfillment. Simply for ease of reference, and not because I wish to take a side on the debate over man's twofold end, I may sometimes refer to the good proportionate to human nature as man's "natural end," but I will more commonly refer to it as man's "natural good" or "natural fulfillment." I in no way intend the terms "end" or "fulfillment" to be taken literally: I have no intention of implying that the attainment of any natural good would fully satisfy human desire.

Finally, although I will assume that Aquinas does recognize a good proportionate to human nature, and although I have views about the most plausible account of that good, I also will not engage in speculation about what Aquinas thinks the good proportionate to human nature is, and I will not enter into any of the debates that surround this question for a very simple reason: I do not believe it is necessary to settle this question in order to offer a clear treatment of Aquinas's account of virtue.

Chapter Outline

Chapters 1 and 2 are concerned with two topics that have to do with Aquinas himself: (1) his explicit theory of virtue, with a focus on what I have called its "structural" features; and (2) his few explicit remarks about the relationship between the infused and acquired virtues. With respect to his explicit theory of virtue, I argue that although many aspects of Aquinas's account of virtue are vague, he is very clear about the *principles* that make natural and supernatural virtue possible. It is clear from that account, moreover, that Aquinas's entire understanding of supernatural virtue builds on and is indebted to his (Aristotelian) notion of natural virtue. Natural virtue provides the framework Aquinas uses to develop his account of supernatural virtue. In chapters 1 and 2, I argue that Aquinas offers a very clear account of the "principles" that enable us to cultivate the acquired virtues, and of how he believes grace transforms those principles. However, he is much less clear about the question of how the virtues that perfect our created human nature are related to the virtues that perfect our perfected human nature. A great many views are attributed to Aquinas, but these views typically have stronger roots in the commentatorial tradition than in Aquinas's own text.

Chapter 3 addresses whether and to what extent Aquinas asserts anything at all about the relationship between the natural and supernatural virtues. Most of the views attributed to Aquinas are insufficiently rooted in his text, but he does make a few isolated remarks about the relationship between the virtues. These remarks do not all imply the same theory of the relationship, but the most consistent implication is that Aquinas envisions what I will call a "coexistence" view of the relationship between the virtues.

Thus chapters 1, 2, and 3 are explicitly concerned with what Aquinas does or does not say. Chapters 4, 5, and 6 are more constructive: they consider what theory of the relationship between the infused and acquired virtues makes the most sense given the clear framework that emerges from my chapters 1 and 2. Chapter 4 considers contemporary defenses of the *coexistence* view; chapter 5 considers three different versions of the most popular contemporary strategy, namely, that the Christian's infused and acquired virtues comprise a single, unified whole, or *unification*. I show that neither the coexistence nor the unification view offers a coherent account of the relationship between the infused and acquired virtues, in particular, or of the Christian moral life, in general. In chapter 6, I propose my own view.

CHAPTER I

The Structure of Natural Virtue

Aristotle understands the human good to consist in the fulfillment of our nature, that is, in becoming most fully the kind of thing we already are. Just as a frog flourishes when it exhibits excellence in doing the unique kinds of things frogs are intended to do (jump, catch flies with its tongue, and so on), so human beings flourish when they exhibit excellence in the activity unique to human beings, namely, when they live a life that exhibits the excellence of reason. Aristotle calls the habits that make such a life possible "virtues." Since Aristotelian virtues are measured by (i.e., make us conform to) the standard set by our human nature, they are commonly referred to as "natural" virtues (this allows us to distinguish them from virtues measured by a different standard, such as heavenly beatitude). And since Aristotle believes that we can cultivate these virtues through our own repeated good acts, they are also sometimes referred to as "acquired" virtues.

Thomas Aquinas accepts much of Aristotle's account. He agrees that human beings have a nature, that they can cultivate virtues ordered to fulfillment of their nature, and that the achievement of such fulfillment is a genuine good. Aquinas also insists, however, that true human fulfillment lies outside nature's grasp. We are truly fulfilled, Aquinas insists, only through the participation in the divine life that occurs in supernatural beatitude. Since natural virtues only order us to the good commensurate with nature, and since supernatural beatitude utterly exceeds our natural good, no amount of natural virtue can order us to the good that truly fulfills us. Aquinas holds that in order for man to be ordered to this higher good, human nature must be elevated and perfected by God's saving grace. He also holds that God, in elevating human nature, bestows new habits on us—the theological and infused moral virtues and the gifts of the Holy Spirit—and these habits enable us to perform acts proportionate to our new status as adopted children of God. Since the habits God bestows along with grace are measured by (i.e., make us conform to) the standard of supernatural beatitude rather than the standard of human nature, they are commonly referred to as "supernatural" virtues. And since these virtues can come from no other source than God's free gift, these virtues are also sometimes referred to as "infused" virtues.

Everyone has always acknowledged that Aquinas "adds" the theological virtues of faith, hope, and love to the list of virtues described by Aristotle.[1] But for much of the twentieth century, possibly out of a desire to emphasize apparent continuities between Aristotle and Aquinas, advocates of Aquinas's "virtue theory" tended to overlook it when Aquinas asserts that God bestows not only faith, hope, and love but also the gifts of the Holy Spirit and *all the moral virtues* along with grace.[2] When I wrote my dissertation in 2004, it was still possible to find Thomistic virtue theorists who were altogether unaware that Aquinas believes that all the moral virtues are bestowed by God along with grace. Many others, though aware of this fact, considered the infused moral virtues to be an extraneous and irrelevant aspect of Aquinas's moral theory. One professor told me, dismissively, that Aquinas's discussion of the infused moral virtues was entirely ad hoc—a gesture to tradition, nothing more. Attitudes like these, though characteristic of twentieth-century Thomist moral philosophers, had already begun to change in 2004, and they are still less common now. Although his *Les sources de la morale chrétienne* was not translated into English until 1995, Servais Pinckaers had already argued in that work, published in 1985, that the Thomism of his contemporaries overlooked the role of grace in the Christian moral life.[3] Jean Porter's important article, "The Subversion of Virtue: Infused and Acquired Virtue in the *Summa theologiae*" (1992), served as an important reminder that the virtues most privileged by Aquinas were a far cry from Aristotle's.[4] In the ensuing decades, interest in the Thomistic notion of infused virtue has only increased.[5] But the very notion that there are virtues bestowed by God still seems strange to the modern ear, unintuitive and in need of defense.[6] Even some of those who defend it still do so apologetically, claiming that divinely given virtues are only virtues in a derivative or "analogous" sense.[7] Such claims imply that even if we add "other" virtues to the mix, the real paradigm is still Aristotelian acquired virtue.

If we are to examine Aquinas's account of moral virtue, it is absolutely vital to understand at the outset that our contemporary attitude toward virtue—an attitude that understands the cultivation of virtue as an exercise in self-perfection and that takes Aristotle's account as basic—is a direct inversion of the understanding Aquinas and his contemporaries had. For them, and indeed for the entire Christian tradition that preceded them, it was the Aristotelian account of virtue that seemed unfamiliar and out of place. The Christian scriptures, to the extent they describe the virtues at all, seem to describe them as divine gifts.[8] Augustine and the other Church fathers certainly understood them as such.[9] Early Christian scholars struggled to accommodate apparent examples of moral goodness in non-Christians, such as the Roman emperor Trajan.[10] István Bejczy, who traces the development of Christian willingness to recognize Aristotelian "natural" virtues, writes that the notion that all virtue was a gift from God "was early medieval orthodoxy."[11] Peter Abelard, sometimes credited with recognizing the possibility of virtue in non-Christians, actually did not: he simply proposed that some non-Christians had unknowingly received God's saving grace, and he credited that divine gift as the source of their good acts.[12]

In Aquinas's world, then, it was *Aristotelian* virtue that was the outlier. In the twelfth century, roughly paralleling the availability of Latin translations of Aristotle's *Nicomachean Ethics* but not obviously because of it, Christian writers began to display an increasing willingness to recognize the possibility that non-Christians (referred to hereafter for the sake of simplicity as "pagans") could display a form of genuine moral goodness and cultivate a kind of genuine virtue, namely, natural virtue.[13] As Bill Mattison and others have shown, however, before Aquinas these attempts were convoluted and unclear. William of Auxerre, Simon of Tournai, Allan of Lille, and others all seem to concede that those outside the life of grace can cultivate a kind of virtue, but they are ambiguous at best about the one question that really matters: How are those genuinely good dispositions related to the Christian moral life?[14]

Aquinas is often upheld as the thinker who first succeeded in integrating Aristotelian and Christian virtue, and for this reason it is often said that Aquinas "baptized" Aristotle. The extent to which such a claim is accurate is in a way the subject of this book. In this chapter and the next, however, I argue that Aquinas integrates Aristotle into the Christian understanding of virtue in at least this much: Aquinas uses the Aristotelian account of nature and virtue as the foundation for his account of how God's grace perfects not only nature but also our natural capacity for virtue. My primary aim in this chapter is to show how Aquinas, appropriating Aristotle's insights about nature and virtue, uses them to offer an account of *natural* virtue. In doing so, this chapter lays the groundwork for chapter 2, where I show how Aquinas uses that same foundation to offer his account of how the gift of grace changes both our nature and our natural capacity for virtue.

In what follows, I first explain why the notions of nature and of the virtues that order us to the perfection of nature are central to Aquinas's understanding of the moral life. With that account in place, I then explain several aspects of Aquinas's account of moral virtue: the foundational role he allots to our natural habitual knowledge of first principles (or *synderesis*), how it is that he believes reason renders those principles specific, and the necessity of the moral virtues. I conclude with some remarks on the debate over the possibility of "pagan" virtue.

"Natural" Virtue

There is a vast conceptual gap between what Aristotle means when he speaks of "virtue" and what the fathers of the early Church mean when they speak of "virtue." Aristotle is speaking of the good habits one can cause in oneself through one's own repeated good acts. Those habits are good because they enable us to act in a way that most fully expresses what we are: beings whose activity can be informed by reason. Aristotle's virtues are habits that allow us to act in ways that express excellent (human) reason. But, as the Christian tradition has always acknowledged, human reason can only take us so far. It is sometimes claimed (often by Catholics) that Protestants reject the notion of virtue altogether.[15] In fact, it was not the idea of virtue itself that many early Protestant writers rejected, but merely the Aristotelian account of virtue, especially the notion that virtue was a *human achievement* rather than a divine gift.[16] Foundational scholars in the Reformed Protestant tradition, including Calvin, Peter Vermigli, and later Jonathan Edwards, all recognized the importance of the virtues that are bestowed by God along with grace. They simply rejected the idea of virtue as a human achievement.

An excellent image of the gap between the Aristotelian and Christian understanding of virtue can be found in Dante's *Inferno*. Dante places Aristotle, Plato, and the other pagan philosophers in the outermost (and most sparsely populated) circle of hell, Limbo. The inhabitants of the outermost circle are not condemned to any tangible punishment, but they "live in longing, without any hope."[17] Dante puts the pagan philosophers in hell because he recognizes that no perfection that is the product of human effort will ever get anyone into heaven. The pagan philosophers have lived the best kind of life that can be lived without God's saving grace. But the best one can hope for from such a life, in Dante's telling, is an eternal, unfulfilled yearning for something more. Without God's grace and the virtues that come with it, true happiness remains out of reach. Dante provides us with a vitally important image of the difference between what Aristotle means when he speaks of virtue and what the early Church fathers mean when they use the same term. Both understand virtue to mean perfection, even perfecting habits, but they understand that perfection in very different ways.[18] Not least among those differences is that Aristotelian virtue is ordered to a purely human kind of perfection and is achieved in a purely human way. Christian virtue is ordered to a supernatural, heavenly perfection, and is necessarily bestowed by God.

16   *Aquinas and the Infused Moral Virtues*

But Dante's image also provides something else: the beginnings of an insight into why a Christian might find the Aristotelian account of virtue relevant after all. In Dante's view, the pagan philosophers have made genuine moral progress; they have achieved a good of sorts. It is just not the kind of moral progress that will get them into heaven. This captures well the traditional Christian understanding of God's "twofold" gift.

The Christian tradition of which Aquinas is a representative holds that God calls man to himself, to participation in the divine life. It also holds, however, that this call is a gift, one that goes beyond the gift that God already gives man merely by creating him. God created man with a distinctive human nature. This distinctively human nature, on the traditional view, has a "proportionate" fulfillment: humans as humans have an internal principle pointing them toward the fulfillment of their created nature and, correspondingly, the resources needed to pursue it. This much—though Aquinas will of course have a rather different account of what man's natural fulfillment consists in than Aristotle does—is in keeping with Aristotle's account of nature.

This same tradition holds that there would have been no injustice on God's part if he had created man for no fulfillment other than that proportionate to his rational, animal nature.[19] It is not of necessity but through God's great generosity that man is called to a still higher perfection—participation in the divine life. When God elevates man to this higher perfection, he bestows a second gift, the gift of sanctifying grace. This higher perfection is not incompatible with man's created nature but a further completion of it. Unless we had our human, created nature, we could not receive the further gift of participation in the divine life, but being human in no way requires that we receive such a gift.[20] The gift of sanctifying grace, however, is nonetheless a perfection and fulfillment of our creaturely nature. This "second gift," as some scholars call it, does not destroy the gift of our human nature, but brings it to a still higher (infinitely higher) fulfillment and completion.[21]

The claim that Aquinas recognizes the "twofold gift" described above is not controversial. Nicholas Healy notes that every serious scholar of Aquinas would concede the points noted above.[22] Indeed, if one wishes to maintain that God gives grace freely, it is necessary that it be a "second gift," something bestowed over and above the gift already given in creation. This, in turn, indicates that it is coherent to discuss the virtues that order man to the perfection of what he "is" prior to the gift of saving grace.

All of this helps to contextualize what it is that we are discussing when we consider Aquinas's account of "natural" virtue. We are discussing virtues ordered to the perfection of man's created human nature—the habits that order man to the perfection of what I have called the "first gift." Original sin stains and impedes both the gift God gives us in creating us and our ability to pursue its fulfillment. As long as original sin does not entirely destroy the gift God gives us in creating us, however, it is plausible to think that even those in a state of original sin can make some progress in the pursuit of the fulfillment of their created human nature (i.e., in the cultivation of natural virtue), even if the "second gift" is out of reach.[23] Moreover, if—as is uncontroversial for the Thomist—the "second gift," sanctifying grace, is not contrary to our created human nature but a further fulfillment of it, then understanding the virtues ordered to our natural fulfillment would seem to be an important preliminary step in understanding the virtues ordered to our supernatural fulfillment. Finally—though I will leave the discussion of this last topic until the second half of this book—if we agree that there are virtues ordered to the perfection of created human nature, then it is only reasonable to wonder whether and how those virtues are affected by the bestowal of the "second gift." For all of these reasons, it seems important to have an account of "natural" virtue.

As we will see, Aquinas does more than merely accommodate nature. In Aquinas's view, God's grace thoroughly transforms nature. But by offering a very detailed account of nature and its capacities, Aquinas is able to offer a very specific theory of just what that transformation involves. In laying out what I call the "structure" of Aquinas's account of natural virtue in the rest of this chapter, I focus first on his account of nature and its inherent capacities, particularly on his claim that the very principles of our created human nature point us toward its fulfillment, and on what exactly Aquinas believes that the moral virtues do. It is the relationship between the principles of our nature and the virtues they enable us to cause in ourselves that will lay the foundation for Aquinas's account of supernatural virtue. In the process of offering this account, I also address how it is that Aquinas believes original sin hinders our ability to pursue our natural fulfillment, and I then offer some general thoughts about whether and how this affects the possibility of "pagan" virtue.

THE SOURCES OF NATURAL VIRTUE

In each of his major discussions of virtue, Aquinas asks the same question: "Is virtue natural to us?"[24] Aquinas's explanation of his answer becomes increasingly more detailed over the course of his career, but his answer is consistently the same. We are not naturally virtuous, Aquinas consistently responds, but we do naturally possess an *aptitudo* for virtue. Translators usually translate *aptitudo* as "aptitude," but the word could also be translated as "suitability" or even "inclination toward." Our ability to cultivate virtue is more than a mere *capacity*, it is more than something we are merely *capable* of. Virtue, for Aquinas, is what we naturally incline toward and something we are naturally suited to. Given this, it is unsurprising that when Aquinas explains our "aptitude" for virtue, he says that although we do not naturally possess the natural virtues themselves, we do naturally possess what he calls the *semina* (usually translated as "seeds") of the virtues, and also the ability to develop those *semina* into genuine virtues.

The goal of this section is twofold. First, I want to clarify what, exactly, the *semina* of the virtues (i.e., our natural inclination, or suitability, or aptitude for virtue) are. I will be concerned with arguing that Aquinas does not equate the *semina* of virtue with our various natural inclinations, but rather with the very principles that make virtue possible: with our natural habitual knowledge of the first principles of practical reason. Second, I want to show that although Aquinas describes several respects in which we possess an *aptitudo* for natural virtue, the *semina* have priority of place: they are the lynchpin of his account of natural virtue. In what follows, I examine his account of both these principles and of how they make the cultivation of virtue possible. With this account in place, I then address the question of whether and to what extent Aquinas believes that original sin impedes our natural capacity for virtue.

The Foundational Role of the "Seeds" of Virtue

Scholars sometimes speak of Aquinas's references to the *semina* of virtue as if they refer to our natural bodily inclinations, or those inclinations we possess as a result of the specific constitution of our nature.[25] This is incorrect. Aquinas means something very specific and precise when he refers to the *semina* of virtue, and he gives them a priority that the other "beginnings" of virtue do not enjoy. In what follows, we'll look at this particular source of virtue and then situate it within the other "beginnings" of virtue that Aquinas describes.

In his discussion of faith in *Quaestiones disputatae de veritate* (*DV*), Aquinas offers an important description of the way in which man is ordered to his natural fulfillment. He offers this description in order to draw a parallel between the way in which we are ordered to our natural good and the way in which we are ordered to our supernatural good. I will return to this latter comparison in chapter 2, but here I want to address his comments on the way in which we are ordered to and capable of pursuing our natural fulfillment because they provide some crucial groundwork for understanding the *semina* of virtue.

In the process of examining the suitability of a certain definition of faith ("the substance of things to be hoped for, the argument of things that are not apparent"), Aquinas articulates a principle that I will quote in full and then unpack:

> Nothing can be ordered to an end unless some sort of proportion to the end preexists in it, a proportion from which there arises in it a desire for the end. And this happens insofar as a sort of inception of the end comes to exist in it, since it desires nothing except

to the extent that it desires some likeness of that [inception]. And so it is that in human nature itself there is a sort of inception of that good which is *proportionate* to [human] nature. For in human nature there naturally preexist (i) principles of demonstration, known *per se*, which are seeds of wisdom, and (ii) certain principles of the natural law, which are seeds of the moral virtues.[26]

This quote contains a number of important claims. First, there is an assertion about a necessary component of having an "end" — a thing cannot be ordered to an end unless a "proportion to the end preexists in it" — and a claim that it is that proportion that produces that thing's desire for its end. Second, there is a claim about what that "proportion" amounts to in human beings: an "inception of the end." Finally, there is a description of what that "inception" is.

In the background of the first claim is the traditional Aristotelian understanding of nature — the view that nature provides things not merely with their goal (*telos*) but also with the very principles that enable them to pursue that goal. Thanks to the "nature" of a frog, we can point to a set of activities that together constitute its fulfillment or flourishing: sitting on lily pads, catching flies with its tongue, jumping in a certain way, and so on. But it is also Aristotle's view that there is something already present in the tadpole that points it toward that kind of life. In the human case, similarly, if there is a good proportionate to our created human nature, a life that would constitute the flourishing of that nature, then we must already have something — thanks to our very nature — that points us toward that kind of life. Moreover, it is thanks to this natural proportionality (whatever it proves to be) that we desire that fulfillment in the first place. I will return to this point shortly.

Having asserted the Aristotelian principle that nothing can be ordered to an end unless it is first "proportioned" to it, Aquinas then proposes an account of *what it is* that naturally points us toward the fulfillment of our created human nature (i.e., an account of how it is that we are "proportioned" to our natural fulfillment). We are naturally ordered to the fulfillment of our created human nature, Aquinas tells us, "insofar as a sort of inception of the end comes to exist in [human nature]." It is that "inception of the end," says Aquinas, that causes us to desire our fulfillment in the first place, "since it desires nothing except to the extent that it desires some likeness of that [inception]."[27] The translation I am using uses the word "inception," which is indeed the best translation of the Latin *inchoato*. Older translations simply translate Aquinas as saying that we possess our end "inchoately." Whatever word one uses, the meaning is the same: we naturally possess some "beginning" of our end, something that gives us some kind of knowledge, however vague and imperfect, of what the fulfillment of our created human nature would be. It is this knowledge, moreover, that makes us desire our fulfillment in the first place.

Finally, we are told that the "inception" or, put differently, the inchoate knowledge of the (natural) end that all men naturally possess consists of the first natural and speculative principles: our natural habitual knowledge of the first principles of demonstration and of the principles of natural law. We are also told that the latter are the *semina* of the virtues. This assertion that our natural habitual knowledge of the principles of natural law (sometimes called *synderesis*) are the *semina* of the moral virtues is a claim that Aquinas repeats again and again throughout his writings on virtue.[28]

Why call our natural habitual knowledge of the principles of the natural law the *semina* of virtue? Aquinas consistently holds that all knowledge, including moral knowledge of good and bad, must come from somewhere: the process of discovery must move forward from something. Whatever it is that the process of discovery begins from must also point us toward what is eventually discovered. This is what the natural habitual knowledge of the first principles of the natural law (*synderesis*) provides, and this is why Aquinas calls the knowledge contained therein an "inception" of our end. We do not naturally know which individual things or actions are good and bad; this knowledge is only gained in and through the cultivation of virtue. But from our first interactions in the world, we *do* have a confused and imperfect knowledge of the good in general, and we *do* know that good is to be done and evil avoided. Aquinas says, moreover, that although our natural knowledge is general, "all the consequences are included as certain seminal principles."[29] Our natural habitual knowledge is indeed *semina* because it contains already, in a general form, all moral knowledge. The task of moral development is to render that general and confused natural knowledge precise.

Thus far I have been focused on the *semina* of the moral virtues. Although it is my contention that the *semina* play a crucial role in the cultivation of virtue, Aquinas also mentions a number of other respects in which human beings have a natural *aptitudo* for virtue. In the process of doing so, he makes a number of distinctions about where those aptitudes are found and about the different kinds of aptitudes. Next, I address each of these distinctions. As I will show, the *semina* of the moral virtues are more basic than any other "beginning" of virtue.

The first central distinction that Aquinas makes has to do with how natural, so to speak, the aptitude for virtue is. An *aptitudo* (aptitude, inclination, or "suitability") for virtue, he notes, can be present in either the *nature of the species* or in the *nature of the individual*.[30] That is to say, some of the things that point us toward virtue are possessed by all of us insofar as we are human beings with a shared human nature: this is the aptitude for virtue that is present in us because of the "nature of the species." Other things that point toward virtue are present in some and not others because of their own particular constitution: some people find acts of temperance easier than others do, and so on. This is the suitability for virtue that is present because of the "nature of the individual" (as we shall see shortly, Aquinas ultimately denies that these latter "beginnings" are actually *sources* of virtue).

The second central distinction is found in the *Quaestiones disputatae de virtutibus (DQVG)*. Here, Aquinas distinguishes two kinds of suitability for virtue: an *active* and a *passive* aptitude. An aptitude is "active" when it actually functions as a *cause*. The "body that can be healed," for instance, has an "active principle" of health because the body is capable of healing itself. Air, on the other hand, has only a "passive capacity" for fire because it can receive the form of fire but not cause it. One can have natural receptivity for virtue, then, either insofar as one naturally possesses the ability to *cause* virtues in oneself or insofar as one naturally possesses the ability to *receive* virtues (a power of the soul's ability to be habituated by repeated acts, for instance, would be an example of such a natural receptivity). So, a natural capacity for or "beginning" of virtue can be understood in a variety of ways. It can be present thanks to our shared human nature or thanks to our specific individual constitution, and it can be something that allows us to cause virtues in ourselves or merely something that renders us receptive to them.

A real cause of virtue has to be at once a cause of *all* the virtues. This is true of the *semina* of virtue. But Aquinas credits our shared human nature with providing us not just with the *semina* of virtue but with other beginnings of virtue too. Next we'll examine Aquinas's account of the other ways in which an aptitude for virtue is present in our shared human nature. These sources are each important in their own right, but they also highlight the importance of the *semina*.

Aquinas says that we all have active and passive capacities for virtue according to our human nature, and that these capacities are found in different ways in the reason, will, and the "lower powers." Human reason has both an active and a passive capacity for virtue. It has an active capacity for virtue thanks to what Aquinas calls the "active intelligence." Reason's capacity for virtue includes both the human capacity to reason and also the things that human reason knows "straight away, without study or inquiry,"[31] namely, the *semina* of virtue. Human reason also has a passive capacity for virtue insofar as it can "receive any intelligible thing."[32] Aquinas likewise ascribes both an active and a passive capacity for virtue to the will. The will has an active principle ordering it to virtue insofar as "the will naturally inclines towards the ultimate end."[33] To the extent that the will itself can be the subject of habits, it also has a passive capacity for virtue. Our lower appetites, however, do not contain an active principle of virtue but only the passive receptivity for it. Our individual nature, even if it inclines us in various ways, proves to be neither an active nor a passive source of virtue.

To summarize all of these intricate distinctions: we can *cause* virtues ordered to the fulfillment of the "first gift," our created nature, in ourselves through our own efforts because (1) our intellect knows some things without investigation and (2) has the ability to discover more things, and because (3) our will naturally desires what the intellect naturally perceives as good. Our repeated good acts can *cause* virtues because the powers of our soul (our intellect, will, or lower appetites) are all naturally susceptible to habituation. In all of this, the *semina* of virtue again play a foundational role. Our intellect has the ability to discover, but that ability rests in an important way on the fact that the process of discovery must begin somewhere; we must know something, or the process of discovery can never get going. The *semina* provide these starting points. Aquinas also indicates, however, that the *semina* of virtue are responsible in an important way for the active principle of virtue that he locates in the will. The will, Aquinas tells us, is an active principle of virtue insofar as it is through the will that we naturally desire the good of reason. Our desire for the good of reason moves us to pursue it. But Aquinas also tells us why it is that the will desires the good of reason: "Nothing can be ordered to an end unless some sort of proportion to the end preexists in it, a proportion from which there arises in it a desire for the end."[34] Our will naturally desires the good commensurate to nature because a "proportion to the end" preexists in us. And that proportion to the end preexists in us insofar as an "inception" of the end is naturally present in all men by nature. To put the same point differently, our will naturally desires our natural good because of the *semina* of virtue. Reason's natural ability to find truth and the will's natural desire for it are important sources of virtue, but both ultimately look back to and presuppose the *semina* of virtue.

Blind Horses: Individual Inclinations

We've examined the sources of virtue that Aquinas believes are present in all men because of their shared nature. But Aristotle tells us, and Aquinas agrees, that some men are just or brave or temperate "from birth." He is referring to an obvious fact of human experience: some people are from birth more inclined to certain kinds of acts than other people.[35] Anyone who has spent time around children knows that some children are naturally timid and others are relatively fearless, some are naturally free with their possessions, others are not, and so on. Aristotle acknowledges, of course, that the qualities we are born with are not yet complete or genuine virtues: they lack the guidance of reason. Aquinas will repeat this, saying that inclinations not guided by reason are like blind horses: they "run more vigorously" and consequently are hurt more seriously when they fall.[36] At the same time, one might well be tempted to use the language of *semina* to describe the relationship between these natural inclinations and the virtues they resemble, and to claim that it is the natural disposition to fearlessness that itself becomes genuine courage, and so on. This is not Aquinas's view. Both in his discussion of such inclinations and in his descriptions of how virtues are caused, Aquinas makes it clear that it would be incorrect to say these natural tendencies are anything more than the matter upon which the real causes of virtue work.

Aquinas affirms Aristotle's claim that there can be "a natural inclination to do what is characteristic of one virtue," but he also insists that "there cannot be an inclination to do what is characteristic of *all* the virtues."[37] This is because, says Aquinas, a natural inclination to do acts characteristic of one virtue is at the same time an inclination to do acts uncharacteristic of another: "Someone who is naturally disposed to be courageous, which is shown in pursuing difficult things, will be less disposed toward gentleness, which consists in restraining the emotions of the aggressive faculty."[38] This is why "the lion, which is naturally daring, is also naturally cruel."[39] A natural inclination that makes acts of one virtue easier makes acts of other virtues more difficult. This is important, because Aquinas like Aristotle believes in the unity of the virtues, and a true source or cause of virtue would be a cause of all the virtues. This is why genuine virtue must "happen in accord with reason: the seeds (*semina*) of all the virtues are in that."[40]

Aquinas makes a similar point in a different text, in the course of explaining the difference between dispositions on the one hand and habits on the other. In his initial discussion of habits in *ST* I-II, Aquinas argues that a habit is "a determinate species of quality," that is, it has its own species and is not merely a disposition that has become deeply ingrained.[41] His explanation is important for present purposes because it indicates that—in his mind, at least—the source of any genuine habit must be reason and not mere bodily inclination.

Aquinas claims that one can understand the difference between habits and dispositions in two ways. On the one hand, habit may be considered a specific kind of disposition, one that has become hard to change, so that dispositions are on their way to being habits "in the way that a boy becomes a man."[42] However, it is better to distinguish habits from dispositions on the basis of their *cause*: dispositions—such as sickness and health—result from changeable causes, while habits—such as knowledge and virtue—result from unchangeable ones.[43] Virtues are not easily changed because they have an unchanging cause, reason.[44]

CULTIVATING NATURAL VIRTUE

Aquinas has given us an account of whether and to what extent an *aptitudo* for virtue is naturally present in all men. I have argued that this aptitude consists of (1) an "inception" or inchoate knowledge of the good proportionate to our nature, (2) a desire for that fulfillment, (3) reason itself, which is capable of moving from that inchoate knowledge and desire to a correct conclusion about what is to be done, and (4) powers of the soul that are naturally susceptible to habituation. A very great deal has been written about the details of habituation and the cultivation of the acquired natural virtues, and this is not the place to revisit that discussion. There are two aspects of the cultivation of acquired natural virtue, however, that do need to be addressed. The first is the sense in which the cultivation of natural virtue is "up to us" or "in our power" or "arises from our own efforts." The second is the question of how we should understand the moral virtues themselves, what they are and what they do.

Virtue as "Up to Us"

The "inception" or inchoate knowledge of the end naturally present in us consists of our natural habitual knowledge of the first practical and speculative principles. Given the discussion so far, one might be tempted to think that reason scientifically "deduces" the right action from those general principles in the way that all of Euclidean geometry is deduced from Euclid's five postulates. This is (luckily) not the case. Anyone who has ever examined Aquinas's account of what the natural principles of virtue are will be aware that the move from those principles to specific moral conclusions is hardly a matter of mathematical precision. But even if it were, it is still unlikely that we would make much progress on our own. How many people other than Euclid have derived his geometry from his postulates? Even in something as certain and unassailable as mathematics, we need help. The same is all the more true of the cultivation of natural virtue. It is likely true that almost anyone who possesses the natural virtues in any degree has had help: parents, role models, and/or teachers who helped them to understand what acts were right and wrong, who encouraged them (or sometimes maybe even compelled them) to do good acts instead of bad ones, and who helped them appreciate and see that certain ways of life were better than others. Natural aptitude for virtue notwithstanding, it is highly unlikely than anyone ever became virtuous in a vacuum. But an essential difference between the natural acquired and supernatural infused virtues is that the former are supposedly of our own making, but the latter are bestowed by God. Thus, it is important for present purposes to say something about the sense in which virtue is "up to us."

In *Quaestiones disputatae de veritate* q. 11, a. 1, Aquinas asks "whether man can teach." His answer is important for understanding just how the cultivation of acquired virtue is "from us." Aquinas reiterates the claim that knowledge and virtue preexist in us to the extent that we naturally possess the beginnings or "seeds" of knowledge and virtue. Knowledge, like virtue, is acquired when we come to know actually those things we already know in a general and confused way: knowledge we already possessed potentially becomes actual. This leads Aquinas to make an important distinction about kinds of potencies.

Aquinas argues that a potency for some perfection can be either "active" or "passive." A potency is said to be active when the thing itself can actualize it through its own power. For example, the body has an active potency for health. When a sick person becomes well, it is the body that restores itself to health. The physician might assist this process, but does not actually heal: he merely ministers to the body so that it is better able to heal itself. A passive potency, by contrast, is a potency for some perfection that the thing cannot achieve on its own: it must be brought about by something other than and external to the thing itself. This, says Aquinas, is the way in which air has the "potential" to receive the form of fire. Air can receive fire, but it is not the cause of it.

Our potential for knowledge and (natural) virtue, says Aquinas, is an active one. Thanks to our created human nature, we already possess what we need in order to actualize our own potential for knowledge and virtue in the same way that our bodies already possess the resources to heal themselves. We possess both the starting points—natural habitual knowledge of the first speculative and practical principles—and reason itself, which can render that general knowledge specific in a concrete instance. When we are taught, the teacher does not simply "give" us our conclusions; indeed, any teacher who did so would at best create opinion. Rather, the teacher ministers to and assists us, helping us to arrive at the correct conclusions on our own. What the teacher does, Aquinas tells us, is help our reason to take the same path it would take if we were to make the discovery on our own. We certainly do need teachers, but when we successfully cultivate knowledge and virtue, that cultivation comes "from us" and not from the teacher. The teacher is merely a sort of midwife who facilitates the cultivation.

What Is a Moral Virtue?

Our natural habitual knowledge of the first practical principles and our consequent desire for them is the most fundamental source of moral virtue. And reason has the ability to move from that knowledge to a correct conclusion about what is to be done. But what about moral virtue as an *appetitive habit*? To have moral virtue is to have rightly ordered appetites, and something about having rightly ordered appetites is supposed to be crucial to acting well. Thus, if we really want to understand moral virtue, we have to say something about moral virtue as an *appetitive* habit: What does it mean to have a rightly ordered appetite, and what does a rightly ordered appetite contribute to morally good action? What do the moral virtues actually *do*?

Aquinas clearly believes that the moral virtues make our appetites responsive to right reason. He makes this claim or a version of it repeatedly and consistently throughout his corpus. But it is not entirely clear what "responsive" means. Is an appetite that has been made responsive to reason one that simply stays out of the way until reason has made a decision, so that the appetite only arises (logically, if not temporarily) after reason has completed its work? Or does an appetite that is rightly related to reason somehow actively assist reason in its work? The latter option seems not only preferable but consistent with some of Aquinas's own remarks about the moral virtues. Yet as recent scholarship shows, defending it is no easy task.[45] For Aquinas clearly holds that any passion experienced prior to reason's judgment (i.e., any passion that is *antecedent*) diminishes the moral quality of an act. This can seem to push us away from the view that virtuous appetites actively assist the reasoning process and toward the view that the appetitive part plays a supporting role at best in acts of moral virtue. It can seem to imply, that is to say, that appetites are virtuous insofar as they stay out of moral reason and come in only once a verdict has been rendered. Such a view, however, is incorrect. It arises out of an overidentification between the activity of the moral virtues and virtuous passions. Ultimately, the key to understanding just how moral virtue assists the process of deliberation is found in a central claim made by both Aquinas and Aristotle: moral virtues have to do with *ends*, not means. First, however, it is important to become clearer on the powers in which many of the moral virtues inhere.

It is easy to describe the activity of the moral virtues in an overly intellectual way, one that can overlook the fact that many of the moral virtues (those that perfect the concupiscible and irascible appetites) are habits that incline the sensitive appetites. A habit in a sensitive appetite is obviously not an intellectual habit: it will not be a habit of, say, *thinking* in a certain way. If we really want to understand what it means for a sensitive appetite to have a morally good habit, we must first say something about the sensitive appetites themselves. In what follows, I will (1) offer a general description of the sentient appetites, (2) offer a hypothesis about the way(s) in which they, and indeed, any appetitive power can be the subject of moral virtue, and (3) address whether and to what extent the mature virtues of the sentient appetites include "natural inclinations."

Aquinas, describing the movement of the sentient appetites, says that "sensual movement is a desire that follows on sentient apprehension."[46] The sentient apprehension presents objects, and those objects "move" the appetites. Aquinas distinguishes two powers in the sentient appetite, one that pursues what is agreeable and avoids what is disagreeable (the concupiscible power) and another that "resists aggressors that pose obstacles to what is agreeable and that inflict harm" (the irascible power).[47] Aquinas claims that the irascible power is the "promoter and defender" of the concupiscible power, and that all the movements of the former originate in the latter.[48]

Since the movement of the sentient appetite follows on sentient apprehension, it might initially seem that reason would have little to do with the movement of the sentient appetite. This is not the case, however. In the first place, in human beings the apprehension of the sensitive appetite is itself informed by reason. Animals are naturally moved by certain apprehensions: a sheep that perceives a wolf naturally flees it. Aquinas explains this by saying that animals possess an "estimative" power: animals naturally (one might say instinctively) apprehend certain objects as dangerous and others as beneficial and so on. But Aquinas holds that in human beings the estimative power is replaced by the cogitative power (which he sometimes calls particular reason): human apprehension can be informed by reason.

Jean Porter, explaining this, has pointed out that for Aquinas the sensitive apprehensions of human beings are initially indeterminate in a way an animal's are not. Animal activity, like human activity, is dependent on sensation. But animals naturally avoid or pursue certain objects. Sheep naturally perceive wolves as something to be avoided. But human beings do not naturally tend to or away from certain objects, at least according to Aquinas, though Porter points to scientific studies that appear to say they do. Children have to learn to avoid touching fire, and so on.[49]

The sentient appetites are thus at least partially subject to reason insofar as a reason can inform sentient apprehension. Aquinas maintains that the sentient appetites are also subject to reason in a second way insofar as human beings, even when moved by their appetites, need not immediately obey them in the way that animals do. When a sheep "becomes fearful of the wolf, it immediately flees, since in sheep there is no higher appetitive act that might resist this movement. By contrast, a man is not immediately moved by an appetitive act of the concupiscible or irascible powers; rather, he awaits the command of the will [*expectatur imperium voluntatis*], which is a higher appetite."[50] Thus, not only is it the case that reason can inform the sensitive apprehensions that move our irascible and concupiscible appetites, it is also the case that we do not necessarily obey those movements.

The discussion so far helps to clarify what the sentient appetites are and how they are moved. But it also, if anything, only seems to highlight their passivity. If there are virtues in the sentient appetites, then those appetites themselves must be capable of habituation, and those habits must somehow play a vital role in morally good action. How should we understand those habits, and what role do they play? In what follows, I will examine some texts where Aquinas describes the contribution of the moral virtues to morally good action. I will argue that those texts indicate that the moral virtues (including those moral virtues in the sentient appetites) help to direct moral deliberation itself.

Moral Virtue as Concerned with "Ends"

Aquinas's remarks about the moral virtues fall into two categories. The first category of remarks describes moral virtue as eliminating appetitive obstacles to right reason. Moral virtues make our appetites subordinate to reason: they cause it to be the case that our appetites do not overcome reason, or distort its judgment, and they cause it to be the case that our appetites readily and easily support reason's judgment once it has been made. But a second, nonnegligible category of Aquinas's remarks indicates that the possession of a moral virtue also *helps and assists the activity of reason*. This latter set of remarks implies that the virtuous person's appetites do more than merely stay out of the way of reason and support its final judgment: they imply that the virtuous person's appetites are part of the process of moral reasoning itself.

Since it is indisputable that Aquinas thinks that the moral virtues enable us to obey reason promptly and that they remove or reduce passionate "rebellion" against reason, I will not rehash that aspect of Aquinas's discussion.[51] Rather, I will focus on the texts where Aquinas seems to indicate that the moral virtues actively assist moral reasoning. First, we can make a general observation about the difference between a *passion* and an appetitive inclination. A passion is necessarily a passion *for* something: it is directed at some concrete thing. It involves, say, a desire for this ice cream cone, or a desire to say something hurtful to this particular person. Inclinations are not particular in this way. We saw this even in our earlier discussion of the inclinations that one possesses thanks to the particular constitution of one's nature. Some people are naturally aggressive; others are naturally timid. One can be *inclined* to aggression or timidity in general, prior to and in the absence of any particular action one does or any particular decision one makes. In what follows, I will argue that an important aspect of what moral virtue does has to do with this: with the general appetitive inclinations it gives us. It is these general inclinations, not any particular passion, that Aquinas believes the moral virtues provide, and it is these general inclinations, not any particular passion, that actively assist reason in its deliberations.

Aquinas clearly believes that we can perform virtuous actions even without the moral virtues, otherwise it would never be possible to cultivate them in the first place. Since we possess an inchoate knowledge of and desire for our natural fulfillment, and since we possess the natural light of reason, which can (at least in theory) render those principles specific in action, we are capable of moving from our general knowledge of our end to a correct conclusion about what is to be done and of acting accordingly. The moral virtues arise when we perform such actions repeatedly. But even if Aquinas is clear that right action is *possible* in the absence of moral virtue, he is equally clear that he thinks we need the moral virtues for the reliable and consistent performance of right actions. He thinks this not merely because the moral virtues keep the appetites in check, but because he thinks that the moral virtues actually help and guide our deliberation.

In *ST* I-II, q. 58, a. 4, in the context of describing the dependence of prudence on the moral virtues (and vice versa), Aquinas describes the different roles of prudence and moral virtue in morally good action. Right action occurs when our reason moves from more universal principles to a correct conclusion about what is to be done in a particular case. But in order for this to occur, Aquinas says, we need to be rightly ordered not only to "universal" but also to what he calls "particular" principles: "With respect to particular matters, reason needs to proceed not only from *universal* principles but also from *particular* principles."[52] Synderesis and "some sort of practical knowledge" secure our right order to universal principles, but Aquinas maintains that we need the moral virtues in order to be rightly ordered to the "particular principles."

Thus it is clear that if we want to understand what Aquinas believes moral virtue is (and what it does), we need to understand what "particular principles" are and what it means for someone to have a "right order" to them. Aquinas offers some limited insights into both questions in the article we have been examining. His remarks are important enough to cite in their entirety:

> Just as a man is disposed toward being correctly related to the universal principles through natural understanding or through a habit of knowledge, so, too, in order for him to be correctly related to the *particular* principles of what is to be done, i.e., the ends, he must be perfected by habits in accord with which it becomes in some sense connatural to the man to judge correctly concerning the end. And this is effected by moral virtue. For the virtuous individual judges correctly about the end of virtue, since, as *Ethics* 3 says, "Such as an individual is, so the end appears to him." (*ST* I-II, q. 58, a. 4)

Two features of this text are to be noted. First, Aquinas equates "particular principles" with "ends." Second, he says that the moral virtues make it "connatural" for us to judge correctly about the "end of virtue."

In the text quoted just above, Aquinas makes a distinction between "universal" and "particular" principles. The reference to universal principles seems clear enough: we have already seen that Aquinas holds that moral reasoning begins from our natural habitual knowledge of the first practical principles. He seems here to include more than just synderesis in our knowledge of "universal" principles, because he says we are correctly related to them either through our natural understanding *or* a habit of knowledge. More important for present purposes, however, are the things the passage implies about "particular" principles.

Even aside from anything more specific, it is clear that a particular principle is a *principle*, and not merely whatever conclusion our reasoned deliberation comes to in a particular case. The moral virtues make us rightly ordered to some set of *principles* that reason takes its departure from: not to the first principles of reasoning (synderesis achieves that) or even to other broad "universal" principles, but to more specific principles. The text even tells us something about what those principles are: they include the "ends" of the moral virtues. Thus, if we can gain insight into the "ends" of the various moral virtues, we should be able to gain insight into the notion of "particular principles."

In his discussion of the individual virtues, Aquinas frequently refers to various "ends" or "goals" that individual virtues seek. He says that temperance holds to the principle that one should "not chase after sensual desires," that the end of civic courage is to establish "man's spirit in human justice, to preserve which he endures mortal danger," that truth "seeks to achieve a due order between our words and deeds and what they signify, i.e., the thing itself," and that justice seeks to render what is due.[53]

It is of course important that the "particular ends" described above should not be understood as independent of more universal ends. Aquinas also indicates in more than one place that differences in more universal ends carry over to differences in particular ends. Both infused and acquired temperance, for instance, regulate the pleasures of touch. But Aquinas argues that each kind of virtue regulates those pleasures in a different way. Acquired temperance sees to it that one's consumption does not "harm the health of the body, or impede the use of reason," while infused temperance helps us to "castigate the body and bring it into subjection."[54]

How should we understand these "particular principles" or "ends"? In the first place, it is important to notice that they are both more specific than the universal goals that synderesis orders us to and more general than the conclusions about what is to be done that we arrive at through deliberation. Aquinas is saying that we need a right orientation to more universal ends *and* to particular ends: a desire to do good and avoid evil does not in and of itself ensure a right order to sensual desires or to establish our spirit in human justice. Something more is needed, and Aquinas believes that the moral virtues provide that something more. Second, and more importantly, Aquinas's remarks about the differences between infused and acquired virtue indicate that there is a link between universal and particular ends: the moral virtues that make us rightly ordered to the particular ends of the acquired moral virtues will not suffice to order us to the particular ends of the infused moral virtues.

The preceding should help to shed some light on the notion of a "particular principle." Aquinas says that the moral virtues help us to judge rightly about particular principles, and that they provide this help insofar as they make it "in some sense connatural" for us to judge rightly about those principles. What does this mean? One thing it cannot mean is that the moral virtues themselves actually *judge*. They cannot, because they are appetitive habits. What an appetitive habit *can* do, however, is incline us to certain general kinds of goals; it can make certain goals seem good. Nicholas Kahm describes this kind of orientation as an "instinctual or intuitive" movement of the appetite.[55] Understood in this way, to possess a moral virtue is to possess an instinctual inclination, not for any specific action, but for certain *ends* of action—an instinctual inclination for the particular principles of the moral virtues or a feeling "in our hearts" that certain goals are good.[56] When we understand moral virtue in this way, we can begin to see both how moral virtue might aid deliberation and how it would diminish moral virtue if we were to understand it merely as rendering our appetites docile to reason's direction.

What does it really mean to be chaste or courageous or honest? Does the possession of those qualities manifest itself only in specific actions, or do certain individuals possess those qualities as general appetitive inclinations, even in the absence of any occasion to act on them? The latter is quite clearly the case. It is one thing to refrain from acts of infidelity to one's spouse and quite another to feel at a deep and instinctual level, "in one's heart," so to speak, that fidelity is an honor and a privilege; one thing to tell the truth in some particular instance and quite another to feel a deep and abiding repugnance for falsehood; one thing to do some particular courageous act and quite another to *want*, in a deep and abiding way, to stand up for what is right. In the first place, we have the latter all the time, even when we are not actually called upon to perform various virtuous acts. In the second place, it is clear that the latter inclinations, precisely because they are abiding and deeply felt, can serve to guide and correct reason's deliberation. When one continually and habitually feels "in one's heart" the goodness of fidelity, one will be more alert to actions that might not be consistent with fidelity, and even to those apparently innocuous acts that, if indulged in now, might pose a threat to fidelity in the long run. It is in this way that an appetitive habit can nonetheless shape and direct our moral reasoning.

"Blind Horses" and Moral Virtue

In addition to making our appetites docile to reason's guidance, the moral virtues give us inclinations for certain "particular ends"; they give us an aversion for dishonesty, or a desire to stand up for what is right, and so on. These general inclinations help to shape and guide the very process of moral deliberation. But a thorough discussion of moral virtues should also consider what, if anything, the moral virtues have to do with the "natural inclinations" for virtue that Aquinas claims can be found in different ways in the appetitive powers of different individuals. I think the account of moral virtue I have been offering helps to further illuminate the gap between the former and the latter.

As we saw earlier in this chapter, Aquinas notes that differences in individual constitution cause some people to find acts of some virtue easier (or more difficult) than others. Someone who is naturally aggressive will find courageous acts easier than will someone who is naturally timid. But, Aquinas maintains, the same natural inclination that makes acts of one virtue easier will make acts of the other virtues more difficult; the person who is naturally aggressive will also find it more difficult to be gentle. What, if anything, do these natural inclinations have to do with moral virtue? Does moral virtue change or alter these natural inclinations? The answer to these questions is not at all obvious, but let's consider two points.

First, although the cultivation of moral virtue would most likely modify a natural inclination, it seems unlikely that it would remove it altogether. Or, to put the same point differently, the particular constitution of one's individual nature might well cause it to be the case that one continues to find some virtuous acts easier and others more difficult, even as one grows in virtue. A natural inclination to aggressiveness, say, will cause it to be the case that one finds it easier to rise up against *whatever* one perceives as an obstacle, and more difficult to back down from a fight or to be gentle, regardless of the reason for it. If Aquinas holds that a natural inclination to overcome obstacles (which I have been referring to, imprecisely, as aggressiveness) makes the acts of some virtues more difficult, then it would stand to reason that as we cultivate those more difficult virtues we will at least somewhat temper that natural inclination. It seems entirely plausible, for instance, that someone who is naturally aggressive will have a harder time practicing the virtue of obedience, and also plausible that to the extent he succeeds in cultivating a desire to obey his superiors, he will have at least somewhat tempered that natural inclination. It seems equally plausible, however, to think that even if a naturally aggressive person makes great progress in cultivating the virtue of obedience, his natural tendencies will never be completely suppressed, that he will always find it easier to rise up against obstacles than to back down from a fight. In short, our natural tendencies, even as they are gradually brought under the control of reason, might well continue to make some virtuous acts easier and others more difficult.

Second, it is plausible that our natural inclinations persist through serious moral change. The natural inclinations that Aquinas describes are something we possess as a result of the particular constitution of our individual nature. Someone with a natural tendency to fight against whatever obstacle arises will find it easier to do so than someone who does not, *whatever* that obstacle might be. A skillful pagan warrior—a Viking raider, say—will most likely have indulged his natural tendency to aggression and curtailed any natural inclination to kindness or gentleness. Were such an individual to cultivate the natural virtues, he would need to order his appetites to different general ends. If he currently fights because he simply enjoys killing, he would need to cultivate instead the desire to fight only in a just cause. But even though I agree that his pursuit of other virtues would necessarily require that his overly indulged natural inclination to aggressiveness be tempered, I see no reason why the same natural inclination that supported his bloodlust could not also support his desire to fight in a just cause. This seems plausible to me because the natural inclinations we are referring to here are just *bodily* inclinations, inclinations that arise merely because of the way the human form inheres in our particular matter. Those natural inclinations can be exacerbated or diminished, depending on how much we indulge them or starve them, but it seems plausible to me that they will nonetheless persist. They are part of who we are.

We have so far considered a "structural" account of natural virtue, focused primarily on the *semina* from which natural virtue grows and on the role of reason in cultivating moral virtues out of those *semina* for a very specific reason—Aquinas envisions a very important parallel between the structure of natural virtue and the structure of supernatural virtue, and this parallel is built on the different *semina* of each type of virtue. Aquinas's remarks about the *semina* and how it is that they enable the cultivation of virtue give us the foundation for understanding the parallels he draws between natural and supernatural virtue. But we have naturally bypassed many of the questions that one might raise about virtue, for instance, about the much-debated question of "pagan" virtue, i.e., whether or not someone outside the Christian moral life can cultivate the natural virtues. An answer to this question is not needed for understanding Aquinas's account of how the natural virtues come to be: neither his account of the *semina* nor his account of how those seeds become virtues nor even his account of what the moral virtues do depends on the answer.

At the same time, however, the question of whether pagans can progress in cultivating the acquired moral virtues is important for the broader purposes of this book. If we wish to give some account of how the natural and supernatural virtues are related, we need to take a stand on the question of whether someone outside the life of grace (i.e., a "pagan") can possess the natural virtues. If he cannot, then many theories of the relationship between the two kinds of virtue will be ruled out at the outset.

THE PROBLEM OF PAGAN VIRTUE

We have examined the resources for virtue that all human beings possess thanks to the "first gift," the gift of our created, human nature, but we've omitted mention of an important caveat about that gift: it is corrupted and impaired by original sin. If it is thanks to the abilities inherent in our created human nature that we are capable of cultivating natural virtue, and if our nature is corrupted by original sin, then it would seem to follow that our ability to cultivate even virtues ordered to our natural fulfillment is also corrupted. Indeed, some might maintain that original sin so corrupts our created human nature that the cultivation of natural virtue is rendered altogether impossible; that even *natural* virtue can only be successfully cultivated by one whose nature has been healed by sanctifying grace. The debate over this question is usually referred to as the debate over the possibility of "pagan" virtue. In keeping with tradition I will use the word "pagan," but the debate is really over whether or not it is possible to make genuine progress in the cultivation of even natural virtue outside the life of grace.

Much has been written about whether Aquinas recognizes the possibility of pagan virtue. In attempting to answer this question, scholars have appealed to a great many different aspects of Aquinas's texts: to his remarks on the end of man, his treatment of the "connection" of the virtues, and to remarks he makes in various places that seem to indicate that virtue is or is not possible for the pagan.[57] In light of our preceding discussion, however, it should be clear that one question is of central importance: What does original sin do to the natural *aptitudo* for virtue that Aquinas so frequently refers to? If original sin altogether destroys that aptitude, then Aquinas cannot really be said to recognize the possibility of pagan virtue. If, on the other hand, original sin merely impairs that aptitude so that the cultivation of natural virtue is rendered more difficult but not altogether impossible, then Aquinas's account can sustain the possibility. Next, we shall examine this question in two parts: (1) Aquinas's account of how original sin affects nature and how Aquinas seems to hold that original sin merely impairs, but does not altogether corrupt, nature; (2) an apparently contradictory text.[58]

When we think of original sin, we tend to think in terms of a contrast between the "uncorrupted" nature given in creation and the nature somehow stained or corrupted by sin. Aquinas's account, however, is a bit more complicated than this because he thinks that before the Fall, Adam and Eve possessed not only the fullness of the nature given them in creation but also another divinely given gift, which he calls "original justice." Original justice, says Aquinas, was a "certain gift of grace given by God to the whole of human nature in the first parent."[59] Thanks to this gift, "reason perfectly restrained the lower powers of the soul, and reason itself was perfected by God and subject to Him."[60] Thus when we consider the effects of original sin, we must consider not only the effect on nature itself but also its effect on the gift of original justice.

Aquinas distinguishes three distinct ways in which original sin might "diminish the good of nature." First, original sin could impair or destroy the very principles of nature itself. Second, original sin could diminish our natural inclination toward virtue. Third, original sin could remove the good of original justice. Aquinas argues that original sin affects human nature in both the second and the third way, but that it leaves the "principles of nature" intact. This will prove important for the question of pagan virtue.

Original sin entirely removes the gift of original justice. After Adam's sin, reason is no longer perfectly subject to God, and the other powers of the soul are no longer perfectly subject to reason. Moreover—though it is unclear whether the diminishment arises simply as a direct result of the loss of original justice or as an additional disorder caused by original sin—Aquinas says that because of original sin, man's natural inclination to virtue is "diminished." However, his view of just how that inclination is diminished is important, especially for present purposes, because the principles of nature are themselves an important source of our natural inclination to virtue. One might assume, then, that when Aquinas says that original sin diminishes our natural inclination to virtue, he means that original sin somehow diminishes the aptitude for virtue that we all possess thanks to our shared human nature. This assumption, however, is precisely what Aquinas denies. He distinguishes two ways in which our inclination to virtue can be diminished: at its "root" (source) or insofar as it is impeded from reaching its end. Since original sin does not destroy the very principles of our nature, it does not destroy the "root" of our inclination for virtue. Rather, original sin places an obstacle between us and the fulfillment of our nature insofar as we are more inclined to sin thanks to original sin. Since like acts cause like habits, the very inevitability of sin means that our inclination to virtue is diminished.

In spite of the obstacles it places between us and the realization of our end, however, Aquinas is abundantly clear about this much: original sin leaves the "principles" of nature intact. Original sin, that is to say, neither destroys nor darkens our natural habitual knowledge of the first theoretical and speculative principles (aka the *semina* of virtue), and it does not destroy the natural desire the "inception" of the end awakens in the will. The loss of original justice and the inevitability of sin means that reason's ability to move from these principles to correct conclusions about what is to be done is impeded, and the disorder in the passions also means that even when we do arrive at a correct conclusion, we are less likely to obey reason's command. But original sin decidedly does not render reason altogether incapable of arriving at correct conclusions, and it decidedly does not render the passions altogether resistant to reason. Even those in the grip of original sin retain their order to their natural fulfillment and retain in principle the resources for acting in a manner befitting that order. Even given all this, of course, there is still room for a broad range of interpretations of just how frequently the pagan will be capable of performing such actions. If the pagan is capable of performing genuinely good acts, but only very rarely, then he certainly will not ever manage to make any real progress in the cultivation of natural virtue and hence pagan virtue will be nonexistent for all practical purposes. Aquinas himself, however, seems decidedly more optimistic: "Even though a man cannot without grace avoid mortal sin in the sense of never committing a mortal sin, this does not prevent him from being able to acquire the habit of a virtue through which he might abstain from bad actions in most cases [*ut in pluribus*] and especially from actions that are strongly opposed to reason [*ab his operibus quae sunt valde rationi contraria*]."[61]

For these reasons, I think one certainly has to concede that the pagan is capable of genuinely good actions. Texts like this one indicate something even more: Aquinas thought the pagan could perform such actions frequently enough to make genuine progress in the cultivation of virtue. But there is obviously a great deal more that could be said (and has been said) about Aquinas's view of pagan virtue, and those who deny the possibility of it obviously have important reasons for doing so. One of those reasons is important enough to merit a brief mention here.

In *ST* I-II, q. 109, Aquinas addresses the necessity of grace. In article 3 of this question, he asks whether a man "can love God above all things by just his natural power and without grace." Aquinas's answer to this question is more important than it might seem at first. In several texts Aquinas appears to affirm that our natural fulfillment (or "end") consists in loving God above all things in the manner appropriate to a creature. This love would not be the love of charity, but the love of a creature for its creator. If this is indeed what Aquinas understands our natural fulfillment to be—and I shall assume for the sake of argument that it is—then any genuinely good act, any act that genuinely counts as an act of natural virtue, would necessarily have to be ordered to the creaturely love of God above all things. *If* it turns

The Structure of Natural Virtue 43

out that Aquinas thinks that no one can order his acts to this end apart from God's saving grace, then we would seemingly be forced to conclude that one cannot perform even an act of natural virtue without the help of God's saving grace.

In his reply, Aquinas seemingly pushes us toward this conclusion. First, he affirms that our natural fulfillment, like that of any created thing, is found in loving God above all things: "To love God above all things is something connatural to man as well as to every creature—not just rational creatures, but also non-rational and even non-living creatures, each in accord with the mode of love that can belong to it."[62] Aquinas also affirms, moreover, that before original sin man did indeed order his acts to such an end: "In the state of uncorrupted nature man referred his love for himself—and, similarly, his love for all other things—to the love of God as his end. And in this sense He loved God more than himself and loved Him above all things."[63] But Aquinas also says that those corrupted by original sin cannot do so: "By contrast, in the state of corrupted nature a man falls short of this as far as the rational will's desire is concerned, since because of the corruption of its nature the rational will pursues its own private good unless it is healed by God's grace."[64]

It is no accident that Aquinas's stark remarks here are so frequently cited as evidence that he would have agreed with Augustine: all that is not of faith is sin. But whatever we make of this text, it is important to read it in the context of Aquinas's other remarks, including remarks he makes in the very same question, which indicate that he either asserts contradictory positions or else does not intend to make as stark a claim as he at first appears to.

Article 8 of question 109 asks whether man is able to avoid sin without grace. If Aquinas's remarks in article 3 of the same question are really to be read as excluding the possibility of rightly ordered acts apart from grace, then the answer to this question should clearly be no. But this is not the answer Aquinas gives; rather, he says that even without grace, man can avoid sin in each individual act, but that because of the disorder sin creates, he cannot avoid sin consistently. Grace is not necessary in order for him to avoid sin, but it is necessary for him to avoid sin consistently: "Each individual act of sinning is such that a man is able to avoid it; but he is not able to avoid all of them together [*non tamen omnes*] except through grace."[65] In the context of elaborating this point, Aquinas explains that even without grace, reason is able to avoid sin, particularly in those cases where the individual is able to engage in deliberation. However, since without grace "man does not have his heart fixed on God in such a way that he wills not to be separated from Him for the sake of any good to be pursued or evil to be avoided," we often choose those subordinate goods over God.[66]

One can certainly take Aquinas's remarks in article 8 to mean that the pagan avoids sin rarely, even so rarely that he never makes much progress in the cultivation of virtue. But however frequently they occur, it is indisputable that Aquinas believes that even pagans can perform acts that are not sinful. And *if* an act is not sinful, then it cannot be ordered to an evil end. So whatever Aquinas means in article 3 of question 109, it does not seem that he can mean that each and every act of those outside the life of grace is necessarily ordered to an evil end, such as pride.

Once we concede that the pagan can perform genuinely good acts, questions about the possibility of pagan virtue reduce to the question of frequency: Can the pagan perform those acts frequently enough to make genuine progress in the cultivation of virtue? If he can perform good acts only very rarely, as isolated exceptions in an otherwise vicious life, the answer will be no. If he can perform them more consistently, a different answer will be possible. The resolution to questions like these, however, is not going to be decisively found in Aquinas's texts. I am also not convinced that the answer to this much narrower question matters a great deal. For as I shall argue in chapter 2, Aquinas's account of the cultivation of acquired virtue matters most insofar as it provides the framework on which he builds his account of infused moral virtue.

AQUINAS'S ACCOUNT OF ACQUIRED VIRTUE IS GROUNDED IN AN Aristotelian account of nature and its capacities. The natural habitual knowledge of the first principles of practical reason give us an initial order to our end, an order that reason is at least in principle capable of rendering specific. Through our own repeated good acts, we cultivate acquired moral virtues that, by ordering our appetites to appropriate ends, help to guide and shape our reason so that we move more easily from the initial ordering of synderesis to a correct conclusion about what ought to be done, and the acquired moral virtues also help us to do that action more readily.

This detailed structure allows us to ask still further questions: What if the first principles were different? What if they were ordered to an end that exceeded our natural resources? How would this alter our account of the virtues that enable us to move from inchoate order to action? These are questions we will address in chapter 2.

CHAPTER 2

Habits of Being

The Structure of Supernatural Virtue

Chapter 1 located our ability to cause natural virtues in ourselves in the sources or principles of virtue that are naturally present in our reason and will. Our natural habitual knowledge of the first principles of thought and action gives us a first, inchoate knowledge of our end. Thanks to that knowledge, confused and general though it might be, our will possesses a natural desire for the good it naturally knows. Our natural ability to reason renders us in principle capable of moving from that general knowledge of our end to a correct conclusion about what to do and of acting accordingly. Though we certainly need the help of teachers and mentors in cultivating them, the natural virtues are nonetheless *our* creation: others can help our reason find the right paths to move along, but habits are formed in our appetites by the repeated motion of the reason by which they are naturally capable of being formed, that is, by *our own reason*. Appetites so formed in turn actively assist our reason insofar as they cause us to possess a general appetitive desire for the various "ends" of the natural moral virtues. The courageous person desires to stand firm for the sake of what is right in a general way *all the time*, just as the temperate person desires in a general way to "eat and drink the amount conducive to bodily health" *all the time*. This is what it means to have rightly ordered appetites. And these rightly ordered appetites are, importantly, *caused* by reason: they are caused when our reason repeatedly moves from the first principles it naturally knows and desires to a correct conclusion.

Aquinas constructs an account of supernatural virtue around these same foundational notions, namely, (1) the idea of principles that orient us to our end and (2) the idea that to act rightly is to render these general principles specific in action. The essential difference is that we are far more dependent on divine help at every stage of the process. Aquinas consistently draws an analogy between the theological virtues (the virtues that give us our first, inchoate order to our supernatural fulfillment) and our natural knowledge of and desire for our natural fulfillment. Although the theological virtues order us to a more perfect end, they are less perfectly possessed by us. Because of that imperfect possession, we cannot create the virtues that order us to our supernatural fulfillment through our own power; we cannot cause the requisite inclinations in our appetites or even reason correctly about what acts are or are not commensurate with our supernatural fulfillment. This is why Aquinas believes that in addition to the theological virtues of faith, hope, and love, God also bestows additional moral virtues (what are commonly referred to as the "infused" moral virtues) and the gifts of the Holy Spirit.

The first section of this chapter deals with the analogy Aquinas draws between the natural principles that order us to (natural, acquired) virtue and the theological virtues. Aquinas maintains that the gifts of faith, hope, and love create in us the "inception" of our supernatural fulfillment—a vague and incomplete knowledge of and desire for participation in the divine life. In the second section, we look at Aquinas's notion of infused moral virtue, with an eye toward explaining two fundamental aspects of it: first, Aquinas's claim that the infused and acquired virtues differ "specifically"; second, what it would mean for the infused virtues to grow or increase. Because the theological virtues are possessed imperfectly, Aquinas does not believe that our possession of the theological and infused moral virtues is sufficient for morally good action. He believes we need additional, continual assistance from the Holy Spirit and that the gifts of the Holy Spirit, also infused along with grace, enable us to receive this assistance. Thus, the third section treats Aquinas's account of the gifts of the Holy Spirit and their contribution to the Christian's morally good acts. The last section compares the respective structures of natural and supernatural virtue.

SUPERNATURAL PRINCIPLES: THE THEOLOGICAL VIRTUES

Aquinas anchors his account of infused virtue in the same foundational notion that shapes his account of acquired virtue: in the idea that we cannot order our acts to an end unless we first possess an "inception" of that end. While our habitual knowledge of synderesis gives us an orienting order to the fulfillment proportionate to our created nature, Aquinas holds that the theological virtues give us a similar order to our supernatural perfection. Thus there is a structural similarity between the respective roles of synderesis and the theological virtues. At the same time, those roles are also importantly different, and those differences may have ramifications for how we ultimately understand the relationship between the infused and acquired virtues.

In what follows, I will first explain the effect that Aquinas believes God's saving grace has on nature in general: i.e., his claim that grace is a habit that perfects the "essence" of the soul. With that account in place, I will examine his claim that grace gives us, so to speak, new "principles" of action. In doing so, I will point out some important ways in which our "inception" of our natural fulfillment differs from the "inception" of supernatural beatitude that Aquinas believes we receive along with the gift of grace.

Aquinas says that God's grace, understood as a special favor that God shows us, is the "special love in accord with which God draws the rational creature beyond the status of his nature to a participation in the divine good."[1] Aquinas also says that in order to "draw us to participation in the divine good," God bestows on us habits that dispose the very essence of our soul. This claim draws directly on the account of natural virtue we saw in chapter 1. Aquinas states that God would not "provide in a lesser way for those creatures whom He loves in order that they might have a supernatural good than for those creatures whom He loves in order that they might have a natural good."[2]

But God gives natural creatures principles that incline them to the types of acts appropriate to their nature, so that "the movements by which they are moved by God become connatural to those creatures and easy for them—this according to Wisdom 8:1 ('. . . and [wisdom] orders all things agreeably' (*suaviter*))."[3] In the same way, then, when God grants human beings participation in the divine life, he infuses into them "certain forms, i.e., qualities, by which they might be moved agreeably and promptly by Him toward attaining that eternal good."[4] Thus, along with grace, which makes us participants in the divine life, Aquinas holds that God also gives us virtues, which order us to participation in that nature. Foremost among the virtues God gives us are the theological virtues.

Aquinas believes that the theological virtues of faith, hope, and love give us a supernatural version of our natural ordering to the good of reason. Throughout his corpus, he consistently begins his discussions of supernatural virtue by reasserting the same principle that guides his account of the natural virtues: a thing cannot be ordered to any end unless it already possesses both an "inception" or "beginning" of that end and an inclination to it. All men naturally possess both an inchoate knowledge of and desire for their natural fulfillment, but they do not naturally possess the same kind of order to their supernatural fulfillment, to the participation in the divine life made possible by sanctifying grace. In his early *Commentary on the Sentences* (*CS*), Aquinas writes: "It should be said that in all things that act for the sake of an end, there must be an inclination to the end and a certain commencing of the end, otherwise they would never act for the sake of an end."[5] In the *Quaestiones disputatae de veritate* (*DV*), he makes the same assertion: "Nothing can be ordered to an end unless some sort of proportion to the end preexists in it, a proportion from which there arises in it a desire for the end. And this happens insofar as an inception of the end comes to exist in it. . . . Hence in order for a human being to be ordered toward the good of eternal life, it is also necessary that a sort of inception of that good should come to exist in the one who is promised eternal life."[6] Aquinas makes similar assertions in both *ST* I-II and in his *Disputed Questions on the Virtues in General* (*DQVG*).[7]

Aquinas clearly maintains that we cannot be ordered to supernatural beatitude unless we receive some supernatural analogue of the principles that order us to the good proportionate to our created nature. But his account of the two sets of principles will differ in two important ways. First, although his account of our "inception" of our natural fulfillment centers around his notion of synderesis, Aquinas will maintain that an entire trio of habits—the theological virtues—are needed to provide the "inception" of our supernatural fulfillment. Second, the habits that order us to our supernatural fulfillment are *virtues*, while the habit that orders us to our natural fulfillment is not. Let's look at each of these points in turn.

Aquinas clearly and consistently asserts that we are given an "inception" of our supernatural fulfillment through the gift of the theological virtues. Just as our natural habitual knowledge of the first principles gives us inchoate knowledge of and a desire for our natural good, so, says Aquinas, do the theological virtues of faith, hope, and love operate as supernatural principles that give us an inchoate knowledge of and desire for our supernatural good: "Since this second sort of beatitude exceeds any proportion to human nature, a man's natural principles, by which he proceeds to act well in a way proportioned to his nature, are not sufficient for ordering man toward this beatitude. Hence principles by which he might be so ordered toward supernatural beatitude have to be divinely added to man—in just the way in which he is ordered by his natural principles toward his connatural end (though not without God's help). And these principles are called theological virtues."[8] Similar statements can also be found in the *CS*,[9] the *Disputed Questions on Faith*,[10] and in the *DQVG*.[11] Aquinas clearly and consistently holds that the theological virtues play the role at the supernatural level that our natural habitual knowledge of the first speculative and practical principles and our natural desire for the good of reason play at the natural level.

Immediately after asserting that we need an "inception" of our supernatural good in order to be ordered to supernatural beatitude, Aquinas tells us in the *DV* that "this inception comes through faith, which on the basis of an infused light holds fast to things that by nature exceed our cognition."[12] And again in the *DQVG*, he states that "by faith, the intelligence may be enlightened concerning the knowledge of supernatural matters, which function just as naturally known principles do at the level of our natural activities."[13] Hence, the infused virtue of faith performs at the supernatural level the role that the first principles of theoretical and speculative knowledge play at the natural level: it gives us an "inception" of the relevant end.

In the case of the natural virtues, the mere fact of our natural habitual knowledge of the first principles of thought and action is itself the cause of our will's desire for its natural fulfillment. At the supernatural level, however, it is seemingly the will that influences the intellect rather than the other way around. Aquinas tells us that "the will, moved by the aforementioned good [eternal life], proposes something that is not apparent to the intellect as being worthy of its assent, and it determines the intellect to that which is not apparent in such a way that the intellect assents to it."[14] The inclination of the will to supernatural beatitude is achieved through the virtues of hope and charity.

The theological virtues therefore play the role at the supernatural level that synderesis plays at the natural level. But it is important to note the differences between the two. Synderesis gives us knowledge, albeit vague and incomplete knowledge, of the good proportionate to our created nature. Aquinas holds that the knowledge of synderesis is itself the source of our desire for the good proportionate to our created nature. If this parallel held in exactly the same way at the supernatural level, then we would expect that God would provide *only* the supernatural equivalent of synderesis, namely, inchoate *knowledge* of our supernatural fulfillment. If so, then it would seem that God should provide only the theological virtue of faith, which is, strictly speaking, the real parallel of synderesis.

Although Aquinas does not directly address this difference, the explanation most likely lies in the difference between the kinds of knowledge in question. Synderesis gives us inchoate knowledge of a good that is fully in our grasp, and one that we are by our very nature capable of pursuing and achieving. The knowledge it gives, however incomplete, is still knowledge of something we are capable of comprehending. The knowledge we receive through the virtue of faith is different. It is not only imperfect and incomplete; it is also knowledge of a good we cannot fully grasp and, perhaps more importantly, knowledge of a good we cannot pursue through our own power. It only stands to reason that that knowledge, first, would have to *follow on* the will's assent, which Aquinas says is achieved through hope and charity.

The other noteworthy difference between the theological virtues and synderesis is this: the theological virtues are *virtues*; synderesis is not. Synderesis consists merely in natural, habitual knowledge. It is a precondition of our pursuit of any good, not a perfection. How should we understand this difference? I raise this question here only to bracket it, but it is worth noting that the right way of understanding this difference might go right to the heart of the question of the relationship between natural and supernatural virtue. If the right way to understand the theological virtues is as perfections of our natural principles, then it would only stand to reason that the former would be virtues and the latter not.

Reason and Virtue

We noted in chapter 1 that the natural active principles ordering us to virtue are capable of being rendered specific in concrete instances thanks to our natural ability to reason, and that the powers of the soul are naturally receptive to habituation. Thus, when one reasons to and performs virtuous acts repeatedly, one cultivates the natural virtues. So far, we have seen that Aquinas insists that grace brings about a change not merely in our end but also to the very principles that order us to that end: the theological virtues do at the supernatural level what synderesis and the desire it awakens do at the natural level. One might expect that Aquinas would leave matters there, that he would claim that reason formed by these new first principles and the will awakened to this new desire would be sufficient, not only for acting in a matter befitting participation in the divine life but also for cultivating moral virtues ordered to that participation. But Aquinas denies that reason formed by the theological virtues is sufficient for producing acts ordered to supernatural beatitude. First, he is quite clear that reason, though in principle capable of rendering its naturally known principles specific in concrete instances, does not have the same ability at the supernatural level: the inception of the end and the desire for it that God gives us in the theological virtues are more perfect than our natural knowledge and desire for our natural fulfillment, but they are less perfectly possessed. Our inception of our supernatural end is still hazier and more unclear than that of our natural end, and our reason has still less of an ability to move from that inception to a correct decision about what is to be done.[15] Even when ordered to participation in the divine life by the theological virtues, then, Aquinas insists that we still need the help and guidance of the Holy Spirit to act rightly.

The second and equally important point is that, as we saw in chapter 1, Aquinas accepts the Aristotelian principle that our appetites are responsive to reason: our repeated good acts can dispose our appetites not just to obey reason but to actually desire the various "ends" of the virtues. Repeated courageous acts create in us a general appetitive inclination to stand up for what is right; when we are consistently conscientious about telling the truth, we create in ourselves a general appetitive inclination to be truthful, and so on. These general appetitive inclinations serve as a help and a guide for reason. But Aquinas is clear that we cannot *cause* the supernatural version of those appetitive inclinations in ourselves, even by repeatedly acting in a manner befitting our participation in the divine life. Any appetitive habit ordered to our supernatural fulfillment must be bestowed by God. Aquinas's reason for holding that those appetitive inclinations must be bestowed by God is something we will unpack in this chapter.

THE INFUSED MORAL VIRTUES

Aquinas is clear that infused theological virtues are only the foundation of our order to supernatural beatitude: they give us the inception of our supernatural fulfillment that is the precondition of any order to supernatural beatitude. But he is also clear that the theological virtues, though necessary, are no more sufficient for the pursuit of supernatural beatitude than our natural habitual knowledge of first principles is for the pursuit of natural fulfillment. Just as we need the further perfection of both prudence and the acquired natural virtues in order to render those general principles specific in action, so, says Aquinas, do we need (infused) moral virtues in order to act in accord with our supernatural fulfillment: "In sum, we need not only the natural principles, but also the dispositions of the virtues, in order to be completed as human beings in the way that is natural to us, as I said above. Similarly, then, we have poured into us by God not only the supernatural *principles* just mentioned, but also certain infused *virtues*, through which we can be completed for doing whatever is ordered to the goal of eternal life."[16] This claim is worth thinking through carefully because it is important to understand both how Aquinas believes the infused moral virtues differ from their acquired counterparts and just how they contribute to supernatural flourishing. Aquinas's own remarks about the infused moral virtues can shed some light here. I focus in particular on two central differences: the difference in the appetitive inclinations themselves and the difference in the ways each type of virtue is cultivated.

The Difference between an Infused Virtue and an Acquired Virtue

In chapter 1, we saw that the acquired moral virtues do not merely make our appetites obedient to reason's command but that they also help to *guide* reason. They do this insofar as they give our appetites a general, "connatural" inclination to the ends of the various moral virtues: they make us "feel in our hearts" that the goals of the moral virtues are the right goals to have. To possess the virtue of truthfulness, say, is to feel a visceral repugnance for falsehood and a desire for the truth. A courageous person, by similarity, *wants* to stand up for what is right, not just in a concrete instance that demands it, but all the time. A similar account can be given of all the other moral virtues. An explanation like this already points to an explanation of why the infused moral virtues are necessary in the first place. There will need to be appetitive inclinations that help and guide reason formed by the theological virtues in the same way that the moral virtues help and guide our natural reason.

In order to better understand the appetitive inclinations that are the infused moral virtues, we will need to examine four things. First, why does Aquinas believe the infused moral virtues are necessary? Why, that is to say, are the appetitive inclinations that guide natural reason insufficient guides of a reason that has been reoriented to supernatural beatitude by the theological virtues? Second, we'll examine Aquinas's account of how the infused moral virtues grow and of how that growth is both similar to and different from the growth of the acquired moral virtues. Last, we take up the gifts of the Holy Spirit.

Aquinas consistently claims that the infused and acquired virtues "differ in species." Understanding what he means by this is vital to understanding what the infused moral virtues are. Aquinas grounds his account of the difference between the infused and acquired moral virtues in two central facts: the infused and acquired virtues arise from different "principles" and are ordered to different ends. Because of these two global differences, it will also be the case that the infused and acquired virtues seek a different "mean": that the infused and acquired virtues, though both having to do with the same "matter" (i.e., moderating the passions), produce different actions. This will be so even in cases where the actions they produce are outwardly indistinguishable.

In his more general treatment of habits, Aquinas asks "whether habits are distinguished by their objects."[17] He replies that a habit "is a certain disposition ordered toward two things, viz., a *nature* and an *operation* that follows upon the nature."[18] Habits can be distinguished in species in three ways. First, they "are distinguished by their active principles"; second, "with respect to a nature"; and third, "they are distinguished by their objects, which differ in species."[19] The establishment of any of these three differences will thus be sufficient evidence that one habit differs from another.

In both his *CS* and *ST* I-II, Aquinas devotes an article to the question of whether the infused virtues and acquired virtues are specifically different, and in both texts he answers in the affirmative. In the *CS*, however, Aquinas focuses on the first cause of specific difference, namely, a difference in active principles. Ends "are as principles in matters of action."[20] Just as a science that did not originate from natural principles would not have the same species as a science that did, so virtues that do not arise from natural principles cannot be of the same species as those that do. Since it has been well established that the virtues that order us to supernatural beatitude *cannot* arise from natural principles, it follows that they must also belong to a different species of virtue: "Since the ends of the infused virtues do not preexist in the seeds of the natural virtues, but exceed human nature, the infused virtues must differ in species from the acquired virtues, which proceed from those seeds."[21] On the basis of this discussion, Aquinas concludes that the infused and acquired virtues are ordered to different kinds of lives. The acquired are ordered to the good of the civic life, and the infused to the life of grace: "Hence acquired and infused virtues also perfect man in different kinds of life: the acquired virtues perfect him in civil life, while the infused virtues perfect him in spiritual life, which is from grace, according to which the virtuous man is a member of the Church."[22]

This early discussion makes no reference to the "mode" of the infused virtues. As we shall see in the next section's discussion of the gifts of the Holy Spirit, there is a good reason for this absence. But when Aquinas discusses the same question in *ST* I-II, he offers the "mode" as a further reason for a specific difference between the infused and acquired virtues. This difference is worth examining, both in its own right and in anticipation of our discussion of the gifts. In the *ST* as in the *CS*, Aquinas asks whether the infused and acquired virtues differ in species. Pointing to the text (I-II, q. 54, a. 1) addressed above, Aquinas reiterates his claim that habits are distinguished in species in two ways: first, "because of the specific and formal characters of their objects"[23]; and second, "according to what they are ordered toward."[24]

Aquinas's explanation of the second point largely reiterates the explanation he offers in the *CS*: a difference in what a virtue *is ordered to* also gives rise to a difference in species. A man's health is not the same as a horse's because their natures are different: men and horses are *ordered to* different things. Similarly, a difference in political regime also gives rise to different virtues. Thus "the infused moral virtues, through which men are related in the right way to being 'citizens with the saints of the household of God' (Ephesians 2:19)[,] differ in species from the other, acquired, virtues, by which a man is related in the right way to human affairs."[25]

In his explanation of the first point—that habits are distinguished by the specific and formal aspects of their objects—Aquinas goes beyond his earlier explanation. The object of a virtue "is the good considered in some proper subject matter." The object of temperance, for instance, "is the good of what is pleasurable in the sentient desires associated with the sense of touch." The formal aspect of temperance comes from reason, which institutes a *modus* in the sensible desires, while the material aspect comes from the sensible desires themselves.[26] The *modus* imposed on sentient desires by human reason, Aquinas insists, is *different* from that imposed by divine rule. With an eye toward our discussion of the gifts of the Holy Spirit in the next section, it is important to note the Latin word that is being used here: "mode." "Mode" is usually translated as "measure," which as we will see is consistent with Aquinas's own description of "mode."[27] The mode human reason imposes on desires is that they do not impede the use of reason, whereas the mode imposed by divine rule is that the desires be "castigated and brought into subjection."[28] Thus, Aquinas concludes that "it is clear that infused temperance and acquired temperance differ from one another in species. And this same line of reasoning holds for the other virtues."[29]

Aquinas's point here is a simple one: because the infused and acquired virtues are measured by a different standard, they each moderate the passions in a different way. This is directly relevant to his most commonly cited claim about the difference between the infused and acquired virtues, namely, that each virtue "seeks a different mean."

An immediate consequence of the different standards that guide the infused and acquired virtues, respectively, is the fact that the acts that are proportionate to those standards will also be different. This is another way of saying that each type of virtue will be found in a different mean: what is moderate by the standard of infused virtue might be excessive or deficient according to the standard of acquired virtue and vice versa. In *DQVG*, Aquinas makes this point explicit: "Infused temperateness and courage do not differ in type from acquired temperateness just in the fact that their actions are governed by charity. The difference, rather, is that reason determines the mid-point for their actions in a way that can order them to the ultimate end, which is the object of charity."[30]

The examples of the different means sought by infused and acquired temperance and fortitude are reiterated in both the *ST* I-II and the *CS*. The rule of reason demands that in our consumption of food we neither harm the body nor impede the use of reason. The divine rule, however, demands "that a man 'castigate his body and bring it into subjection' (1 Cor. 9:27)" through fasting from food and drink and other things of this sort.[31] That is to say, what is moderate according to the standards of acquired temperance is deficient according to the standards of infused temperance. Even in the *CS*, where (as we will see in our discussion of the gifts of the Holy Spirit) Aquinas does not appear to believe that the infused virtues involve a different "mode" of action, he nonetheless says that what is excessive according to the standards of civil (i.e., acquired) virtue, such as offering oneself "voluntarily to death for the sake of defending the faith," might be moderate according to the standards of infused virtue.[32]

In the context of explaining how the infused virtues and acquired virtues differ, Aquinas consistently refers to a respect in which they are the same: they have to do with the same "matter." In some places he seems to assert that individual *acts* of the infused and acquired virtues are the "same materially."[33] Elsewhere (and more consistently), Aquinas asserts that the infused and acquired *virtues* have the same "matter."[34] These claims are important, not least because scholars have interpreted them in various ways.[35] We will first look at Aquinas's claim that the infused and acquired virtues themselves "have the same matter," and then address the sense in which he believes that individual acts of infused and acquired virtue might have the same "matter."

The "matter" of a virtue, for Aquinas, is the power that the virtue habituates, a claim he makes explicitly in *DQVG* in response to the objection that infused and acquired virtues "agree in both matter and form" and hence cannot differ from each other.[36] The objector appeals to the example of temperance, arguing that infused and acquired virtues have both the same matter and the same form: "The activities of acquired and infused temperateness agree in their matter, for they both deal with things that are pleasurable to touch. They also agree in form, because they both consist in a mid-point."[37] Aquinas responds that infused and acquired temperance "agree in their matter, for they both deal with things that are pleasurable to touch,"[38] but argues that they do not have the same form: though each seeks a mean, each does so according to a different rule. Infused temperance looks for the mean that "accords with the reasons of God's law," while acquired temperance "takes a mid-point according to lesser reasons, ordered toward the good of this present life."[39]

Aquinas offers a similar explanation in the *CS* in the context of explaining why the acts of the infused and acquired virtues differ. Here he claims that acts of infused and acquired virtue "agree materially," but they have different forms because each seeks the midpoint according to different reasons. This is why each gives rise to different acts, and why what is excessive according to the standards of acquired virtue might be moderate according to the standards of infused virtue.[40]

It is clear from the context that when Aquinas says that the infused and acquired virtues "have the same matter," he means no more than that the acts of a given type of virtue, whether they are acts of infused or acquired virtue, moderate the same power of the soul. To say that infused and acquired temperance have the same "matter" merely means that they both habituate the pleasures of touch. Some scholars, however, take Aquinas's assertions about the "shared matter" of infused and acquired virtues to mean far more. For, in at least one text, Aquinas seems to indicate that not merely the infused and acquired *virtues* themselves but also their individual acts are "materially" the same. To say that acts of infused virtue are "materially" the same as acts of acquired virtue seems to imply not merely that they arise from the same power, but that they in fact also give rise to outwardly identical actions, that the same thing is done in each case, albeit perhaps for a different final goal. When we look at this text, however, it is clear that Aquinas is making a much more minimal claim. He is simply conceding that what infused virtue requires can *sometimes* be outwardly identical to what acquired virtue requires.

Even in making this concession, however, he reiterates that even when this outward identity is present, the acts themselves are still different.

In *CS*, in the context of arguing that the infused and acquired virtues are specifically different, Aquinas raises and responds to the following objection. Habits, the objector argues, "are specified by their acts and objects."[41] Since the infused and acquired virtues have the same act and the same object, they must belong to the same species of virtue.[42] Aquinas responds by arguing that *even when* acts of infused and acquired virtue are "materially the same" (outwardly identical), they are still different acts: "To the second it should be said that although the act of infused virtue and of acquired virtue is the same act materially, it is not the same act formally; for by acquired virtue the circumstances are limited according to proportion to the civil good, but by infused virtue according to proportion to the good of eternal glory."[43] Considered in isolation, this text could reasonably be read in more than one way. It could be read as saying either that (1) the acts of infused and acquired virtues are *always* materially the same or that (2) the acts of infused and acquired virtues are *sometimes but not always* materially the same. But when we read the remainder of the objection, the ambiguity is erased. Elaborating on the formal difference, Aquinas points out that infused and acquired virtues do not necessarily require us to perform outwardly identical acts: "Hence also something that is excessive according to civil virtue is moderate according to infused virtue, as for example that a man fast, and that he offer himself voluntarily to death for the sake of defending the faith."[44]

Infused virtues and acquired virtues, then, have the same matter: they both moderate the same power of the soul. Infused and acquired temperance both moderate the pleasures of touch. Infused and acquired courage both moderate feelings of fear and daring. But because infused and acquired virtues moderate those powers in a different way, the acts they give rise to might or might not be outwardly identical (i.e., materially the same). This conclusion is further evident in Aquinas's descriptions of the "proximate ends" or "objects" of each type of virtue. Acquired courage seeks to "establish man's spirit in human justice,"

62 *Aquinas and the Infused Moral Virtues*

while infused courage "strengthens the mind in God's justice."[45] The same is true of temperance. Similar accounts could be given of the other virtues. I will return to this point at the end of this chapter. First, it is important to address another important difference between the infused and acquired virtues, namely, that Aquinas believes the former not only can but should increase.

Growth in Infused Virtue

We've seen Aquinas's account of the difference between the infused and acquired moral virtues. Aquinas maintains that the former, unlike the latter, must necessarily be bestowed by God. He also maintains that they are bestowed all at once. This can give the (erroneous) impression that this is all there is to be said about the Christian moral life: we receive infused moral virtues from God, and then all that is left to do is practice them. In Aquinas's view, however, the divinely given gift of infused moral virtue is the true *beginning* of the Christian moral life, not its culmination. The infused moral virtues give us an initial appetitive inclination for their respective proximate ends. But Aquinas also maintains that (1) this gift is given differently to different persons, and (2) it is a gift that can be made use of or neglected. If we use it well, God will (typically) cause those initial appetitive inclinations to deepen and grow. Let's unpack these general claims, focusing specifically on (1) Aquinas's account of the gift of infused virtue itself, (2) the much-discussed question of whether and what kind of "facility" the infused virtues give, and (3) the question of what it means for the infused virtues to "increase." An increase in infused virtue is not to be confused with the degree of facility we experience in its acts. Far to the contrary, Aquinas understands "increase" to be a deepening in the "rootedness" of the appetitive inclination itself, and he describes this deepening in much the same way he describes the growth of an acquired habit.

Aquinas claims that the infused virtues are bestowed along with the gift of saving grace and remain as long as grace remains. This means that the infused virtues can come and go not only quickly but also—potentially—frequently. If, as he also holds, grace is lost in mortal sin and regained through repentance, someone who struggles with serious sin might gain and lose the infused virtues several times over the course of a month or a week or even a few days. A deeper and more important question, however, concerns the "amount" of infused virtue one possesses.

In his discussions of both charity and penance, Aquinas indicates that the gift of grace depends entirely on God's generosity, not on any human contribution. It is not merely that grace and the infused virtues are God's to bestow, but also that God does not bestow them equally. Nor does the "amount" we receive necessarily correspond to anything in us.

In *ST* II-II, q. 24, a. 3, Aquinas asks whether charity is infused in proportion to one's natural powers. He responds that the "quantity of any given thing depends on its cause."[46] Since charity exceeds all proportion to human nature, it "does not depend on any human power but only on the grace of the Holy Spirit who infuses it."[47] Thus, the gift does not depend on anything in us. Aquinas concludes by quoting scripture: "Every one of us is given grace according to the measure of the giving Christ."[48] The "amount" of charity we receive depends entirely on God, not on us. This is true even though Aquinas also holds that we can "dispose" ourselves to receive the gift of grace because he holds that it is the Holy Spirit who also "initiates this disposition or effort."[49]

Although Aquinas makes these comments in the context of explaining why the amount of charity we receive depends on God's gift rather than our own effort, nothing in his reply is specific to charity itself. To the contrary, his answer—which focuses on the fact that the cause is entirely external to us—holds true of all the other infused virtues, both theological and moral. It is therefore reasonable to conclude that he would give the same account of them.

We cannot really understand what it means to say that God bestows "more" infused virtue on some people than on others unless we understand what it means to possess more or less infused virtue. When scholars discuss the notion of growth in infused virtue, they often make much of the notion of "facility" and particularly of Aquinas's acknowledgment that we do not—at least at first—experience the same kind of facility in acts of infused virtue that we do in acts of acquired virtue. He does indeed make this claim, but it is also important to note that he does not equate growth in infused virtue with an increase in facility.

Aquinas holds that the infused virtues can exist alongside vicious dispositions in a way that their acquired counterparts cannot. Unlike Aristotle, Aquinas holds that even the acquired virtues do not completely remove conflicting desires. However, the acquired virtues do cause conflicting desires to diminish, and this diminishment is caused by the very process through which we acquire virtue: "When someone becomes accustomed to virtue through repeated actions, they then become unaccustomed to obey [vicious] emotions, and accustomed to resist them. The consequence is that they feel less troubled by them."[50] In the case of the acquired virtues, then, their very acquisition causes the struggle of the flesh against the spirit to be "felt less." The infused virtues, on the other hand, operate in a different way. The infused virtues cause it to be the case that we are in no way determined by the passions we feel, so that "if emotions of this sort are felt, they do not take control."[51] So long as the infused virtues are possessed, they enable us to "refrain totally from obeying sinful desires."[52] Rather than removing conflicting desires, then, the infused virtues allow us not to be ruled by the desires we feel.

Even if the infused virtues do not remove vicious desires, Aquinas gives some indication that vicious desires will diminish as one progresses in the life of infused virtue. In his reply to objection 15, which argues that the absence of pleasure is a sign of the absence of virtue, Aquinas modifies his earlier claim somewhat. Instead of saying that the infused virtues do *not* remove vicious dispositions, he says that they do "not always remove the experience of the emotions straight away in the way that acquired virtue does."[53] The implication is that with the continued practice of the infused virtues, contrary emotions *will* be removed or diminished. What is not found at any point in Aquinas's discussion, however, is a claim about precisely how those emotions are removed. I will return to this point in chapter 3.

Also ambiguous in Aquinas's account is the question of precisely *which* residual passions are potentially in conflict with the infused virtues. It is clear that he thinks residual vicious dispositions will impede the activity of the infused virtues. Yet if the infused and acquired virtues are found in a different mean, then it would seem that passions habituated to the activity of acquired virtues might *also* conflict with the activity of the infused virtues. If I habitually desire to eat the amount acquired virtue dictates (the amount conducive to bodily health and the optimal use of reason), then mightn't this too conflict with an infused temperance that seeks to castigate the body and bring it into subjection? Some scholars argue that it is *only* vicious dispositions that impede the activity of the infused virtues, but this seems to me to go considerably beyond Aquinas's text.[54] We will return to this point in chapter 3.

The important point for present purposes is that an increase in the "facility" with which one performs acts of infused virtues would seem to correspond to the removal of the obstacles that oppose such acts, namely, the obstacles presented by preexisting habits. The mere removal of an obstacle, however, does not *increase* the habit it opposes; it merely removes impediments to the practice of that habit. A good night's sleep does not make me smarter; it merely enables me to put the intellectual ability I already possess to the best use possible. And Aquinas is clear that he believes the infused virtues actually *increase* in a manner that parallels our attempts to cultivate them.

Aquinas devotes an entire article of *DQVG* to the question of how the infused cardinal virtues "increase." The language of size is unavoidable, but Aquinas argues that the "increase" of charity and the other infused virtues must be understood in terms of what they are: qualities. The "increase" of a quality, he argues, is "nothing other than a subject's sharing to an increasing degree in that quality," with the result that "the quality becomes more strongly active."[55] Charity and the other infused virtues "increase," then, insofar as they become "more strongly active" in us. This "increase" occurs when "the subject is brought to actualize them more fully, through the activity of the agent that causes them."[56]

In this last quote Aquinas repeats the same assertion he consistently makes elsewhere: not only are we unable to cause habits ordering us to supernatural beatitude in the first place, we are also unable to bring about their increase. If the theological and infused moral virtues grow in us, it will be thanks to God's free gift and not our own efforts. At the same time, however, Aquinas does hold that growth in the life of grace typically does at least *parallel* our own efforts. In his detailed discussion of charity in *ST* II-II, Aquinas claims that growth in charity "is in some way similar to a corporeal increase."[57] Plants and animals do not continually grow at each moment in time. To the contrary, "for a time nature operates to dispose the plant or animal for the increase and does not increase anything in actuality, and afterwards it produces the effect that it had disposed the subject for by increasing the plant or animal."[58] In the same way, each act of charity disposes us for an increase in charity, so that "by one act of charity a man is rendered more prompt to act out of charity once again."[59] As we become more prompt in our acts of charity, "man breaks out into a more fervent act of love by which he strives to make progress in charity, and it is at this point that charity increases in actuality."[60]

Aquinas's description of growth in charity (and by extension the other infused virtues) warrants our careful consideration. First, it is clear that Aquinas *does not* consider the increase of the "facility" with which we perform acts of infused virtue to itself be *growth* in infused virtue. Growth in charity occurs when we "break out into a more fervent act of love": to have more charity is to love God more fervently. The same, *mutatis mutandis*, would apply to the other acts of infused virtue. The promptness or easiness with which we perform these acts is thus in principle separable from the "amount" of infused virtue we possess. With practice, we find it easier to perform acts of infused virtue. But even if we perform them more easily, that ease is not itself an indication that our infused virtues have increased. Infused virtue does not actually increase until our appetitive inclination is itself intensified: until we break out "into a more fervent act of love."

The second important point to note about Aquinas's account is just how closely it parallels his account of growth in acquired habits. He here compares growth in charity (and by extension the other infused virtues) to the growth of a corporeal body. But what is easily overlooked is just how similar Aquinas's account of the growth of infused virtue is to his account of the growth of any habit whatsoever. In *ST* I-II, q. 52, he considers the growth of habits. Just as he will later do with charity, he asks whether habits can increase and whether they increase with every act. And just as he later does with charity, he asserts that growth in a habit (1) corresponds to the intensity with which one acts and (2) is similar to animal growth. When the intensity with which we act is proportionate to or even exceeds our habit, "then each such act either makes the habit grow or disposes one toward its growing."[61] The result, says Aquinas, is that "we speak of the growth of habits in a way similar to an animal's growth. For not every instance of food that is actually taken makes the animal grow, just as not every drop of water hollows out a rock; instead, as the food is multiplied, the growth comes in the end. So, too, as the acts are multiplied, the habit grows."[62]

A similar point can be made about Aquinas's account of the loss and diminishment, respectively, of the infused and acquired virtues. When he describes the increase and decrease of natural habits, he links growth in a habit to the "intensity" with which one acts. The mere possession of a habit is no guarantee that we will always act in a manner fully proportionate to it. Even those who are kind sometimes act with less kindness than they are capable of, and those who are unkind sometimes do kind things in spite of their overarching inclination. Aquinas claims that when our acts display less virtue than we are capable of, we dispose ourselves to a decrease in virtue: "If the act's intensity falls proportionately short of the habit's intensity, then such an act does not dispose one toward the growth of the habit, but rather disposes one toward a diminution in the habit."[63] He says more or less the same thing about the infused virtues, with this difference: our acts do not diminish the infused virtues, but they can dispose us to sin and thus to the loss of infused virtue altogether.

Aquinas, then, does not understand growth in infused moral virtue to merely consist in an increase in the "facility" with which one acts. Far to the contrary, facility can be present without an actual increase in virtue. An increase only occurs when we break out "into a more fervent act": when our appetitive inclination for the good increases. As importantly, Aquinas seems to understand growth in infused virtue in much the same way he understands growth in acquired virtue. This reaffirms our earlier observation: the initial gift of infused virtue marks the

THE GIFTS OF THE HOLY SPIRIT

The account offered thus far suggests a neat contrast between the infused and acquired moral virtues. The principles known through synderesis order us to the good commensurate to our created, human nature. It is in principle possible, albeit difficult, for reason to move from the general knowledge of synderesis to a correct conclusion about what is to be done and to act accordingly (this is what makes it possible for us to cultivate the acquired moral virtues in the first place). The acquired moral virtues, by inclining our appetites to the ends of the acquired moral virtues, help to guide reason. By making our appetites docile to reason's directives, the moral virtues also help to see to it that reason's commands are carried out. It would seem to follow that if we have both new first principles (thanks to the theological virtues) and correspondingly new appetitive inclinations (thanks to the infused moral virtues), our picture of action ordered to supernatural beatitude will be complete: we will perform acts ordered to supernatural beatitude when reason, helped and guided by the infused moral virtues, moves from the theological virtues to a correct conclusion about what is to be done. But any such claim would be not only premature but also an incorrect representation of Aquinas's view, for he is clear that unlike synderesis, we possess the theological virtues incompletely. They order us to a more perfect good, but our imperfect possession of them allows us to see that good only "through a glass darkly." The result is that reason is impaired in its ability to recognize what acts are proportionate to supernatural beatitude. The remedy for this deficiency, for Aquinas, is the Holy Spirit. Even after we receive the theological and infused moral virtues, Aquinas believes, we still need the help and guidance of the Holy Spirit if we are to act in a matter befitting supernatural beatitude. And he believes that the gifts of the Holy Spirit make this help and guidance possible. In Aquinas's view, even those who have received the theological virtues cannot perform acts ordered to supernatural beatitude without the additional and continual help and prompting of the Holy Spirit, but these promptings in no way diminish the freedom with which we act.

I now examine Aquinas's account of the gifts of the Holy Spirit. It should be noted, however, that the interpretation I offer is drawn primarily from Aquinas's mature treatment of the gifts. Aquinas's understanding of not just the gifts but also of the infused virtues evolves in important ways between his early *CS* and his later works. Thus, after offering an account of what I take to be Aquinas's mature understanding of the gifts, I will address the discrepancies between my account and the discussion found in his *CS*.

Aquinas's Mature Treatment of the Gifts

Aquinas discusses the gifts of the Holy Spirit in *ST* I-II, q. 68. Article 2 of that question asks whether the gifts are "necessary for salvation." Aquinas responds by returning to the distinction that led him to posit the theological virtues in the first place: our need for principles that order us to our end. He states that the theological virtues give us a perfection that is greater than that conferred by the knowledge of synderesis, but which at the same is possessed in a less complete way: "Even though this second sort of perfection is greater than the first, nonetheless, the first is had by a man in a more complete way than is the second. For the first sort of perfection is had by a man as a full possession, so to speak, whereas the second is had as an incomplete possession, since we know and love God in an incomplete way."[64] Our incomplete possession of the theological virtues forms the basis of Aquinas's assertion of our need for the gifts.

When something possesses a "nature or form" completely, says Aquinas, "then it can operate in its own right in accord with that nature or form," but when it possesses that nature or form incompletely, then "it cannot operate in its own right without being moved by another."[65] Since we possess the theological virtues incompletely, it follows that on Aquinas's account, we cannot operate in accord with them "in [our] own right": to act in accord with the theological virtues, we need to be moved by another. The examples Aquinas offers in support of this claim are dramatic and striking:

> If a thing has a nature or form (or virtue) incompletely, then it cannot operate in its own right without being moved by another. For instance, because the sun possesses light in a complete way, it can give light in its own right, whereas the moon, in which the nature of light exists incompletely, does not give light without itself being illuminated. Likewise, a physician who has complete knowledge of the art of medicine can work in his own right, whereas a student of his who has not yet been completely instructed cannot work in his own right without being instructed by the physician.[66]

Aquinas claims that our inability to act in accord with the theological virtues is akin to the moon's inability to give off light without the sun and the medical student's inability to work without the guidance of a teacher. Since we possess the natural principles that order us to our natural fulfillment perfectly, reason alone allows us to act in accord with our connatural end: "With respect to what falls under human reason, i.e., in relation to man's connatural end, a man can operate through the judgment of reason."[67] But since we imperfectly possess the supernatural principles that order us to our supernatural end, our reason is insufficient: it cannot on the basis of the theological virtues alone order our acts to supernatural beatitude. We need further assistance, and this assistance is provided in the form of the gifts of the Holy Spirit: "On the other hand, with respect to man's ultimate and supernatural end, toward which reason moves one insofar as it is formed in an incomplete way by the theological virtues, the movement of reason is not sufficient without the prompting and movement of the Holy Spirit from above."[68]

One could of course interpret the assertion that the movement of reason "is not sufficient without the prompting and movement of the Holy Spirit" in different ways. One might think "not sufficient" means not *always* sufficient (i.e., that reason formed by the theological virtues generally does a fairly good job moving toward one's supernatural end but sometimes needs extra help). Alternatively, one might think that Aquinas means that reason formed by the theological virtues is *always insufficient*. The first analogy Aquinas offers, that of the moon's inability to give off light without the sun, certainly implies that the latter is the case. The second analogy is less clear. Initially, a physician's student would seemingly be in almost the same position as the moon, unable to do anything at all without careful supervision. But the physician's student will become increasingly more capable of autonomous action. Aquinas is clear that the student in question "has not yet been completely instructed" but does not give any additional details. I think there is good reason, however, to assume that he thinks our need for the gifts is most akin to the moon's need for the sun and a beginning medical student's need for the physician's supervision.

Article 2, objection 2 argues that the gifts are unnecessary for salvation. Salvation requires that man "act well in relation to both divine matters and human matters."[69] Acting well in the latter is made possible by the moral virtues, and acting well in the former is made possible by the theological virtues, and hence the gifts are not necessary for salvation.[70] Aquinas's response indicates which of the two options described above he is inclined to accept. Aquinas replies that for the reasons he has already given, "a man is not perfected by the theological and moral virtues in such a way that he does not *always* need to be moved by the higher prompting of the Holy Spirit."[71] This reply seems to indicate that Aquinas clearly intends his assertion about our need for the gifts in the second sense: reason formed by the theological virtues is not just occasionally but *continually* in need of the prompting and movement of the Holy Spirit.

One further remark about the sense in which we are "always" in need of the guidance of the Holy Spirit is appropriate here. We can distinguish between the question of whether our reason might in fact reach the appropriate conclusion on its own and the question of whether we ought ever to be *confident* in our reason's ability to do so—whether we should ever be so confident that we feel no need to subject whatever our reason tells us to the guidance of the Holy Spirit. Even an advanced medical student should still look to the guidance of his teacher and seek his teacher's approval in all he does. An important upshot of Aquinas's treatment of the gifts, then, is this: we should always seek the Holy Spirit's guidance and always distrust the dictates of our own reason.

Aquinas believes that we are continually in need of the prompting of the Holy Spirit and thus that the gifts of the Holy Spirit, which make this prompting possible, are "necessary for salvation." But we have still not said very much at all about what the gifts are or what they do. Aquinas holds that the gifts of the Holy Spirit are divinely infused habits that make us receptive to the movement or "instinct" of the Holy Spirit. Let's consider his description of the gifts as "habits" and then the more important and more central claim, namely, that they render us amenable to the *instinctus* of the Holy Spirit.

Aquinas compares the way in which the gifts render us receptive to the movement of the Holy Spirit to the way that the moral virtues render the appetites of the soul receptive to the command of reason. Just as the moral virtues dispose our appetites to obey reason promptly, so too do the gifts of the Holy Spirit dispose us to be receptive to the Holy Spirit's promptings. Just as it is by a habit that our appetites are made receptive to the command of reason, so too is it by habits—albeit divinely infused ones—that we are made receptive to the promptings of the Holy Spirit.

Because Aquinas says that the gifts of the Holy Spirit are divinely given habits, it can be tempting to think of them as virtues, or to think that they are somehow identical to or interchangeable with the infused moral virtues. This would be a mistake. When Aquinas addresses the difference between virtues and gifts, he agrees they are similar in at least one respect: gifts, like the virtues, are habits that perfect us for acting well.[72] But, says Aquinas, whereas a virtue perfects us with respect to our *own* motion, a gift perfects us with respect to God's motion.[73] We need divine counsel in order to act rightly, and the gifts make us receptive to this help. The gifts, says Aquinas, make us "promptly moveable by God's inspiration."[74] Virtues, then, are habits that perfect us with respect to what we ourselves do, but gifts make us receptive to God's help. Obviously the two sets of habits will interact. A fundamental point of our discussion here has been the insufficiency of the theological and infused moral virtues: we cannot on the basis of them alone deliberate correctly about what acts are befitting our order to supernatural beatitude. The gifts, by enabling us to receive God's help, remedy this insufficiency.

It is worth noting that the habits that enable us to receive the promptings of the Holy Spirit are found not merely in the intellect, but in *all* the powers of the soul. Speculative reason is perfected for the apprehension of truth by the gift of understanding, and practical reason by the gift of counsel. Speculative reason is perfected in its ability to judge correctly by wisdom, and practical reason by the gift of knowledge. The appetitive powers, on the other hand, are perfected by the gifts of piety, fortitude, and fear. The fact that the gifts inhere in more than merely our intellectual powers is important, for two reasons. First, gifts do not merely enable us to receive some kind of intellectual or propositional knowledge. Second, the metaphor of sight, which is sometimes used to describe what it is the gifts of the Holy Spirit enable, is inadequate. The gifts of the Holy Spirit make us receptive to its promptings. The Holy Spirit may well prompt our deliberation, but it might well also prompt our appetites.

How should the "prompting" of the Holy Spirit be understood? Aquinas's account of this prompting is informed by scripture, which refers not to "gifts" but to "spirits": "Upon him will rest the spirit of wisdom and understanding."[75] On the basis of this understanding of scripture, Aquinas proposes that the spirits referred to "exist in us by divine inbreathing [inspiration]."[76] Since "inbreathing" implies that we are moved by something outside of us, Aquinas proposes that we need something in us that is receptive to that motion, namely, habits (the gifts) that dispose us to receive them.

It is worth unpacking how the Holy Spirit "inspires" us.[77] Servais Pinckaers has noted that Aquinas's account offers a way in which the Holy Spirit can prompt and guide us in our actions without destroying our own free will in acting: "This is the peculiar effect of inspiration or of the gifts: to achieve the unity of action between the superior principle, which is God's Spirit, and the interior principles which are virtues, at the level of our free and reasonable will, at the source of our actions."[78] The Holy Spirit offers counsel, helps our judgment, and helps us experience the right appetitive movements, but it does not act

74 *Aquinas and the Infused Moral Virtues*

or choose for us. Aquinas's use of the word *instinctus*, Pinckaers argues, is perfectly suited for this idea: "It refers to an interior impulse, whose origin is nevertheless exterior, or rather superior ... it is a spiritual instinct, a Spirit that inclines us in a very personal way toward truth and the divine goods that are revealed to us."[79] In providing us with this spiritual instinct, the Holy Spirit goes beyond what our reason and our appetites can do on their own and helps us to experience what we are otherwise unable to see or feel.

Gifts in the *Commentary on the Sentences*

This chapter is devoted to the "structure" of supernatural virtue. Supernatural virtues parallel the natural virtues in important ways, but because the theological virtues are less perfectly possessed, reason formed by them cannot determine us to act in a manner commensurate to supernatural beatitude without assistance, even though reason formed by the natural principles *can* order us to our supernatural fulfillment. This additional assistance comes through the movement, or *instinctus*, of the Holy Spirit, which the gifts make possible. In order to highlight this point, I have focused entirely on the account of the gifts found in *ST* I-II. Those familiar with the literature on the gifts, however, will be aware that many Thomists have historically offered a very different interpretation of the gifts of the Holy Spirit. According to that interpretation, the gifts of the Holy Spirit are not present in every action ordered to supernatural beatitude, but only assist us occasionally in a special, spiritual way.

Réginald Garrigou-Lagrange, in particular, maintains that acts of the theological and infused virtues are completely separate from acts of the gifts of the Holy Spirit. He compares the activity of the former to "rowing" toward the goal through our own power and the latter to "sailing" toward it, moved by the "wind" of the Holy Spirit.[80] Garrigou-Lagrange argues that the infused virtues and the gifts represent different "modes" of action. When we act according to the former, we act according to human reason. The reason that guides acts of infused virtue is formed by faith, but it is still *human* reason: we deliberate and act on the basis of our own power, just as we might row a boat toward a goal. The gifts, on the other hand, are like sails: they enable us to be propelled by a different kind of motion altogether. In Garrigou-Lagrange's telling, the Christian is like a boat with both oars and sails: we can pursue supernatural beatitude through our own efforts (the oars), or we can catch a favorable wind in our sails.[81] He acknowledges that one might row while also catching wind, but he clearly does not think this is the typical case. He also insists that the gifts are "latent" in all but the mystical life, that in the typical case the motion of the Holy Spirit is both rare and hidden.[82] And although it seems quite plausible that the motion of the Holy Spirit would be hidden, that is, that we might be unaware of its motion, it is less clear that its motion would be rare. Such a thesis seems hard to reconcile with scripture, for Christ tells us that the Holy Spirit is our inheritance: the guide that will be with us when He cannot. It also seems hard to reconcile with Aquinas's claims that the gifts are bestowed along with grace, that they are necessary for salvation, and that we "always" need the motion of the Holy Spirit in order to act in a manner befitting supernatural beatitude.

The most central claims made by Garrigou-Lagrange are based on remarks that Aquinas makes in *CS*. Everyone agrees that there is a shift in Aquinas's account of the gifts of the Holy Spirit between the *CS* and *ST*. In the *CS*, Aquinas is concerned with the "mode" of action the gifts make possible, but in the *ST* he is primarily focused on what the gifts do, namely, allow us to receive the *instinctus* of the Holy Spirit. What everyone disagrees about is whether those differences mean that Aquinas's understanding of the gifts changes between the two works.[83]

I next offer my own view of this shift. Against those who explain the difference by arguing that the mature Aquinas discards the notion of a "mode" of action that features so prominently in *CS*, I argue that the notion of "mode" in fact takes on an even more central role than it previously did, so that it is not just the gifts of the Holy Spirit, but in fact all the supernatural virtues that operate according to a different mode. In Aquinas's mature account, the gifts of the Holy Spirit aren't themselves the different mode of action but are instead necessary components of the different mode of action itself.

In his early *CS*, Aquinas describes the gifts as making a different "mode" of action possible. In *CS* III, d. 34, a. 1, Aquinas asks whether the gifts are virtues. He replies that the gifts are given "for higher acts than the acts of the virtues" and proceeds to explain what he means by "higher." An act is called human because (1) it is elicited or commanded by human reason, (2) it has human "passions or actions" as its matter, or (3) "by reason of its mode."[84] An act is said to be above the human "mode" when one "carries out human things in a way that is above the human mode."[85] When this occurs, "the act will be not simply human but in a certain way divine."[86] This third way, says Aquinas, is the way in which the gifts are given for acts that are "higher" than the acts of the virtues. Aquinas returns repeatedly to the notion that the gifts make a higher "mode" of action possible in his discussions of the individual gifts. For instance, he says that virtues such as justice, liberality, and magnificence regulate our passions well in accord with reason, on the basis of the good of those with whom we interact, and thus help us to act well in the human "mode." But for the same interactions to be regulated "on the basis of the divine good, and thus not limited only to granting so much to the other as is due him or as is beneficial for the one who gives, but as much as the divine good that shines out in himself or in his neighbor is pleasing to God—this is above the human mode."[87] In order for our actions to achieve this higher mode, then, Aquinas posits that we need the gift of piety, which allows us to be moved by the Holy Spirit.[88] He offers similar accounts of the other gifts.

Since the term "mode" figures so prominently in Aquinas's account, it is important to understand precisely what he means by it, especially in this particular context. Aquinas uses "mode" in a variety of places, and he is clear about what he understands the word to mean. "Mode," Aquinas states earlier in his *CS*, "implies a measuring."[89] Reason is said to place a "mode" on the moral virtues insofar as it orders and directs the appetites, making them commensurate with its own rule. Aquinas claims that reason directs "the very passions and actions in themselves, insofar as it brings them to a mean according to a certain commensuration, and thus it is said to place a mode in them, since mode implies a measuring."[90] It would follow, therefore, that to bring passions and actions to a mean according to some other commensuration would be to place a *different* mode in them.

At this point, Aquinas's mature description of the difference between the infused and acquired moral virtues falls into place, for Aquinas in his mature writings distinguishes the natural and supernatural (or acquired and infused) virtues on *precisely the same grounds*— each brings man into conformity with a different rule; each is measured by a different standard. The natural virtues are measured by the rule of reason, while the supernatural virtues are measured by God's rule. The infused virtues, that is to say, are ordered to and make possible a different "mode" of action, because they are measured by a different rule. Aquinas does not appeal to this distinction in *CS* but only to the different lives each type of virtue belongs to. If we carry the line of reasoning through, it would seem to follow that the mature Aquinas believes that simply by being ordered to supernatural beatitude and therefore being measured by a different rule and hence lying in a different mean, all of the infused moral virtues already belong to the higher mode described in the *CS*. The mature Aquinas simply realizes that that higher mode of action still cannot take place without the continual guidance and prompting of the Holy Spirit.

STRUCTURAL SIMILARITIES

We have necessarily taken a narrow focus in this chapter, but it is also helpful to take a step back and summarize the general parallels between the infused virtues and the acquired virtues.

It is abundantly clear that Aquinas believes the theological virtues give us a knowledge and desire for supernatural beatitude that is analogous to the knowledge of our natural fulfillment given by synderesis and the subsequent desire for that fulfillment it causes. But the former knowledge and desire, though more perfect, is less perfectly possessed: we cannot render it specific in action in the way we can render our natural, habitual knowledge of synderesis specific.

Our imperfect possession of the theological virtues has another consequence: reason, even when formed by the theological virtues, cannot by itself incline our appetites to supernatural beatitude. At the natural level, repeated good acts create an inclination in our passions, which causes them not merely to be obedient to reason, but to actually desire in a general way the ends of the moral virtues. My repeated acts of acquired courage cause me to become the sort of person who *wants* to fight for what is right in a general way all the time. My repeated acts of acquired temperance cause me to become the sort of person who wants, again in a general way, to eat and drink the amount conducive to the good of reason. The same will hold true of all the other moral virtues. As we saw in chapter 1, even when we receive assistance in our deliberations, at the natural level reason is the *cause* of the move from our general, natural knowledge of first principles to a correct conclusion about what is to be done. Reason, even formed by the theological virtues, is not a cause in the same way. Not only our reason but even our appetites need the help and guidance and prompting of the Holy Spirit in order to act in a manner commensurate with supernatural beatitude. Just as importantly, our repeated acts cannot cause our appetites to incline to acts befitting our supernatural good, nor can they make our appetites appropriately responsive to supernatural reasons. This is why Aquinas posits not only the gifts of the Holy Spirit but also the infused moral virtues.

We now have a general picture of the respective structures of the infused and acquired moral virtues. Aquinas's account of infused virtue clearly relies on the framework of the acquired virtues in important ways. It centers around the foundational notion that we have principles pointing us to our ends, that right action requires not just reason but also the right ordering of our appetites. Aquinas's account of infused virtue also reveals just how deeply he believes human beings need divine assistance. The Christian moral life is not simply a matter of redirecting natural abilities to a new end; it is in every sense a *rebirth*. And even as we are reborn, our steps are uncertain and unsure: we need divine guidance at every turn.

All of this raises an important question. Aquinas's Aristotelian account of nature's capacity for natural virtue clearly plays a foundational role for his account of infused virtue. But do the acquired virtues play *any other* role? Does he envision a place for them in the Christian moral life at all? Do they somehow assist the work of the infused moral virtues? Would such assistance even be coherent? A great deal of ink has been spilled on such questions, and we will examine some of that discussion in chapters 4 to 6. First, however, it is important to get clear on what Aquinas himself does and does not say about such questions.

CHAPTER 3

Relating the Virtues

Aquinas's Texts

So far I have compared the "structure" of Aquinas's accounts of natural and supernatural virtue and argued that Aquinas's account of infused virtue looks to and grows out of his Aristotelian understanding of nature. We are still left, however, with the question of whether and to what extent Aquinas believes the infused virtues and acquired virtues interact. In spite of the many claims attributed to him, Aquinas himself says very little about this topic. In what follows, I will first make some general remarks on what it would mean for the infused and acquired virtues to be "related." Then I will examine two sets of texts: (1) texts typically cited as evidence of Aquinas's views about the relationship between the infused and acquired virtues and (2) the scattered texts where Aquinas does directly refer to the relationship between the infused and acquired virtues. I will argue that the first set of texts falls far short of establishing the claims it is cited in support of, and that the second set—to the extent it implies anything at all—implies that Aquinas believes the Christian's infused and acquired virtues are each operative in distinct arenas of the Christian moral life.

RELATING THE VIRTUES

Aquinas maintains that the infused theological and moral virtues and the gifts of the Holy Spirit are bestowed all at once, along with grace, in baptism. This means that some people—those baptized in infancy—receive all the infused moral virtues before they ever attempt to cultivate the natural virtues. It also means that others—those who convert as adults—receive the infused moral virtues after they have spent a life cultivating other habits, good or bad. Moreover, if one also holds—as Aquinas does—that one can receive and lose (and, in repentance, receive again) an order to supernatural beatitude over the course of a life, then this means that the virtues that are gifts of grace can be lost and bestowed repeatedly.

All of these possibilities raise a series of questions. First, does Aquinas think that someone who possesses the infused virtues also needs to cultivate the acquired natural virtues? If he does, what role do those virtues play in the Christian moral life? Second, what does Aquinas believe happens to any existing natural virtues in conversion? Are they somehow transformed or "taken up" into the supernatural virtues, so that the Christian possesses one and only one type of virtue, namely, infused virtue? Or do they remain distinct? If they remain distinct, then how, if at all, do the two types of virtue interact? I will refer to questions like these as questions about how the infused and acquired virtues are "related."

The work of chapters 1 and 2 indicates two broad paths a theory of the relationship between the infused and acquired virtues might take. Aquinas holds that we cannot be ordered to supernatural beatitude without a change in our natural habitual order to our commensurate good—a change in the very principles that enable us to act in the first place. Aquinas also maintains that the virtues we can acquire through our own repeated good acts arise from the principles of, and are ordered to the good commensurate with, our created human nature. We cannot produce acts ordered to supernatural beatitude without "new" principles of action ordering us to that further end, namely, the theological virtues. Aquinas believes that even with these new principles we still need the guidance of the Holy Spirit and need appetitive inclinations ordered to our supernatural good. It is clear, then, that the answers to the questions raised above will depend heavily on the relationship between our natural principles of action and the supernatural principles we receive along with the gift of grace. But we can understand that relationship in different ways.

On the one hand, we could take Aquinas to mean the natural principles that order us to the good proportionate to our nature are themselves transformed by grace. On this view, both our natural habitual knowledge of the first principles of speculative and practical reason and our consequent natural desire for the fulfillment commensurate with our created nature are formed by faith, hope, and love. What we naturally know and desire is not lost; it is simply known and desired in a new way, in the context of a higher and infinitely more perfect end. If this is what Aquinas envisions, then it would seem to follow that there is also only one kind of virtue that is relevant to the Christian moral life: the virtue that enables us to act in a manner befitting our transformed first principles. One could, of course, give any number of explanations of what "happens" to any preexisting natural virtues or of whether and how natural virtue might reappear after the loss of grace, but if the principles that order us to virtue are indeed transformed by grace, there would seem to be no coherence to the idea that there is a role for the cultivation of natural virtue in the Christian moral life. I will refer to this view as the "unification" view.

On the other hand, we could take Aquinas to mean that the new principles given in the gift of grace do not replace but somehow exist alongside our natural principles. On this view, the Christian would have two sets of principles and hence be capable of two different kinds of virtuous action. When acting from his natural principles, the Christian could perform acts ordered to his natural fulfillment, and when acting from his supernatural principles (and the habits given to assist acting in accord with them), he would perform acts ordered to his supernatural fulfillment. On such an interpretation, grace also removes the effects of original sin so that when we cultivate the natural virtues we do so without the impediments the pagan experiences. I will call this view the "coexistence" view.[1]

Whether one opts for a coexistence or a unification view of the relationship between the virtues is directly and necessarily related to whether one thinks that the principles given in grace transform our natural principles or simply exist alongside them. And on this latter question Aquinas says virtually nothing. He says in some places that the supernatural principles are given *in loco quorum* or *supra*, which could be taken as an indication he holds the unification view.[2] But he also says in other places that supernatural principles have to be "added" [*superaddantur*], which could be taken to imply a coexistence view.[3]

Aquinas is ambiguous about how he envisions the relationship between the natural and supernatural principles, but he is slightly less ambiguous about how he envisions the relationship between the infused and acquired virtues themselves. However, he is much more ambiguous about this question than many scholars claim. In what follows, I will examine some claims commonly attributed to Aquinas. Although most of them establish next to nothing about how he envisions the relationship between the infused and acquired virtues, some texts do imply a view. That view, however, is one that few contemporary scholars (myself included) would want to defend. I divide the texts I consider into two groups: those that are overinterpreted and commonly but incorrectly used as "evidence" that Aquinas ascribes to a certain view about the relationship between the infused and acquired virtues; and then texts that do genuinely seem to imply something about Aquinas's view.

THE ACQUIRED VIRTUES AS SUPPORTING ACTORS

Scholars commonly argue that Aquinas believes the acquired virtues support the infused virtues in some way. As these scholars interpret him, Aquinas makes one or more of the following assertions: (1) the practice of the infused virtues "strengthens" the acquired virtues, (2) the cultivation of acquired virtues "facilitates" the activity of infused virtue, or (3) the cultivation of acquired virtues "fills out" the infused virtues.[4]

ST I-II, q. 51, a. 4, ad 3, and *DQVG* a. 10, ad 19

Many scholars, citing either *ST* I-II, q. 51, a. 4, ad 3, or a parallel text, have argued that Aquinas believes that acts of infused virtue "strengthen" existing acquired virtues.[5] Those who make this claim typically seem to mean that the infused virtues "perfect" existing acquired virtues. John

Inglis, for instance, after stating that Aquinas holds that the infused virtues "strengthen" the acquired virtues, proposes that this text means that the infused virtues make existing acquired virtues more perfect. One might, for instance, have already acquired moderate eating habits. Infused temperance, he proposes, would add to these habits an infused strength.[6] Gilson, citing the same text as Inglis does, claims that the infused virtues "add to" the acquired virtues and "bring them to their perfection."[7] It is worth noting that if it could indeed be shown that Aquinas holds such a position, we would have come a long way toward solving the question of how he understands the relationship between the infused and acquired virtues; for an answer like this implies that the infused virtues simply serve to make existing acquired virtues more perfect and do not have a separate, independent role or function. However, any such claim goes far beyond the details of the text itself.

The text most commonly cited in defense of this claim is *ST* I-II, q. 51, a. 4, ad 3, but since the remarks Aquinas makes there are virtually identical to those he makes in *Disputed Questions on the Virtues in General (DQVG)* and in his discussion of the increase of charity in *ST* II-II, I discuss all of these texts together. What Aquinas consistently asserts is *not* that acts of infused virtue strengthen the acquired virtues, but rather that acts of infused virtue strengthen the infused virtue that produced those acts in the first place.

ST I-II, q. 51, a. 4, asks "whether any habits are infused into man by God."[8] Objection 3 argues that habits are not infused by God, for the following reason. If we received a habit from God, then we would be able to make use of it in our actions. But repeated acts of that divinely given habit would in turn also cause us to acquire a habit, with the result that we would have an infused and an acquired version of the same habit.[9] Since this is impossible, the objector argues, it cannot be the case that God infuses habits in us. This is virtually the same objection that appears in objection 19 of article 10 of *DQVG*.[10]

In both texts, Aquinas offers similar replies. In the *ST* I-II text, he replies that the infused virtues "strengthen the preexisting habit" in the way that medicine strengthens existing health: "The acts that are produced by an infused habit do not cause any habit but instead strengthen the pre-existing habit, in the same way that medicine given to a man who is through his nature healthy does not cause health but instead strengthens the health that was had beforehand."[11] In *DQVG*, he responds that acts of infused virtue strengthen a preexisting habit in the same way acts of acquired virtue do: "The activities of infused virtues do not bring about any disposition but strengthen a pre-existing disposition. Indeed, not even the actions of an acquired virtue actually generate a further disposition; otherwise, our dispositions would be multiplied indefinitely."[12] Although each reply is clear enough in its own right, when both replies are considered together and in the context of the objections they are replying to, it seems clear that Aquinas is *not* claiming that acts of infused virtue strengthen the acquired virtues, but instead making a more minimal and moderate claim: acts of infused virtue strengthen the infused virtue that produced them.

The question at issue is whether the "preexisting disposition" that acts of an infused virtue strengthen is the infused virtue itself: the virtue that originally produced the act, or some other acquired disposition? Even apart from considerations of context, the former interpretation seems far more plausible than the latter. In the first place, there is no reason to assume that the agent performing the act of infused virtues possesses a corresponding acquired disposition that *could be* strengthened. In the second, Aquinas's supporting remarks also go against such an interpretation. Medicine does not create a *new kind* of health but strengthens the health that already exists. Even acts of acquired virtue do not create *a new disposition*, but strengthen an existing disposition. In both cases, Aquinas seems to be talking about one and only one disposition and asserting that the disposition is itself strengthened. When we consider Aquinas's remarks in the context of the objections they are replying to, this is even more apparent.

Aquinas is replying to the objection that acts of infused virtue would create not just an acquired virtue, but an acquired virtue that would be *of the same species* as an infused virtue, which is impossible. Aquinas responds that acts of infused virtue don't create a virtue at all. Indeed, even acts of acquired virtue don't create a new virtue. They strengthen the virtue that produced them. Far from asserting that acts of infused virtue strengthen an entirely different species of virtue, the most logical interpretation of these remarks is that Aquinas is merely making a point about how any virtue—infused or acquired—increases. Acts of a virtue don't create a new virtue, or else virtues would be multiplied indefinitely. Acts of a virtue simply strengthen the virtue that produced them.[13]

ST I-II, q. 65, a. 3, ad 2, and *DQVG* a. 10, ad 14

Interpreters of Aquinas frequently claim that he believes the acquired virtues support or "facilitate" acts of the infused virtues; that the infused virtues are somehow completed by or reliant upon the acquired virtues for their successful action.[14] The infused virtues, they argue, make right action possible, but not easy. In order to experience the kind of pleasure and ease that one typically expects of a virtue, they argue that one must cultivate the acquired virtues. A Christian who has successfully cultivated the corresponding acquired virtues will experience the pleasure and ease that would otherwise be absent from his acts of infused virtue. Only these individuals can truly be called virtuous. Indeed, some scholars even argue that without the support of the corresponding acquired virtues, the infused virtues cannot really be considered virtues at all. Andrew Dell'Olio, for instance, says that "infused virtues, without the facility or ability that comes with acquired virtues, are habits only in an analogous sense. For they lack the ease or facility of operation that characterize a habit in the strict sense."[15]

The text most commonly cited in support of the claims above is *ST* I-II, q. 65, a. 3, ad 2. Since this text is very similar to *DQVG* a. 10, ad 14, I consider them together.[16] Both texts address the question of whether all the moral virtues are infused along with grace.[17] The same objection is raised: if the moral virtues were infused all at once along with grace, then those in a state of grace ought to find acts of moral virtue easy and pleasant. But it is clear that many of those in a state of grace do not experience ease and pleasure in their actions. Therefore, the moral virtues are not bestowed along with grace.[18]

In both places, Aquinas offers a similar reply. It is possible, Aquinas argues in his *ST* I-II response, to possess a habit and yet, because of some "external impediment," not experience ease and enjoyment in the acts it produces. Someone with the habit of scientific knowledge, for instance, can have trouble understanding because he is tired or sick.[19] Similarly, habits acquired by previous acts can impede the activity of the infused virtues: "Habits of the infused moral virtues sometimes experience difficulty in acting because of certain contrary dispositions that are left over from previous acts."[20] This problem does not arise for the acquired virtues, however, because the very process of their acquisition drives out contrary desires: "This sort of difficulty does not occur in the same way in the case of the acquired moral virtues, because contrary dispositions are removed through the exercise of the acts by which those virtues are acquired."[21]

Aquinas's response in the *DQVG* is similar but more detailed. Neither the acquired nor the infused virtues, Aquinas argues, completely remove opposing desires, for "the flesh lusts against the spirit and the spirit against the flesh."[22] But both the acquired and infused virtues — albeit in different ways — cause it to be the case that we are not moved by our desires "in an unrestrained way."[23] The very process of acquiring the natural virtues means that we feel opposing desires less because "when someone becomes accustomed to virtue through repeated actions, they then become unaccustomed to obey those emotions, and accustomed to resist them."[24] But the infused virtues cause it to be the case that even if we *feel* those desires, "they do not take control."[25]

I have examined both of these texts in detail because it is important to notice what claims they do and do not commit Aquinas to. In both, Aquinas offers a contrast: the acquired virtues allow us to overcome sinful emotions in one way, while the infused virtues allow us to overcome them in another. Aquinas also asserts that the mere presence of sinful desires is not itself evidence of an absence of infused virtue. But in neither text does Aquinas make the claim so frequently attributed to him: that the cultivation of the acquired virtues makes the practice of the infused virtues easier.

ST II-II, q. 47, a. 14, ad 1, and *DQVC* a. 2, ad 3

The final texts to examine in this section are those cited in support of the claim that Aquinas believes the acquired virtues somehow "complete" the infused virtues.[26] This general claim is rooted in a claim that

Aquinas makes in his discussion of prudence. Many scholars interpret Aquinas as saying that prudence is "fuller" in some people than it is in others, and that the "fullness" of prudence consists in a union of infused and acquired prudence. Josef Pieper, for instance, says that: "It is true that every Christian receives in baptism, along with the new life of friendship with God, a supernatural 'infused' prudence. But, says Thomas, this prudence granted to every Christian is limited solely to what is necessary for his eternal salvation; there is, however, a different, 'fuller' prudence, not immediately granted in baptism. . . . This is that prudence in which supernatural grace has united with the 'prerequisite' of a naturally perfected ability."[27] Other scholars make similar claims.

Precisely what it means to say that an acquired virtue "completes" or "fills out" an infused virtue is unclear, of course, because one would first need some account of the relationship between the virtues. If Aquinas believes that the Christian cultivates one kind of virtue in one area of life and another kind of virtue in another, then one could see how a "full" or "complete" virtue would mean the full possession of both types of virtue. If the infused and acquired virtues play supporting roles in each individual act, then the cultivation of the one would also "complete" the other, but in a different way. If the acquired virtues are altogether transformed by grace, so that the Christian possesses *only* infused virtues, the claim would have to mean something still different (though what, I am not sure). For the moment, however, we will simply consider the texts themselves. Far from asserting that the acquired virtues complete the infused, the texts in question are not concerned with *virtue* at all but with the abilities it presupposes. Moreover, any assertion they make about infused virtue could be made equally about acquired virtue.

In his treatment of prudence in *ST* II-II, Aquinas asks whether all who have grace also have prudence. Objection 1 argues that not all those who have grace have prudence, for the following reason: a person cannot have prudence unless he also possesses "a certain sort of diligence [*industria*]."[28] Since many of those who have grace lack this *industria*, it cannot be the case that they possess prudence. Aquinas replies that there are two kinds of *industria*. One kind, which "suffices for what is necessary for salvation," is given to all who have grace.[29] Another "fuller" kind of *industria*, however, enables its possessor "to provide for himself and others not only in those matters that are necessary for salvation, but also in everything that pertains to human life."[30]

The first crucial point to make about this text is that neither the objector nor Aquinas is focused directly on prudence itself, let alone on a "fuller" prudence. Each is focused on *industria*, something they both agree is a necessary prerequisite of prudence. If we are to accurately evaluate this text, we first have to understand what Aquinas means by *industria*.

Aquinas's varied uses of *industria* indicate that it refers to what we might call "purposeful action," the kind of effort we exhibit in a deliberate effort. For instance, Aquinas sometimes contrasts sins committed through *industria* from those committed in passion.[31] He also argues that those not naturally inclined to modesty can alter that inclination through *industria*.[32] Thus, *industria* seems simply to refer to conscious, deliberate effort. We can, as Aquinas indicates in the text at hand, exhibit this effort in any number of areas of life. We can exhibit *industria* in improving our golf swings, in keeping our homes clean, or in being good students. Some people exhibit more *industria* than others. What is required for the possession of the infused virtue of prudence, however, is not *industria* in everything, but only in those matters "necessary for salvation," and Aquinas tells us that this kind of *industria* is given to all who have grace. But there is, he tells us, also a "fuller" *industria* that allows one to provide well for oneself in all areas of life, and this is not in all who have grace.

A considerable leap is required to move from Aquinas's remarks about this precondition of virtue to the claim commonly attributed to him, namely, that the cultivation of acquired prudence "fills out" infused prudence. To see just how dramatic this leap is, it is helpful to notice that we could potentially make a virtually identical claim about *industria* and acquired prudence. When we say that an individual possesses acquired prudence, we mean that he deliberates and acts in a manner commensurate with his natural fulfillment. In order to do so, he clearly needs to exhibit the necessary *industria*. But does an individual who possesses acquired prudence need to exhibit similar *industria* in everything he does? Does he need to possess the *industria* that "enables him to provide well for himself in all areas of life"? Surely not, unless we wish to narrow the domain of the virtuous to the vanishing point. Is it possible to possess a high degree of prudence and be absentminded or unorganized? We all have acquaintances who, in spite of being clearly unable to "provide well" for themselves in many areas of life, also clearly seem to possess a high degree of prudence. An inability to provide well for oneself in an area of life is *only* evidence of a lack of virtue—natural or supernatural—if that inability prevents one from acting in a manner commensurate with one's natural or supernatural fulfillment. And Aquinas's own texts seem to indicate that he does not understand virtue in this way.

In his general discussion of virtue in *ST* I-II, Aquinas asks whether it is possible to have moral virtue without intellectual virtue. In response to the objection that many of those who are virtuous have deficient reason, Aquinas argues that virtue does not require that one be able to reason well in *all* areas of life, but "only with respect to what has to be done in accord with virtue."[33] It is only with respect to this—with respect to what is in accord with virtue—that "the use of reason is strong in all virtuous individuals."[34] Aquinas claims that this is why "even those who seem simple because they lack worldly wisdom [*carent mundana astutia*] can be prudent."[35] Aquinas makes this statement again in his *Disputed Questions on the Cardinal Virtues* (*DQVC*) in response to the objection that not all who are baptized are prudent. The objector points out that many of those who have been baptized, such as infants, the mentally handicapped, and those who are "simple," are not good at taking counsel. In this latter text, Aquinas is clearly referring to infused prudence. But Aquinas's earlier statement is found in *ST* I-II, q. 58, three questions *before* Aquinas's assertion in question 61 that the natural virtues are what he has been discussing "up until now." So there is strong reason to think that Aquinas intends this earlier assertion to apply to natural virtue.[36]

Regardless of what Aquinas does or does not say, the more important point is that *industria* is driven by the end, and not vice versa. If I want to appropriately pursue a given end, then I need to exhibit *industria* in cultivating those habits that are ordered to that end. This is true whether the end is good or bad. Adolf Eichmann exhibited quite a great deal of *industria* in his efforts to see that genocide was carried out in a timely and effective manner. Similarly, if I want to be a successful thief or if I want to successfully pursue the end of vanity, then I clearly need *industria*. But I don't need to exhibit *industria* constantly; I only need to exhibit it in those things ordered to that end. I am *not* claiming that some of an individual's pursuits are not ordered to the end of virtue and that it is therefore unnecessary for him to exhibit *industria* in those pursuits. Rather, I am arguing that a virtuous person need not pursue all things. Some virtuous people simply never try to perfect their golf swing or organize their closets, and it is not at all clear that there is any moral failure involved in this.

Explicit References to the Relation between the Natural and Supernatural Virtues

In the preceding section, I examined three pairs of proof texts where Aquinas supposedly makes claims about how the natural and supernatural (i.e., acquired and infused) virtues are related. In each case the actual text does not support those claims. In fact, there are only three or four places where Aquinas directly references the relationship between the infused and acquired virtues. Two of those references occur in his early *Commentary on the Sentences* (*CS*). Aside from the *CS*, Aquinas makes only two, contradictory, allusions to his view of the relationship between the infused and acquired virtues. I will first address some texts from Aquinas's *CS* and then his mature references to the relation between the infused and acquired virtues: his reply to objection 4 in article 10 of *DQVG* and his discussion of the kinds of virtue in *ST* I-II, q. 61, a. 5. Although Aquinas does not articulate a definitive "theory," he seems to lean toward the view that the Christian cultivates acquired virtues in some areas of the moral life and the infused virtues in others.

CS III, d. 33, q. 1, a. 2, qa. 4

Aquinas devotes an article of *CS* to the question of whether the infused and acquired virtues are specifically different. He argues there, as he will in later texts, that the infused and acquired virtues differ in species because they arise from different principles and are ordered to different ends. The acquired virtues are ordered to the good proportionate to our created human nature and arise from the natural principles that order us to that good, namely, our natural habitual knowledge of the first speculative and practical principles. The infused virtues are ordered to our supernatural good and arise from the additional principles God bestows on us with grace, namely, the theological virtues. Because they are each ordered to different goods and each arise from different principles, what is moderate according to the standard of acquired virtue might not be moderate according to the standard of infused virtue, and vice versa. In the context of establishing all this, however, the Aquinas of the *CS* offers some strong indications that he believes the Christian can possess both infused and acquired virtues and that each type of virtue is ordered to supernatural beatitude in a distinct way.

The first indication that Aquinas believes the Christian can simultaneously possess both infused virtues and distinct acquired virtues is found in the *sed contra* of *CS*, d. 33, q. 1, a. 2, qa. 4. The infused and acquired virtues differ in species, says Aquinas, because we possess them both at once, and there can't be two different "forms" of the same species in the same person: "There cannot be two forms of the same species in the same subject. But infused virtue is together with acquired virtue, as is evident in the adult who approaches baptism already possessing acquired virtue—he does not receive less of the infused virtues than a child does. Therefore acquired virtue and infused virtue differ in species."[37] Aquinas thus clearly says that the Christian in a state of grace can possess *both* infused virtues and distinct acquired virtues. He asserts this claim so clearly that it would be hard to interpret it any differently. Someone who has already cultivated the acquired virtues and who is baptized not only receives the infused virtues but receives no less of them than a baptized infant does. Thus, the infused and acquired virtues have to differ in species; if they did not, such an individual would possess two forms—one infused and one acquired—of the same virtue, which is impossible.

We have, then, an assertion in the *sed contra* that the Christian can possess both infused and acquired virtues, and an assertion in the body of the text that the infused and acquired virtues arise from different principles and are ordered to different ends, one natural and one supernatural. The obvious question is why a Christian ordered by grace to supernatural beatitude would need to cultivate virtues ordered to a purely natural end. Aquinas seems to indicate an answer in his replies to the objections, and to indicate that the Christian's acquired virtues *are* ordered to supernatural beatitude and *do* produce meritorious acts; they just are not ordered to supernatural beatitude in the same way that the infused virtues are.

Objection 3 argues against a particular reason for asserting a difference in species: that acts of infused virtue are meritorious, while acts of acquired virtue are not. A virtue is meritorious, the objector argues, insofar as it is formed by charity. But being formed or unformed does not change the species of a virtue, because "it is a difference according to something extrinsic."[38] This objection thus makes two key claims: virtues are meritorious when they are "formed" by charity, and charity's formation is "extrinsic"—it does not change the species of the virtue.

Aquinas's reply is significant for what he does not say. He does not deny that charity can "form" the acquired virtues or that its formation is "extrinsic." Instead he says merely that the infused and acquired virtues "do not differ in species with regard to being meritorious, except insofar as the infused virtues are closer to merit on account of the end to which they are ordered."[39] Aquinas therefore seems to *agree* that the acquired virtues can be formed "extrinsically" by charity and that they are meritorious when so formed: he simply argues that it is not merit that is responsible for the specific difference, but the end to which the virtues are ordered.

But all this raises a still further problem. Aquinas's entire rationale for asserting that the infused and acquired virtues differ in species stems from the different *ends* to which they are ordered. If, as his *sed contra* and his reply to objection 3 seem to imply, he also thinks that the Christian can possess *meritorious* acquired virtues, then the Christian's infused and acquired virtues are ordered to the *same* end, namely, supernatural beatitude. For an act can only be m eritorious if it is ordered to supernatural beatitude. But if the Christian's acquired and infused virtues are both ordered to the same end, wouldn't they end up being indistinguishable from each other?

Aquinas's reply to objection 4 offers a way out of this circle: he distinguishes between a virtue's *actual* relation to an end and its *original* relation to an end. Objection 4 argues that a virtue's species comes not from its end but from its object. Since the infused and acquired virtues have the same object, they do not differ in species.[40] Aquinas replies that although virtues do not belong to the same species merely because they have the same end, a difference in end can make a difference in species. However, it is not a virtue's *actual* relation to an end that causes the difference in species, but rather its *original* relation: "It should be known that an actual relation to the remote end does not make the aforesaid difference, but the original relation to it, inasmuch as a difference of end makes a different proportion in the act and habit."[41]

What does Aquinas mean by distinguishing a virtue's *actual* relation to an end from its *original* relation to an end? There is a way of interpreting these remarks that accommodates not only this distinction but also Aquinas's earlier claims that the Christian's acquired virtues are meritorious and that charity forms the acquired virtues "extrinsically." We could say that the infused virtues are *originally* ordered to supernatural beatitude and that that original order is responsible for their "different proportion in act and habit" and hence for the specific difference between the infused and acquired virtues. On the other hand, in the Christian the acquired virtues retain their original proportion in act and habit but are formed *extrinsically* by charity, so that they receive a further direction to supernatural beatitude. Grace would also remove the debilitating effects of original sin, so the Christian's acquired virtues would be both "perfectly" ordered to man's natural fulfillment and yet also meritorious thanks to charity's further, "extrinsic" direction. Supernatural beatitude would then be the *actual* end of the Christian's acquired virtues and the cause of their merit. This further direction and subsequent merit, however, would be entirely external to the virtues themselves.

On such an interpretation, the Christian would simply be able to possess two kinds of virtue: (1) "perfect" natural virtues made meritorious by grace and (2) supernatural virtues. Each, consonant with Aquinas's claims in the *CS*, would enable him to act well in a different arena of life. The natural virtues would enable him to act well in civic life, and the supernatural virtues would enable him to act well in his spiritual life.

As will become clear in subsequent chapters, I think this account of the relationship between the infused virtues and acquired virtues is problematic in important ways, not least because it marginalizes the life of grace. But I think that this interpretation may well be the view Aquinas is committed to in the *CS*. It accommodates all of the distinctions he raises, and it seems supported by his surrounding remarks. It seems to me that older Thomists who interpret Aquinas in this way likely do so on the basis of the texts examined above.

Indications of a Shift?
CS III, d. 33, q. 1, a. 4 versus *ST* I-II, q. 61, a. 5

A plausible reading of the account in *CS* of the specific difference between the infused and acquired virtues is that Aquinas believes the Christian can cultivate both acquired and infused virtues. Although each type of virtue produces acts that are meritorious, each produces very different acts, and each produces acts relevant to a very different area of life. In light of this possibility, it is interesting to note how Aquinas's description of moral progress changes between the *CS* and *ST* I-II. In both texts, Aquinas appeals to Macrobius's descriptions of the kinds of virtue—political, purifying, perfect, and exemplar virtues—to explain moral progress. In *ST* I-II, however, he seems to imply that an individual's virtues begin as political virtues and become perfect virtues. Additionally, he seems to imply that political virtues are acquired virtues, and perfect virtues are infused virtues. This of course implies a rather different account of the relationship between the infused and acquired virtues than the one we have just addressed. Nor can this later discussion be dismissed as an attempt to accommodate Macrobius, for Aquinas also appeals to Macrobius's divisions in the *CS*, but in that earlier text he makes use of those divisions in a very different way. This variance raises the possibility that Aquinas has one view of the relationship between the infused and acquired virtues in the *CS* and another by the time he writes *ST* I-II.

ST I-II, q. 61, is devoted to the cardinal virtues. Article 5 asks whether the virtues are appropriately classified. Given the topics that Aquinas discusses in the first four articles of question 61 (what makes a virtue "cardinal," how many cardinal virtues there are, which virtues are cardinal, and how the cardinal virtues differ), one would expect that article 5 would again focus on the cardinal virtues themselves—prudence, justice, fortitude, and temperance. But the "classification" that article 5 examines is rather different; it asks instead whether the cardinal virtues are "appropriately classified as political virtues, purifying virtues, virtues of a purified mind, and exemplary virtues."[42] Article 5 asks not about the cardinal virtues themselves, but more broadly about what *kind* of virtues the cardinal virtues are. Aquinas's response seems to indicate that one kind of cardinal virtue becomes another kind of cardinal virtue as the moral life progresses.

In his reply, after asserting that the exemplars of the virtues exist in God, Aquinas considers the various ways that virtues exist in man. Since man "is by his nature a political animal," the virtues that exist in him by nature "are called political virtues insofar as by these virtues a man behaves uprightly in conducting human affairs."[43] Aquinas's next remark seems particularly telling: "This is the way in which we have been speaking of these virtues up to now."[44] The natural reading of this is that to this point in *ST* I-II, Aquinas's discussion of virtue has been a discussion of the virtues that perfect man's created nature (i.e., the virtues that are political and acquired). But, Aquinas claims that since man "must also draw closer to divine things as much as he can," we must also "posit certain virtues that fall between the political virtues, which are human virtues, and the exemplary virtues which are divine virtues."[45] These are the "purifying" and "perfect" virtues and are distinguished by their "movements and endpoints." Purifying virtues are the virtues "that belong to those who are 'passing through' and who are tending toward a likeness of God," while the virtues of "those who have already attained the likeness of God," the kind of virtues possessed by "the blessed in heaven or of those who are the most perfect in this present life," are perfect virtues.[46] Both purifying and perfect virtues, says Aquinas, leave behind worldly matters and look to divine things.

It is clear that perfect virtue refers to infused virtue because Aquinas says that the perfect virtues are those possessed by the blessed in heaven, and he consistently maintains that only the infused, not the acquired, virtues remain in heaven. Since purifying virtues are virtues that are in the progress of becoming perfect (aka infused) virtues, these would seem to be infused virtues. And since moral progress is described as a move from political to perfect virtue, it would be natural to assume that Aquinas is saying that acquired virtues somehow become or are replaced by infused virtues as the moral life progresses. This implies a rather different view of the relationship between infused and acquired virtues than does the *CS* text examined above and thus raises the possibility that Aquinas's view of the relationship between the infused and acquired virtues has shifted. This possibility is supported in that Aquinas appeals to Macrobius's same divisions in a distinctly different way in the *CS*.

In *CS* III, d. 33, q. 1, a. 4, Aquinas asks whether the virtues remain in heaven. As he will also argue in later texts, Aquinas responds that only the infused, not the acquired, virtues remain in heaven. In support of this claim, he makes two distinctions.[47] First, he distinguishes the act a virtue has in regard to "its proper matter" from the act it has "when it has reached its end."[48] This distinction establishes that a virtue might still be present and operative, even if it produces different acts than it previously did. But—and this anticipates Aquinas's second distinction—if the end to which a virtue is ordered is no longer present, then the virtue will not be either.[49]

Aquinas's second distinction has to do with the difference between the infused and acquired virtues. Since the acquired virtues "have the civil good as their end," and since earthly citizenship does not remain in heaven, the acquired virtues will not remain in heaven either. But since the infused virtues perfect man with respect to the spiritual life and as a citizen of the kingdom of heaven, this citizenship is not lost but perfected in heaven. The infused virtues, then, will remain, but they will not have the same act.[50]

This reply is roughly consistent with Aquinas's other remarks and potentially consistent with a number of different accounts of how the infused and acquired virtues are related. But in his reply to objection

2, Aquinas appeals to Macrobius's divisions, and he does so in a rather different way than he does in his later *ST* I-II discussion.

Objection 2 operates from the presupposition that the division between the active and passive lives applies to the virtues as we possess them on earth and in heaven, respectively. On this basis, the objector argues that the moral virtues, which have to do only with the active life, will not exist in heaven, because in heaven there is only contemplation. In his reply, Aquinas does two things. First, he reiterates his earlier claim that a virtue produces different acts on the way to the end than it does when the end has been attained: "The virtues that perfect in the active life, even the acquired virtues, need not be taken away when someone crosses over to the contemplative life. But they have different acts, insofar as they now attain to their proximate end; for the contemplative life is the end of the active life."[51] But Aquinas then introduces Macrobius's divisions as an account of how progress in *acquired virtue* occurs. The acquired political virtues first make man "right in civil works." At the purgative stage of the acquired virtues, the man who "[uses] civil affairs" "longs for contemplative rest." At the third and final stage, he "rests in contemplation."[52] Even at this last stage, when contemplation has been achieved, Aquinas argues that the acquired political virtues remain. It is merely that, having attained their end, they simply now produce different acts. But it is also clear, given the body of the article, that the end the acquired virtues rest in is a *this worldly*, natural end because they are not ordered to heavenly beatitude and do not remain in heaven.

In the *CS*, then, Aquinas seems to think that Macrobius's divisions simply refer to what it means to progress in virtue. They do not represent a progression *from* one kind of virtue to another as his *ST* I-II discussion implies, but rather represent what it means to make progress *within* a given kind of virtue, whether it be acquired or infused.

DQVG a. 10, ad 4

On the basis of the texts examined so far, one could plausibly maintain that the early Aquinas believes the Christian possesses and cultivates two very different types of virtue, each operative in a different area of life. It could also plausibly be maintained, on the basis of the shift in the way that Aquinas appeals to Macrobius's divisions, that the later Aquinas has begun to entertain a different view: that moral progress entails a gradual move from acquired to infused virtue.[53] This possibility is bolstered by the fact that the mature Aquinas does not make the same distinctions with regard to a virtue's "original" and "actual" end, or repeat his *CS* claim that charity only "extrinsically" forms the acquired virtues. But proving exactly what the mature Aquinas believes about the relationship between the infused and acquired virtues is no easy matter. This difficulty is evidenced by the final text where Aquinas alludes to the relationship between the infused and acquired virtues.

Aquinas does make one very clear remark about the relationship between the infused and acquired virtues, albeit only in a reply to an objection. This remark occurs in article 10 of *DQVG*, which asks "whether some virtues are infused into us."[54] I will argue that this text, written at roughly the same time as *ST* I-II, seems to imply the position taken in the early *CS* rather than the position implied in *ST* I-II. Objection 4 argues that infused virtues are unnecessary. Virtue, the objector argues, "orders human beings toward the blessedness of eternal life insofar as it consists of meritorious activity."[55] But "the activity of acquired virtues can merit eternal life if it is informed by grace," so the infused virtues are unnecessary.[56] Since Aquinas's reply has been interpreted in very different ways, I will quote it here in its entirety:

> Since we can merit nothing without charity, the actions of an acquired virtue cannot have merit without charity. However, the other virtues are infused in us together with charity; that is how the actions of an acquired virtue can be meritorious only by means of [*mediante*] an infused virtue. For a virtue that is ordered towards a lower end can only bring about actions that are ordered to a higher end if this is done by means of a higher virtue. For example, the courage that is a virtue of a human being *qua* human being does not order its actions to the civic good except by means of [*mediante*] that courage that is the virtue of a human being *qua* citizen.[57]

Although this quote is frequently cited as evidence of Aquinas's view of the relationship between the infused and acquired virtues, it is cited in support of drastically different interpretations.[58]

The above quote certainly asserts something about the relationship between the infused and acquired virtues, but exactly what it asserts is not immediately clear. The quote consists of a claim and a supporting analogy. The claim is that the acquired virtues merit only *mediante* the infused virtues. The supporting analogy compares the way the infused virtues order the acquired virtues to the way that the courage of a "human being *qua* citizen" orders the courage of a human being qua human being. When this text is cited in support of a given theory of the relationship between the infused and acquired virtues, the vague *mediante* is made to do all the work. This is unproductive, because the term is vague enough to support any number of interpretations. To achieve real clarity about the meaning of this text, we have to look at Aquinas's supporting analogy. But the supporting analogy is itself confusing.

Aquinas's analogy hangs on a comparison between the courage of man "as a citizen" and the courage of a "human being as human being." It compares civic courage to infused virtue and the courage of a "human being as human being" to acquired courage, and asserts that the former is *higher than* the latter. This comparison is in itself surprising. At a minimum, it means that Aquinas understands something different by "civic virtue" than Aristotle does, since Aristotle says that a citizen's virtue is regime-specific and coincides with the virtue of a good man only in the best regime.[59] In order to understand the analogy, we have to first understand how Aquinas understands the relationship between civic virtue and the virtue of "man *qua* man." Moreover, we have to understand the relationship between the two kinds of fortitude mentioned here. But Aquinas does not make the distinction between "civic" fortitude and the fortitude of "man *qua* man" in his discussion of fortitude. Thus, if we want to understand his analogy, we will have to find some indirect way of understanding that relationship.

Although Aquinas never discusses a "higher" civic fortitude, he does discuss something very similar. He identifies a "political" version of the virtue of prudence, and he says both that political prudence is higher than prudence *simpliciter* and that political prudence guides and directs prudence *simpliciter*. It is reasonable to think, then, if we examine the way in which civic prudence guides and directs prudence *simpliciter*, we will be able to gain clarity about the analogy Aquinas intends to draw.

Prudence finds fitting means to a "due end." But because the "due ends" that prudence finds fitting means to can differ, so too can prudence. The ability to find fitting means to one's own individual good, for instance, is different from the ability to find fitting means to the good of one's household or city.[60] Aquinas thus distinguishes prudence *simpliciter dicta* (simply so called), which enables one to deliberate well about one's *bonum proprium* (one's own individual good), from the prudence that enables one to deliberate well about the good of one's household (economic prudence) or city (political prudence).[61]

Since it is the ruler of a city who is primarily entrusted with directing it to a due end, political prudence primarily belongs to the ruler.[62] But insofar as citizens have a share in the laws and must act rightly in obeying the laws, citizens too have a share in political prudence.[63] What is important for present purposes, however, is Aquinas's account of how the two forms of prudence are related. Individual and political prudence each have different concerns. Yet just as horsemanship can be ordered to the ends of war, so too can the lower form of prudence be ordered to the higher. When this happens, Aquinas says that the virtue concerned with the higher end will be the superior virtue, and that it will command the lower virtue.[64] In the case of prudence, this means that political prudence, which is concerned with a higher good, will be superior to the other forms of prudence and command them. Individual prudence and economic prudence will therefore be subordinate to and directed by political prudence.

Although Aquinas makes it clear that individual prudence is subordinate to political prudence, he also makes it clear that political prudence can only exist in the context of a just regime. A virtuous individual, whether ruler or citizen, cannot exhibit political prudence if he is a member of an unjust regime. So as the regime changes, the same individual might or might not possess political prudence. Perhaps more importantly, Aquinas is clear that when political prudence *is* present, it does not contradict the other, subordinate, forms of prudence but rather orders and directs them. The pursuit of one's own individual good is never contrary to the pursuit of the common good. Far to the contrary, whatever is good for the community will also be good for the individual.[65]

All of this can help to shed light on what it might mean for individual prudence to be "ordered" to the common good *mediante* political prudence. First, although the two forms of prudence ideally exist together, they can certainly exist apart. Second, when the two forms *do* exist together, each will still perform a distinct role in a distinct arena of life. The mere fact that one is a citizen of a just regime, or even exercises political prudence in one's own right, will not eliminate the need for one to deliberate about fitting means to one's *bonum proprium*. Third, it is clear that for the citizen of a just regime, individual prudence must be conducted *in light of* political prudence: in light of his status in that regime and in the context of his obedience to its laws. This means that the exercise of individual prudence, though distinct from political prudence, might still nonetheless be shaped and guided by it. Finally and importantly, both forms of prudence are ordered to the same ultimate end. This, indeed, is *why* individual prudence must look to and be guided by political prudence and why there can ultimately be no contradiction between the two. Both types of virtue are ultimately ordered to the common good of the universe as governed by eternal law. The individual good is most properly pursued, not in isolation, but in the context of a community.

An Interpretation of *DQVG* a. 10, ad 4

Our examination of the parallel case of prudence yields a possible interpretation of Aquinas's comparative analogy. As we saw above, the relationship between political prudence and prudence *simpliciter* has the following features. First, prudence *simpliciter* remains a distinct virtue with its own distinct act. It is not taken up or subsumed by political prudence. Rather, it guides man in one domain of life, and political prudence guides him in another. Second, prudence *simpliciter*, even while remaining distinct, is nonetheless directly affected by the higher virtue of political prudence: prudence *simpliciter*, when exercised in light of and constrained by political prudence, may give rise to different acts than it otherwise might. The prudent citizen of the just regime will be guided by individual prudence, but his individual prudence will itself be informed by the laws of the just regime he is a citizen of. At the same time, it is crucial that Aquinas does not simply *identify* the various kinds of prudence. Individual prudence, household prudence, and political prudence each have different tasks and are exercised in distinct domains. The higher forms certainly do direct the lower, but they do not supplant them. In the exercise of household prudence, for instance, the citizen of the just regime will necessarily be constrained and guided by political prudence: zoning laws, for instance, will constrain his prudential deliberation about how best to pursue the good of his household. But such deliberation, though conducted in a manner that is attentive to the requirements of political prudence, will still be an example of household prudence.

The preceding implies an interpretation of Aquinas's view of the relationship between the infused and acquired virtues. First, Aquinas thinks the infused and acquired virtues each have to do with distinct arenas of life. Second, even in those arenas of life that have specifically to do with acquired virtues, the acquired virtues are nonetheless "guided and directed" by the infused, and one's reasoning is always altered and constrained by the dictates of the infused virtues. Third, the Christian's practice of the acquired virtues will therefore differ from the non-Christian's practice of the same virtues: the Christian's deliberations about his natural good will always be "mediated" by his higher, supernatural good.

I do not like this interpretation of the relationship between the infused and the acquired virtues. Indeed, as I argue in chapter 4, I do not think it is even coherent. But it is the interpretation most consistent with the comparative analogy that Aquinas offers.

Where does all this leave us? In this chapter, we've seen that Aquinas says very little about the relationship between the infused and acquired virtues. Most of the texts cited as proof of his view actually prove nothing at all. Aquinas does, however, make a few isolated remarks that could be taken to imply a thesis about the relationship between the infused and acquired virtues. Most of these occur as asides: in replies to objections or in a *sed contra*. Anything we can decisively say about Aquinas's view of the relationship between the infused and acquired virtues has to be gleaned from these remarks. When we consider all of them together with his surrounding text, the best we can say is that Aquinas appears to lean toward the view that the Christian possesses and cultivates both infused and acquired moral virtues and that both are operative in distinct arenas of the Christian moral life.

Taken together, the texts from the *CS* and the *DQVG* imply that Aquinas envisions both types of virtue as relevant to the Christian moral life, but that he also envisioned each type of virtue as operative in a different arena of life, with the activity of the acquired virtue attentive to and constrained by the activity of infused virtue but nonetheless distinct. If this is how Aquinas envisions the relationship between the infused and acquired virtues, then something like his vague *CS* remarks about charity's "extrinsic" direction of the natural virtues to supernatural beatitude must be a correct account of his view. It must be the case, that is to say, that even in the Christian, the acquired virtues will order one to one's natural, not one's supernatural, fulfillment. They simply receive an "extrinsic" further ordering from charity, one that does not alter the norm that measures them. Such an account of the relationship between the infused and acquired virtues is difficult to reconcile with the account of the progression of the virtues that Aquinas describes in *ST* I-II, q. 65, a. 1. There, he seems to describe progress in the moral life, even in this life, in terms of a move from political acquired virtue to infused virtue, not in terms of the cultivation of both. But more importantly, some defense of the intuitive plausibility of his implied account needs to be offered. I will return to this point in more detail in chapter 4. For the moment, I merely state the main challenge that the "coexistence" view needs to meet.

I noted at the beginning of this chapter that the view that the Christian cultivates two distinct kinds of virtue in two distinct areas of life directly implies a thesis about the Christian's natural and supernatural principles of action, namely, that the latter do not inherently shape the former but simply exist alongside them, making an alternative way of acting possible. In order for such a view to be consistent with the claim that Christians have a single, supernatural end, it would also have to be the case, on this view, that acts arising from the Christian's natural principles receive an "extrinsic" direction to supernatural beatitude. This conclusion is consistent with what Aquinas implies (albeit indirectly) in some scattered texts, especially in *CS*. But in order to make an account like this intuitively plausible, one needs to give some account of when, why, and how each "set" of principles is operative. When and why is it appropriate for a Christian to cultivate purely natural virtues? This question becomes particularly pressing because Aquinas believes the Christian possesses all the infused moral virtues and could in principle perform an act of infused virtue, arising from his supernatural principles, at any time. If this is the case, why would it ever be appropriate *not* to act out of those principles? This is the primary question the coexistence view will have to answer.

CHAPTER 4

Interpretive Options, Part I
Coexistence

Thus far I have argued that although Aquinas is clear about how he envisions the different "structures" of the infused and acquired virtues, he makes only a few scattered references to any "relation" between the infused virtues and acquired virtues. It follows that any theory of that relationship will necessarily go beyond the text of Aquinas. In this chapter and the next, I examine different ways in which one could attempt to formulate a theory on the basis of Aquinas's scattered remarks. I focus here on a theory that would accommodate the implications of Aquinas's remarks in his *Commentary on the Sentences* (*CS*) and in his *Disputed Questions on the Virtues in General* (*DQVG*). In chapter 5, I focus on theories that would accommodate the implication of *ST* I-II, q. 61, a. 5. I argue that all of these theories fall short in different ways. In chapter 6, I propose my own view of the relationship between the infused and acquired virtues.

In chapter 3, we saw that Aquinas's few, scattered references to the relationship between the infused and acquired virtues, particularly the references that occur in *CS*, could be taken to imply the following things about the Christian's infused and acquired virtues: (1) the Christian can possess both infused and acquired virtues, (2) even in the Christian, each virtue continues to produce acts proportionate to its respective end (the acquired to man's natural fulfillment and the infused to man's supernatural fulfillment), (3) the Christian's acts of acquired virtue, though proportionate to his natural fulfillment, receive a further "extrinsic" order to supernatural beatitude through the mediation of the infused virtues, and (4) the infused and acquired moral virtues are relevant to and operative in distinct spheres or "domains" of the Christian moral life.

Of the four claims listed above, (3) and (4) are both the most crucial and the most difficult to defend. By definition, acquired virtues produce acts proportionate to man's natural fulfillment. Typically, to speak of what a virtuous act is ordered to is to speak of that virtue's "end." This, after all, is what it means to possess a virtue. Virtues make us rightly ordered to our end. But (3) seems to indicate that in the Christian, the acquired virtues produce acts proportionate to one end (man's natural fulfillment) and are yet at the same time also ordered to another end (supernatural beatitude). In the first section below, I examine (3) and the standard defense of it, namely, the claim that the infused virtues order and direct the acquired virtues in the same way that one natural virtue orders and directs another. I will argue that the analogy does not go through unless (4) is also true — one cannot make sense of the idea that the Christian's acquired virtues both produce acts proportionate to one's natural flourishing and are yet also "ordered" to supernatural beatitude by the (very different) infused virtues unless it is also the case that the infused and acquired virtues are operative in different domains of the Christian moral life.

Having established that (4) is central to the coexistence view, I devote the second section to a consideration of the claim that the infused and acquired virtues are relevant in distinct "domains" of the moral life. We shall see that the most frequently proposed way of understanding this division is untenable, and that other attempts are likely to be unsatisfactory. Thus, even if Aquinas's few, scattered remarks imply something like the coexistence view, it is not a viable theory of the relationship between the infused and acquired virtues.

"Healed and Elevated" Acquired Virtues

On the traditional Christian view, grace both heals and elevates nature. Thesis (3)—that the acquired virtues receive an "extrinsic" order to supernatural beatitude—implies that it is not just nature itself that is elevated and healed by grace but also any natural virtues that may have been acquired prior to conversion. Original sin damages nature. Though it does not destroy the principles of nature, it does bring disorder into our appetites. Insofar as grace heals the effects of original sin, it follows that a Christian attempting to cultivate the acquired moral virtues (for the purposes of this chapter I am assuming that it is both possible and appropriate to do so) would not face the same kinds of obstacles a non-Christian would. "Perfect" acquired virtues would thus be possible for the Christian in a way they could never be possible for the pagan.[1] But if the notion of a Christian who cultivates acquired virtues is to make sense at all, it must be the case that those virtues are not merely "healed" but also elevated.

Aquinas clearly and consistently maintains that the infused and acquired virtues are distinguished by their different *ends*. Each type of virtue produces acts proportionate to a distinct end, one natural and one supernatural. Aquinas also clearly and consistently maintains that the Christian only has one end: supernatural beatitude.[2] Any attempt to carve out a role for the cultivation of the acquired virtues in the Christian moral life must therefore accommodate both of these claims. One way of accommodating both claims is by asserting something like (2) and (3) above: in the Christian each type of virtue still produces acts proportionate to a different end, but acts of the lower virtue receive a further, "extrinsic" direction to supernatural beatitude from the corresponding higher virtue. This means that acquired virtue, even though remaining an acquired virtue in every sense of the word (it both produces acts proportionate to our natural good and is acquired by means of our own repeated good acts), is nonetheless "elevated" by grace and the infused virtues. The Christian's acts of acquired virtue, on this view, are nonetheless ordered—not of their very nature, but thanks to the further, extrinsic, direction provided by the infused virtues—to supernatural beatitude.

This explanation is complicated, unintuitive, and unwieldy, but it warrants our careful consideration. In the first place, Aquinas's few, scattered remarks indicate that he may have held something like this. Second, one very frequently encounters the claim, even if it is often made without much explanation or context, that existing acquired virtues are somehow "directed" to supernatural beatitude by the infused virtues. For both of these reasons, it is important to see what, if anything, can be said for this view.

If (3) is correct, it must somehow be the case that the acquired virtues both remain acquired virtues and are nonetheless ordered or directed to supernatural beatitude. Defenders of this view typically claim that this reordering is achieved by means of the theological and infused moral virtues. It is not at all obvious, however, how virtues ordered to one end can "order and direct" virtues ordered to a different end. Those who argue for this view typically cite *DQVG* a. 10, ad 4. As we have seen, in that text Aquinas draws an analogy with the case of natural virtue, arguing that just as one natural virtue can order and direct the act of another natural virtue, so too can charity and the infused moral virtues order and direct the acts of the acquired virtues. The implication is that just as a natural virtue remains ordered to the same end despite its further ordering by another natural virtue, so too does natural virtue remain the same and continue to produce acts proportionate to man's natural fulfillment, even while it is ordered to a higher, supernatural end by charity and the infused moral virtues.

In exactly what way does one natural virtue order and direct another, and exactly how is what occurs between two natural virtues supposed to translate to the case where a supernatural virtue orders a natural virtue? In what follows I will look at two examples of attempts to offer such an explanation: first, Aquinas's apparent comparison between the way that one natural virtue orders another and the way that the supernatural virtues order natural virtues; second, an example offered by John Bowlin, a contemporary defender of this view. In both instances, the features that make the ordering of one virtue by another coherent at the natural level are absent at the supernatural level.

We saw in chapter 3 that (for Aquinas) political prudence can guide and direct the other forms of prudence, including prudence *simpliciter*—that is, the prudence of man qua man. This ordering and directing is made possible because each type of prudence has its own distinct concern. Prudence *simpliciter* enables its possessor to deliberate well about fitting means to his own good. Household prudence enables one to deliberate well about household management. Political prudence enables one to deliberate well about fitting means to the civic good. The same account can be given of all the other types of prudence. Moreover, deliberating about the one is not the same as deliberating about the other. Deliberating well about fitting means to one's own good is not the same as deliberating well about the good of the household or about deliberating well about the civic good. Each concerns the making of a distinct kind of decision, so it requires a different version of the same virtue. But these concerns, though distinct, are also clearly related. Considerations about the higher aims of political prudence can affect and even alter what it means to deliberate correctly about the good of the household, and so on.

It is because of the clear relationship between the different kinds of prudence that it makes sense to think that one kind of prudence can order and direct another kind of prudence. In theory, deliberation about one's own individual good could happen in a vacuum. But we do not live in a vacuum. In reality, our pursuit of our own good is tied up with a host of other pursuits, and all of those pursuits are in turn tied up with our ultimate end. Moreover, the ends of one pursuit might well be subordinate to the ends of another. As we have seen in chapter 3, Aquinas (following Aristotle) points out that this is true not just of virtue but of every aspect of life. The art of bridle-making has its own ends, but those ends are themselves subordinate to the ends of a distinct pursuit, horsemanship. The ends of horsemanship are in turn subordinate to the ends of battle, and so on. In the same way, my deliberation about fitting means to my own good is both distinct from and subordinate to my deliberation about fitting means to the household good, and both of those are distinct from and subordinate to my deliberation about fitting means to the civic good. This subordination makes sense because the goods sought are subordinate to each other and because they are all sought for the sake of the same end.

I have been considering the example of how the different kinds of prudence can order and direct each other, but there is no reason to limit our consideration to prudence. John Bowlin, who also argues that the acquired virtues are "elevated" and directed by the infused virtues, points to the example of how different kinds of justice can order and direct each other. Bowlin uses the example of someone who is both a professor and a parent and whose son enrolls in his class. Insofar as his son is a student in his class, the professor owes his son the kind of justice he owes any other student. Insofar as this particular student is also his son, the professor owes him the kind of justice a father ought to show his son.[3] The latter kind of justice can order (and guide and direct) the former, but it does not replace or nullify it.

These examples of cases where one natural virtue orders another are both plausible and perfectly reasonable. However, if the analogy is to work, the features that make them plausible will have to be present in the hypothetical situation of a supernatural virtue ordering a natural virtue. The examples offered above have two central features. First, in each case the virtue that orders and the virtue that is ordered operate in distinct arenas of life. Second, both virtues are subordinate to the same ultimate end. The virtue that orders is "closer," so to speak, to the ultimate end than the virtue that is ordered, and it is that hierarchical relationship that makes the ordering of the one virtue by the other plausible. Let's address each of these points in turn.

Prudence *simpliciter*, or individual prudence, does not involve the same kind of deliberation as household prudence does, and neither individual prudence nor household prudence involves the same kind of deliberation as political prudence does. Deliberating well about one's own good involves a very different kind of deliberation than deliberating well about household management or the civic good. Though all of these goods are importantly linked (a point I will return to shortly), a person could conceivably be relatively good at one kind of deliberation and bad at another. Some people, for instance, keep a household running smoothly while making terrible decisions about their own health. The same can be said about Bowlin's example of the different kinds of justice. The justice a father shows his son is importantly different from the justice a professor shows a student:

each involves a different kind of reasoning and stems from a different kind of relationship. As in the previous case, one could conceivably treat one's students justly while neglecting one's children, or vice versa. One virtue can and should order the other because (1) both virtues are ordered to the same end and (2) one can't be fully proficient in the lower virtue without also being attentive to what higher virtues demand.

We have seen that individual prudence is the ability to deliberate well about the means to one's *bonum proprium*, one's own individual good. But because we do not live isolated lives, we cannot truly deliberate well about our individual good if we simply ignore other, higher goods. The individual good is pursued in the context of other relationships: we are individuals, but we also are members of households and cities. And we if we neglect those larger contexts, we will not adequately pursue our individual good. If something appears to be consistent with my individual good but is destructive of the good of my household or city, then it cannot actually advance even my individual good. Why? Because as Aquinas understands it, all these goods are ordered to the same ultimate end, and hierarchically so. What advances my individual good *necessarily* also advances the good of the household and the city. So, although the individual good is logically distinct from the good of a household or city, our deliberation about the one must also take into account the other.

The same point can be made about the different kinds of justice. In the abstract, it might seem that what one owes one's students is entirely distinct from what one owes one's children. I owe it to my students to be fair, to return their papers in a timely fashion, to prepare well for class, and so on. The things I owe my children are different: I owe them love, encouragement, and quality time. But everything I owe is owed in the context of my life as a whole. When considered in the context of a life as a whole, my just relationship to my students is subordinate to my just relationship to my family and my society. I cannot *really* serve my students while neglecting how justice demands I treat my country or family. Hence, some of the things that seem just in the abstract, such as returning papers within a certain amount of time, say, can prove unjust in the concrete. If my child is deathly ill, I should not neglect his well-being to go and grade papers. I should not because it would be unjust to my child and it would also be unjust to my students. Accurate deliberation about what I owe my students must take into account what I owe others. And it is clear that I do not owe it to my students to grade their papers when my child is dangerously ill.

The two features I have been describing are equally important to a coherent account of virtue. Life involves a variety of different activities, and the different virtues are a way of explaining what it means to act well in all of them. But none of life's various pursuits are pursued in isolation: they are all pursued in the context of one's ultimate end. No virtue is in principle independent of any other. Just as the most important pursuits in life affect our pursuit of lesser goods, so will the virtues that have to do with those most important pursuits inform what is and is not a virtuous way of pursuing those lesser goods. The problem, though, is that it is not at all clear how any of this is supposed to translate to an account of the relationship between the infused and acquired virtues.

We saw above that in the examples where one natural virtue orders another natural virtue, each virtue has what we might call its own "domain." Each virtue is concerned with or has to do with a distinct subject matter. Because the subject matters in question are hierarchically related, so too are the virtues. But this is not, or at least not obviously, the case with natural and supernatural virtue. As we shall see in what follows, the very rationale Aquinas offers for distinguishing the natural and supernatural virtues has this consequence: there is a supernatural version of *every* natural virtue. So although each natural virtue has a distinct "domain," there will be a supernatural version of every natural virtue, no matter what its domain. The absence of distinct domains means that if the supernatural virtues do order and direct the natural virtues, they cannot do so in the same way that one natural virtue orders and directs another. That is to say, rather than household prudence directing individual prudence, as occurs at the natural level, it would have to be the case that *infused* household prudence directs *acquired* household prudence, and so on.

In his general explanations of virtue, Aquinas repeatedly asserts that a virtue is an "ultimate" of a power. What Aquinas means by this is merely that a virtue is the fulfillment of a capacity. A power that has been habituated by a virtue is able to operate in a way that fulfills its potential; it is fully actualized. It is important to understand just what it means for a power to be "fully actualized," not least because the full actualization of a power has a direct relationship to the *telos* of the thing in question.

Consider for the moment a simple capacity, such as the human capacity of sight. What does it mean for the human power of sight to be "fully actualized"? The human power of sight is fully actualized when the human eye sees well: when it can see things clearly both up close and at a distance, when it can detect differences in color and shape, and so on. But it is also clear that the end (*telos*) of the thing in question is inherent in the very notion of "seeing well." The full actualization of the human power of sight will be rather different than the full actualization of the cheetah's or the bat's power of sight. The human eye will not see well if it sees only those things a bat or a cheetah sees. Hence if we really want to understand what it is for a power to function at its "utmost," we need to understand the power in terms of the end of the being that possesses it. This understanding of capacity has clear implications for how we understand the claim that a virtue is the "utmost" of a power.

The moral virtues enable the appetitive powers to function at their "utmost" insofar as they enable those powers to act in a manner commensurate with the fulfillment of the individual who possesses them. All the virtues that have to do with the right ordering of the irascible appetite, for instance, together enable that appetite to operate at its "utmost," which is merely to say that through those virtues the irascible appetite is enabled to act in a manner commensurate with the human end.

The clear relationship between the "utmost" of a virtue and the end to which the possessor of the virtue is ordered means that a change in a thing's end will of necessity alter how we understand the "utmost" of the power in question. If the irascible appetite operates at its "utmost" when it produces acts ordered to man's fulfillment, and if we agree that man's natural fulfillment is not identical to his supernatural fulfillment, then virtues that produce the acts ordered to the former fulfillment will not produce acts ordered to the latter fulfillment, and vice versa. This means that if our appetitive powers are to function at their "utmost" in the person ordered to supernatural beatitude, he will need to possess supernatural versions of all the natural virtues. To truly act in a manner befitting the end of supernatural beatitude, one will need not merely infused "individual" prudence but also infused household prudence and infused political prudence; one will need not merely the infused virtue of justice, but also infused versions of the justice that enables one to give one's children and one's students their due. . . . The list goes on.

The consequence of this is that the way in which one natural virtue orders another does not have any clear implications for the way in which a supernatural virtue might order a natural virtue. When one natural virtue orders another, a virtue that has to do with one area of life is ordered and directed by a virtue that has to do with another area of life. Each natural virtue has its own distinct role, and there is a clear necessity for each natural virtue. It is merely that because those areas of life are also hierarchically ordered, the virtue concerned with the higher pursuit guides and directs the lower. But, as we have seen, there are natural and supernatural versions *of every virtue*. The Christian should possess infused political prudence, infused household prudence, infused individual prudence, and so on. This creates a problem for the analogy. If I am a Christian ordered to supernatural beatitude, then it seems that the actions that will be virtuous for me to do will be acts proportionate to the end of supernatural beatitude. Certainly, my infused household prudence will need to be guided and directed by infused political prudence, and so on, just as it would in the case of natural virtue. But it is not at all clear why I would need to continue to cultivate a *natural* household prudence, a *natural* political prudence, and so on. And if I did, it is not at all clear how a natural household prudence would be or could be "guided and directed" by a supernatural household prudence. When there are no distinct "domains" and the virtues in question produce acts proportionate to different ends, the rationale for the claim that the one type of virtue "orders and directs" the other is lost.

There is, however, a way of saving the analogy — if it is the case that it is only sometimes appropriate to act in a manner proportionate to supernatural beatitude. If the moral life can be divided so that in some areas of life it is appropriate to cultivate virtues ordered to one's natural fulfillment, while in others it is appropriate to cultivate virtues ordered to one's supernatural fulfillment, then one could envision a version of the kind of "ordering" described above. Suppose, for instance, that it were only appropriate to perform acts of infused virtue when explicitly engaged in religious activity. It could then be the case that there are infused versions of every acquired virtue, that the infused and acquired virtues remain distinct, and that the latter are guided and directed by the former. The clear problem, though, is that it is not at all clear how to make that division. The infused virtues are surely not something that we ought to practice only in church on Sunday or during Lent. If we grant that and if we still wish to include a role for the cultivation of distinct acquired virtues in the Christian moral life, we need some account of how the infused and acquired virtues divide.

DIVIDING THE CHRISTIAN MORAL LIFE

It should be clear from the preceding that a successful defense of (3)—the claim that the natural virtues are extrinsically ordered to supernatural beatitude by the infused virtues—will depend on our ability to offer a coherent defense of (4)—the claim that each type of virtue is operative in a different domain of the moral life. Aquinas himself, however, offers very little indication of how one might offer such a defense. Throughout his corpus, Aquinas consistently links the infused and acquired virtues to distinct kinds of "lives." In both his early *CS* and his late *Disputed Questions on the Cardinal Virtues (DQVC)*, he tells us that the acquired virtues perfect man in the "civic" life, but the infused virtues perfect man in the spiritual life.[4] If it is also the case, as he seems to imply in the scattered remarks examined above, that on earth the Christian pursues perfection in *both lives*, then this seems to offer the kind of general answer we have already indicated. There are infused and acquired versions of every virtue, but which virtue is appropriate depends on which "life" one is engaged in. When one is pursuing the civic good, one will practice acquired virtue. When one is pursuing the spiritual life, one will practice infused virtue. The latter pursuit is higher than and directs the lower, and thus one's pursuit of the civic good will be guided and directed by one's (distinct) pursuit of the spiritual life. Just as the goods are ordered but distinct, so too will be the virtues. Linking this to the examples examined above, there will be an acquired individual prudence, an acquired household prudence, and an acquired political prudence, all of which will be cultivated in the service of the civic good. But there would, on this view, *also* be an infused individual prudence, an infused household prudence, and an infused political prudence, which one would cultivate and exercise in the service of one's spiritual good.

Vague references to different kinds of "lives," however, do not shed much light on the content of those lives or on the question of when the cultivation of each type of virtue is appropriate. To really evaluate the view, we need something more concrete. When does the Christian who possesses both infused virtues and acquired virtues perform an act of acquired virtue? When does he perform an act of infused virtue? What different criteria make it appropriate to perform an act of infused rather than acquired virtue, and vice versa? Scholars commonly approach this question by arguing that the distinction has to do with "things necessary for salvation." Those actions that have to do with "what is necessary for salvation" require the infused virtues, but others do not. Although many scholars assert this in passing, at least some have offered hypotheses about how this distinction plays out in practice. Next we'll look at a few such accounts. There is indeed something intuitively appealing about the idea of what is "necessary for salvation," but the notion cannot be used in an intuitively appealing way to distinguish acts of infused from acts of acquired virtue.

Bonnie Kent argues that the answer to these questions is tied to Aquinas's recognition of two distinct kinds of happiness. The infused virtues are the virtues necessary for happiness in the afterlife, and the acquired virtues are the virtues necessary "to be happy in the ordinary human society of this life."[5] Kent argues that Aquinas considers both kinds of happiness to be important, and hence that he considers the cultivation of both kinds of virtue to be important. The infused virtues, says Kent, confer a very specific kind of ability. Infused prudence "does not enable one to deliberate well about everything under the sun, but only about things related to salvation. People must learn from experience how to succeed in business, deploy troops in combat, and exercise judgement in other worldly affairs."[6] The acquired virtues more generally, Kent argues, have to do with other ends that are "good in themselves." In the Christian, that right order to a genuinely good end receives a further direction, so that the Christian's acquired virtues are also meritorious: "Those with the virtue of charity might nonetheless develop the natural virtues and exercise them both for their intrinsic worth and for the sake of God. When they do, Thomas says, the acts of these naturally acquired virtues are meritorious. Thus a Christian's daily conduct in selling cars, caring for patients, or teaching philosophy, and likewise her routine behavior with family and friends, can express both her love for strictly human goods *and* her love for God."[7]

If we combine Kent's claim about what infused prudence does with her claim about what the acquired virtues more generally do, we get something like the following account. The natural virtues are ordered to goods that, though not necessary for salvation, *are* necessary for the ordinary Aristotelian happiness that is possible in this life. Aquinas thinks that the Christian should cultivate such virtues because the happiness of this life matters and that, in the Christian, charity (and ostensibly the other infused virtues) makes it possible for one to order those natural virtues to a further end. *But*, the Christian also needs infused virtues for those things "necessary for salvation."

Kent's reference to what is "necessary for salvation" is not unique. Josef Pieper, acknowledging that God infuses prudence and the other moral virtues along with grace, hastens to add that the prudence given with grace is limited not only in the kinds of actions it extends to but also as a virtue. "It is true," writes Pieper, "that every Christian receives in baptism, along with the new life of friendship with God, a supernatural 'infused' prudence. But, says Thomas, this prudence granted to every Christian is limited solely to what is necessary for his eternal salvation."[8] Virtually the same claim is made by Michael Sherwin, who says that Aquinas "specifies that the infused moral virtues do not concern all actions, but only those actions necessary for salvation."[9] Sherwin also proposes a way of understanding how acts "necessary for salvation" differ from other acts. Aquinas, says Sherwin, claims "that the infused moral virtues pertain to a narrow band of action: they pertain only to those acts necessary for the agent's personal salvation."[10] Like Kent, Pieper and Sherwin understand Aquinas to hold that the infused virtues—considered in their own right—concern only a very "narrow" area of the moral life, and specifically those "acts necessary for personal salvation." Kent, Pieper, and Sherwin all claim that the infused virtues, properly speaking, only concern those acts "necessary for salvation." Several other scholars make similar claims.[11]

Aquinas does refer to what is "necessary for salvation" in a number of different places. Kent cites the reply to article 2, objection 3 of *DQVC*, while Pieper and Sherwin cite the reply to *ST* II-II, q. 47, a. 14, obj. 3. I argued at length in chapter 3 that the actual textual support for this identification is thin. Aquinas certainly does distinguish between what is necessary for salvation and what is not, but he offers this distinction *not* in support of a claim about prudence or indeed any other virtue but about prerequisites of those virtues, and typically about *industria*, a quality whose possession is as compatible with vice as with virtue.[12] To read a claim about something not itself even a virtue but only a prerequisite of it as applying to prudence itself is to vastly overinterpret Aquinas's text.

Even absent any textual support, one might still argue that the distinction between what is necessary for salvation and what is not offers a promising way of characterizing the scope of the infused virtues: that the infused virtues enable us to act virtuously in "matters necessary for salvation." This line of argument, however, is problematic. For although the distinction between what is necessary for salvation and what is not can have intuitive appeal, scholars who use it to distinguish acts of infused virtue from acts of acquired virtue do not use it in an intuitively appealing way.

The distinction between what is necessary for salvation and what is not offers an appealing way of understanding how it is that a flawed human being can be a saint. It is impossible to become acquainted with the lives of the saints without becoming aware that many of them were flawed, sometimes in serious ways. St. Louis IX may have been devoted to God, but he also squandered his countrymen's money and lives on ill-advised crusades. St. Thomas More died a martyr's death, but he also burned heretics at the stake (or at least caused them to be burned). St. Junipero Serra built missions, but many claim that he drove his Native American workers too hard and treated them poorly to boot. Mother Teresa's critics claimed that she provided inadequate and unsanitary treatment to those under her care, and that she worried more about coercing deathbed conversions than about making her patients' last days comfortable. St. John Paul II, whose holiness seems beyond dispute, appears to have been an absolutely terrible judge of character. The list goes on.

One possible way of responding to the deep flaws of saintly individuals, of course, would be to deny that they were saints after all.[13] But another more reasonable response is to acknowledge their flaws but maintain that they were saints nonetheless: in spite of their clear flaws, they had what was "necessary for salvation." Used in this way, I think a reference to what is "necessary for salvation" has a clear intuitive appeal. But it is important to be clear about how the term is being used. First, as used here, "necessary for salvation" is an assessment made of *a life as a whole*: it is a claim that the life of the individual in question, whatever its ups and downs, exhibited something sufficient for salvation. Second, it is vitally important to notice that a very wide range of lives will potentially fit the bill. After all, all that is really "necessary for salvation" is that God grant it to us. This means that the lifelong thief who died next to Christ will also have exhibited what was "necessary for salvation." Used in this way, "necessary for salvation" is intuitively appealing but also uninformative.

It is vitally important to notice, however, that the scholars cited above do *not* use "necessary for salvation" in the intuitively obvious but uninformative way. Far to the contrary, they use "necessary for salvation" as a means of distinguishing the agent's *individual acts*. The unavoidable implication of their usage is that some of a Christian's acts are necessary for salvation, and others are not. This inevitably raises the question of how we distinguish those acts that are "necessary for salvation" from those that are not, and it is not at all clear that a question like this has an obvious answer.

Both Kent and Sherwin offer examples of how they understand the difference between those acts that are "necessary for salvation" and those that are not. Sherwin argues that Louis IX possessed infused but not acquired prudence because, in spite of possessing "great personal sanctity," he ignored his wife and made poor decisions about the running of his country.[14] This, says Sherwin, helps to explain how an individual of great holiness might also neglect the needs of his wife and country. So if the infused virtues only "pertain to a very narrow band of action: they pertain only to those acts necessary for salvation," then Louis exhibited the infused virtues within that narrow band, but not elsewhere.[15] Kent's examples are less dramatic, but they have a similar implication. She proposes that one exhibits acquired virtue in daily activities such as "selling cars, or caring for patients, or teaching philosophy," and even in "routine behaviors with family and friends."[16]

Both Kent and Sherwin, then, seem committed to the claim that the way one treats one's family and friends, governs one's country, or does one's job is not relevant to one's salvation; at the very least, they are committed to the claim that one can fail in these aspects of life without failing in what is "necessary for salvation." This seems manifestly incorrect. One's treatment of one's spouse would seem to be very relevant to salvation, as would the way one runs one's country or even sells cars. I suspect, however, that what at least Sherwin and perhaps also Kent has in mind is this: well-meaning and holy people can make mistakes. But, Sherwin seems to be arguing, they don't make mistakes about "things necessary for salvation," insofar as they don't make mistakes about what their faith teaches or requires of them. Their mistakes stem from failures of *human reason*—from a failure to understand what *natural flourishing* demands of them. Flawed saints, the claim seems to be, get supernatural flourishing right and natural flourishing wrong. Moreover, in Sherwin's telling, a failure of human reason results from a failure in acquired virtue and can be remedied by the cultivation of the same. Why did Louis IX mistreat his wife? Because he didn't cultivate acquired prudence. Why did he launch a disastrous crusade? Because he didn't cultivate acquired prudence. And so on.

The problem with this view is that it seems manifestly false. Historians tell us that Louis's decision to launch the Seventh Crusade resulted from a promise made to God during an illness, and that his decision was reinforced by his miraculous recovery from the same illness. They also tell us that Louis was well aware that the crusade would not be particularly beneficial for his country, but that he launched it anyhow, because he believed it was more important to serve God than to serve man. If this is truly the case and if Louis genuinely did make a bad decision in launching the Seventh Crusade, it seems more like a failure in infused prudence than a failure in acquired prudence. Moreover, if it is the case that Louis's long hours at prayer and other devotions were a partial cause of the neglect he showed his wife, then this too sounds more like a failure to rightly exercise infused virtue than a failure in acquired virtue: a failure to understand that a devotion that requires neglect of one's loved ones is not the right kind of devotion at all.

If we consider other saintly moral failures, I suspect we will find, similarly, that the things saints are criticized for doing, in the typical case, are things they believed their love for God required them to do. It is unlikely that considerations about *natural* flourishing led Thomas More to condemn heretics to death. There is every likelihood that he acted as he did because he believed his love for God required it. Similarly, if Mother Teresa was overzealous in her pursuit of deathbed conversions, it clearly was not because she misunderstood how best to pursue the *natural* flourishing of those in her care. It makes more sense to say that their attempts to act out of infused prudence fell short than it does to say that their acquired prudence fell short.

This leads to the most important problem inherent in attempts to draw a line between what is necessary for salvation and what is not. The possessor of infused virtue, this view seems to imply, *doesn't need to grow in infused virtue.* He just needs to "fill out" the rest of his life (or, in Kent's language, also secure earthly happiness) by cultivating the acquired virtues. It is the latter, not the former, that will lead to Christian moral perfection, that will "fill out" the Christian moral life. But this is directly contrary to what Aquinas himself says. On Aquinas's account, it is the *infused virtues* that need to grow and to become more deeply rooted. And an account like this does not accommodate that understanding.

IF SOME FIRM DISTINCTION CAN BE DRAWN, *WITHIN* THE CHRISTIAN moral life, between the life of civic (acquired) virtue and the life of supernatural virtue, and if it can be shown that *both lives* are crucial to Christian moral growth, then some version of the "coexistence" view of the relationship between the infused and acquired virtues will have to be correct. Aquinas's few scattered remarks can reasonably be taken to imply that—at least at some point—he may have held both views. My objection is simply that the coexistence view yields an untenable account of the Christian moral life: first, it is not coherent; second, it does not fit well with Aquinas's own more foundational account of the infused virtues. That is to say, even if Aquinas held a pure coexistence view of the relationship between the infused and acquired virtues, it is not the view that best accommodates his own structural account of the virtues.

Aquinas believes there are infused versions of every natural moral virtue. This means that in any given instance, I *could* act in a manner proportionate to supernatural beatitude. But if this is the case, why would it ever be appropriate for the Christian *not* to act in that way? Why would it ever be appropriate to merely act in a way proportionate to one's natural fulfillment when one could instead act in a manner proportionate to an adopted child of God and adopted sibling of Christ? It is certainly true that citizens of the world must consider the good of their city. But someone who has been ordered to supernatural beatitude through the gifts of grace should surely now consider his city's good and every other natural pursuit in light of the new life he participates in. To say otherwise would imply that the new higher life of grace is only sometimes relevant or is only sometimes appropriate to participate in. It would be one thing to maintain that the Christian *should* always act in a manner proportionate to supernatural beatitude but sometimes or even often fails to do so. That is not, however, what the scholars we examined above seem to propose. They rather seem to say the Christian should deliberately cultivate dispositions to perform acts that are not proportionate to supernatural beatitude, and that such dispositions are an important component of a "full" Christian life.

The attempt to divide the Christian moral life is similarly unconvincing when considered in light of our initial discussion of the respective "structures" of natural and supernatural virtue. In chapter 1, we saw that Aquinas believes we can cultivate the natural virtues because we all naturally possess the "principles" that enable us to cause virtue in ourselves. We possess a natural habitual knowledge of the first speculative and practical principles that gives us an inchoate knowledge of and desire for the fulfillment of our created human nature. Because we also possess reason and appetites susceptible to reason's formation, not only can we act in a manner commensurate with our natural fulfillment but, when we do so repeatedly, we can create habits ordered to our fulfillment in ourselves. This, as we saw in chapter 2, provides the natural foundation that not only makes the infused virtues possible but also enables us to make sense of what the infused virtues are and of what the infused virtues do.

The principles of our nature are sufficient to order us to our natural flourishing, but—as Aquinas clearly insists—they are *insufficient* to order us to the higher, supernatural flourishing made possible by the gift of God's saving grace. To be appropriately ordered to the kind of flourishing grace makes possible, the very principles of our nature must be transformed. Since we cannot act in a manner befitting an end unless we somehow know and desire that end, we must receive supernatural analogues of both our natural inchoate knowledge and our inchoate natural desire. These supernatural analogues are what Aquinas believes we receive in the gift of the theological virtues: an inchoate knowledge of (thanks to the theological virtue of faith) and desire for (thanks to the theological virtues of hope and charity) our supernatural fulfillment.

If grace is truly in harmony with nature (if it is not contrary to nature but instead truly shapes and perfects it), then it would be natural to assume that those new supernatural principles shape and form our natural principles. It is plausible to think that after the gift of grace we have not two sets of principles perhaps hierarchically ordered in some way, but in fact natural principles that have themselves been shaped and fulfilled by grace. But such a view is inconsistent with the version of the coexistence view described above.

The account of the relationship between the infused and the acquired virtues that we have been concerned with in this section implies that the principles of natural and supernatural virtue remain completely distinct, even in the Christian moral life. By Aquinas's own account, the natural virtues arise from natural principles and are ordered toward a natural end. That natural ordering must remain if the virtues that arise from them are to be accurately designated as natural. If the Christian's acts of natural virtue necessarily proceed from natural principles rather than supernatural ones, then this must mean that the natural principles remain capable of their own independent operation, even after God bestows new principles in the form of the theological virtues. The new principles, if they do anything at all, might give a kind of "further direction" to the acts the natural principles produce. But the natural principles themselves would not, on this view, be themselves fundamentally transformed by the gift of grace.

The implication of the pure coexistence view is that our natural principles, rather than being transformed by the gift of grace, simply operate alongside the principles that order man to supernatural beatitude, so that each produces a different kind of act, and so that each act is (primarily) ordered to a different kind of end. The upshot is that grace and nature do not really seem to be in harmony with each other. To the contrary, on this view grace certainly does seem to heal nature, but it does not seem to perfect it. We rather seem to possess two sets of principles, which exist alongside each other in some kind of complicated relationship.

If the coexistence view is unsatisfactory, the clear alternative is to argue that the Christian possesses one and only one kind of virtue. In chapter 5, we will look at arguments to this effect.

CHAPTER 5

Interpretive Options, Part II

Unification

In chapter 3, we saw that Aquinas's scattered remarks about the relationship between the infused and acquired moral virtues can be interpreted in two different ways. His remarks in his *Commentary on the Sentences* (*CS*) and in his *Disputed Questions on the Virtues in General* (*DQVG*) seem to indicate the view we examined in chapter 4: the Christian can and should cultivate both the infused and acquired moral virtues. But—as we saw in chapter 3—Aquinas makes a remark in *ST* I-II, q. 61, a. 5, that does not square neatly with his other remarks. Here, Aquinas could be interpreted as referring not to the Christian's simultaneous cultivation of two distinct kinds of virtue, but to a progression: a gradual shift from the life of acquired virtue to a life of infused virtue. Since he also says that the acquired virtues are what he has been speaking of "until now," it raises the interesting possibility that this article marks a shift: Aquinas is about to stop describing acquired virtue, which has been the topic "until now," and to begin discussing the infused virtues. In this chapter, I examine the view implied by this reading of *ST* I-II, q. 61, a. 5, namely that the Christian's good acts are always of a single, unified kind. Advocates of this view, which I will refer to as the "unification" view, maintain either that all the Christian's virtues are infused virtues, or that the Christian (typically) performs a single unified good act that contains contributions from both the infused and acquired virtues.

In this chapter I will address three different versions of a unification view. The first version holds that grace does not so much change an individual's virtues as the individual himself. Any previously cultivated virtues remain, but they are stronger than they were, and they are now practiced from a new "perspective." On this view, infused virtues are more or less the acquired virtues, as they exist in the person who has received God's saving grace. Moreover, this view holds that as grace is gained and lost, infused virtues become acquired, and vice versa. Although this account preserves the continuity of the Christian moral life, it is problematic. It does not really preserve a place for infused virtues as *virtues*, and it does not accommodate the fundamental differences that Aquinas insists exist between the infused and acquired virtues.

The second view is a more sophisticated version of the first. It too holds that existing acquired virtues become infused virtues, but it offers a much more dramatic account of the transformation. On this latter view, the infused virtues are not merely acquired habits practiced "in a new perspective" but different habits altogether. This view holds that *something* persists through that transformation, but it does not hold that the something that persists is the acquired virtue itself. It also denies that infused virtues become acquired virtues again when grace is lost. Although this view has much to recommend it, I argue that it leaves some important questions unanswered.

The third view maintains that the Christian's infused and acquired virtues, though distinct, can and for the most part do work together, so that each morally good Christian act typically includes the activity of both infused and acquired virtues. This proposal has been defended in different ways by different scholars, but I will focus primarily on what are the most sophisticated versions of that view—those put forward by David Decosimo and George Klubertanz.[1] Although they do an excellent job of anchoring their claims in Aquinas's text, their interpretations minimize his account of the fundamental difference between the infused and acquired virtues.

Interpretive Options, Part II   129

Same Virtue, Different Agent?

In the *Catechism of the Catholic Church* (CCC), which is in other respects deeply informed by the thought of Thomas Aquinas, the infused moral virtues typically receive no mention at all.[2] The same is true of the brief references to or overviews of Aquinas's moral theory offered by moral philosophers of the same period. Philippa Foot, for instance, tells us that "by and large Aquinas followed Aristotle— sometimes even heroically—where Aristotle gave an opinion, and where St. Thomas is on his own, as in developing the doctrine of the theological virtues of faith, hope and charity, and in his theocentric doctrine of happiness, he still uses an Aristotelian framework where he can."[3] The difference between Aristotle and Aquinas, says Foot, is merely that Aquinas emphasizes different things, introduces a few new elements, and "works things out in far more detail than Aristotle did."[4]

What is noteworthy about such accounts is that the acquired moral virtues are made to shoulder all the work of the Christian moral life. One can offer different explanations for this. Foot may simply have been unaware that Aquinas posited the infused moral virtues. But even if she was unaware of them, the authors of the CCC surely were not. A more charitable and more likely explanation is that they simply thought it unnecessary to mention the infused moral virtues. This would be the case if, for instance, the so-called infused virtues simply *are* acquired virtues as they exist in a Christian in a state of grace. If so, then there is really no need to make the discussion murky by introducing the complicated vocabulary of "infused" virtues. Since the "infused virtues" will simply be the acquired virtues as they exist in the individual who has received God's saving grace, it will only really be necessary to consider the process through which the moral virtues are acquired, on the one hand, and grace, on the other. Although an account like this is appealing in its simplicity, I argue that it cannot accommodate Aquinas's most fundamental insights about the virtues.

One scholar who is credited with holding that the infused virtues are simply the acquired virtues as they exist in the Christian in a state of grace is Étienne Gilson.[5] There is good reason for attributing this view to him, for he seems to directly assert it in some places. He says, for instance, that in the Christian, "the natural virtues remain what they were; it is the one who possesses them who has changed" and that "every moral virtue residing in man through charity is a supernatural infused moral virtue."[6] Because Gilson's surrounding discussion is at best unclear, however, I will examine a clearer and more recent defense of this view, that offered by Harm Goris in his "Moral Virtues in Wounded Nature."[7]

Goris's account of the relationship between the infused and acquired virtues is motivated by a laudable concern, namely, to preserve the coherence and unity of the Christian moral life. On an account such as Aquinas's, where the infused virtues are lost with mortal sin and regained with repentance, and where mortal sin is a constant possibility even for the believer, it will necessarily be the case that even most Christians frequently transition in and out of a state of grace. Goris wishes to offer an account that can accommodate those frequent transitions, one that does not depict the Christian moral life as "a chain of radical, discontinuous breaks, of absolute peaks and rock bottoms, like a kind of moral and spiritual rollercoaster."[8] In view of this goal, Goris proposes two theses about Aquinas's account of virtue. First, he argues that Christians in a state of grace "are not *per se* morally better off."[9] As Goris interprets Aquinas, the Christian in a state of grace practices the same virtues he previously possessed but simply with "a different perspective."[10] Second, Goris wishes to argue that for Aquinas, grace transforms existing acquired virtues into infused virtues. When grace is lost, infused virtues become acquired virtues again. When the same individual repents, his acquired virtues are once again transformed into infused virtues.[11]

In support of the first thesis, Goris rightly points out that for Aquinas the cultivation of the acquired moral virtues is itself a preparation for grace. Grace elevates our nature and orders us to a supernatural end, but there is an important continuity between the respective ends of the natural virtues and supernatural virtues. The infusion of grace casts the goods we previously sought in a new light and—Goris argues—transforms the acquired moral virtues into infused virtues. Goris insists, however, that the transformation should be understood as a "qualitative" change: existing acquired virtues, he argues, should be understood not as being replaced but as strengthened: "We could also label this 'transformation' as a 'strengthening' of the acquired virtues, which brings out better that there is also continuity: the acquired virtues are not destroyed or replaced, but somehow remain virtually present, though in a different form because of a different perspective and a different rule: the supernatural instead of some natural end and the rule of divine law, in particular the New Law, instead of the (mere) rule of natural reason."[12] The infused virtues, Goris concludes, should thus be understood as "the supernatural perfections" of the acquired virtues.

Several scholars have proposed accounts similar to Goris's.[13] If an account like this is to be understood, however, two aspects of it need further development. First, we need a fuller understanding of what it means to say that the "same" virtues are present before and after the infusion of grace, that it is merely their possessor who has changed. Second, the claim that the acquired virtues constitute some kind of core or component of the infused virtues would have to be defended in a way compatible with Aquinas's clear and consistent claim that the amount of infused virtue one possesses depends only on God. An account like this would need to explain how the infused virtues can be both fully gratuitous and still contain some kind of acquired "core."

With respect to the first claim, I think that what Goris and Gilson and others who make similar claims have in mind is something like the following. Grace might give new goals and new reasons, but one makes use of the same habits in pursuing those new goals. I think they intend to claim that if temperance, say, is informed by new or different reasons, or directed by new or different motives, this doesn't require any change in the *habit* itself: my habit still causes me to act in accord with right reason. Suppose, for instance, that I habitually exercise because I rightly realize that doing so is conducive to my bodily health and that health is conducive to a flourishing life. If, after years of doing so, the circumstances of my life change — I have a child or my spouse is sick — I might realize that it is no longer appropriate for me to devote as much attention to my physical health as I previously did. I might realize that it is in fact appropriate to be less physically fit so that I can be a better spouse or a better mother. I think what Goris and others have in mind is that when I make this change, the *same* temperance is at work: indeed, it is the very presence of temperance that enables me to realize that it is now appropriate for me to exercise less than I previously did.

With respect to the second claim, I think Goris and others might argue that one should distinguish the *amount* of an infused virtue one possesses from the *ease* with which one practices that virtue. They could argue that the amount of infused virtue one possesses depends on God's free gift, but that the ease we experience in the practice of that virtue stems from previously acquired virtues. We might think, for example, of two different martyrs. Suppose that martyr A lived a life of natural virtue and cultivated a high degree of acquired courage prior to his conversion, but that his faith is weak. As a consequence, he possesses a very limited degree of charity and the other infused virtues. Suppose on the other hand that martyr B converted wholeheartedly from a life of vice and cowardice: he had cultivated no acquired virtue whatsoever, but he possesses a high amount of charity and the other infused virtues. I think that what Goris and others have in mind is something like the following. B's martyrdom would exhibit a great deal of infused virtue, far more than A's would, but B would also (on this account) find his far more virtuous act far more difficult to carry out because he would lack the "strength" that A's acquired courage supplied. A, by contrast, would exhibit a far lesser degree of infused virtue, but he would find his martyrdom far easier than B would.

Both of these responses, however, misunderstand moral virtue. Consider first the claim that previously cultivated acquired virtues provide the "ease" that the infused virtues would otherwise lack. We certainly have to concede that an individual who receives infused virtue will still be able to make use of many previously cultivated abilities. We should agree, for instance, that someone who is self-disciplined and attentive to detail will remain self-disciplined and attentive to detail after his conversion. And traits like self-discipline and attention to detail do make it easier for one to achieve whatever goal one happens to have. But they are not *virtues*. They cannot be, because they also facilitate our pursuit of evil ends. They are traits that facilitate the pursuit of *any end whatsoever*. The acquired moral virtues, by contrast, cause our appetites to be rightly ordered to appropriate ends. They give us a general affective inclination to stand firm in human justice, or to eat and drink the appropriate amount, and so on. Those general affective inclinations both help to direct our moral reasoning and help us to follow through on our decisions. They do not provide some kind of general, portable "strength" that facilitates the pursuit of any end whatever. Thus *if* it is the case that previously cultivated acquired virtues make the activities of the infused virtues easy, it will have to be the case that general appetitive inclinations to the ends of the natural virtues make it "easy" to pursue the ends of the infused virtues. I address this point in more detail in my discussion of the example of infused and acquired courage in chapter 6, but for the moment it suffices to say that it is by no means obvious that this is the case.

A deeper problem for this account is that infused virtues are not recognizable in it as *virtues* in any sense of the word. In our example above, where B performs an act of great love with great difficulty, where is B's infused courage? It is easy to see him as performing a *virtuous action*, but it is less coherent to claim that he is *acting virtuously*. Goris and others who defend such accounts acknowledge this, saying that the infused virtues are only virtues in an "analogous" sense. But it is hard to see why, on such an account, there would be infused virtues at all. Why wouldn't acquired virtue and charity suffice?[14] More importantly, such an account does not square well at all with Aquinas's more general account of moral virtue. As we saw in the preceding chapters, the moral virtues are inclinations that inhere in the appetites. By making us well ordered to the various ends of the moral virtues, they guide and direct our reasoning and help us to adhere to reason's judgment. It is hard to see how B's act, as described above, captures any of this. I will return to this point in chapter 6.

A similar point can be made about the claim that it is not the previously acquired virtue itself that changes, but merely the "perspective" of the one who possesses it. The possession and practice of infused virtue is not merely a matter of having additional reasons. The infused moral virtues dispose the appetites to be appropriately ordered to a good that reason cannot fully comprehend. An affective desire for a good that reason cannot fully comprehend is not the same as an affective desire for a good that reason *can* fully comprehend. An appetitive inclination to defend one's faith, even in the face of death, is not merely a matter of taking an inclination to defend one's country and adding some additional presuppositions. It is the difference between an inclination to risk one's life for a fully comprehensible, tangible good and an inclination to risk one's life for something one cannot fully comprehend. And the latter does not easily translate to the former. I will address this point in more detail in chapter 6.

"Trans-formation"

The version of the unification view examined in the previous section is successful in this respect: it offers a unified account of the Christian moral life and especially of the Christian's transition from sin to grace and back again. One might well argue, however, that this is not so much an asset as a defect, that it characterizes Christian moral goodness more as the result of effort than of grace. In this section, I examine a rather different version of the unification view, that defended by Bill Mattison. As Goris does, Mattison holds that the Christian possesses one and only one kind of virtue, infused virtue. Mattison, however, characterizes the transformation brought about by grace in a much more dramatic way. He does not argue that the change is merely one of "perspective," or credit previously acquired virtues with providing any ease that one might experience in the activity of infused virtue. And, although Mattison does hold that any previously existing acquired virtues are transformed by the initial gift of grace, he does not believe that infused virtues become acquired virtues again when grace is lost. To the contrary, what persists through the loss of grace are not virtues, but dispositions akin to the kind of dispositions that originate through custom.[15] Although I am sympathetic to this last claim, I do not examine it here, because the truth of it is not central to the unification view.[16]

Mattison has addressed the question of the relationship between the infused and acquired virtues in several articles. The two most relevant for present purposes are "Can Christians Possess the Acquired Cardinal Virtues?" and "Revisiting the Relationship between Infused and Acquired Cardinal Virtues."[17] The first article argues for the general thesis: any acquired virtues are necessarily transformed with the infusion of grace; the second offers a proposal about how, precisely, that transformation should be understood.

Mattison's argument that the Christian cannot possess any acquired moral virtues is based on his interpretation of two central texts: *ST* I-II, q. 51, a. 4, ad 3, and *DQVG* a. 10, ad 4. After rightly arguing that *ST* I-II, q. 51, a. 4, ad 3, does not make any assertions whatsoever about a continued role for the acquired virtues in the Christian moral life, Mattison offers his own proposal regarding how grace affects any preexisting acquired virtues: "If an acquired virtue did exist before the infused virtue, the infused virtue has either replaced the acquired habit — or, if one prefers, has (literally) trans-formed it — into a new ('strengthened') habit, now directed toward a supernatural last end with the resulting formal difference in species of action and habit."[18] The hyphenated "trans-form," as Mattison argues in a footnote, is used to emphasize the dramatic nature of the change that would necessarily occur: not just a change in end, but a change in *form*. In the same vein, Mattison argues that Aquinas's own account of the differences between the infused and acquired virtues makes it impossible to interpret *DQVG* a. 10, ad 4, as defenders of the coexistence view do.[19] Aquinas holds that the infused and acquired virtues produce acts proportionate to different ends and as such seek a different mean — they do not produce the same acts. But if this is the case, it is not at all clear how infused temperance could guide and direct a distinct acquired temperance: How could a virtue that in itself requires one kind of action guide and direct a virtue that requires something altogether different? How could a virtue that requires that I castigate my flesh and bring it into subjection, as infused temperance does, "guide" the virtue that directs me to eat the amount appropriate to bodily health?[20] Mattison argues that a better interpretation of *DQVG* a. 10, ad 4, would take it as the assertion that the infused virtues altogether "trans-form" the acquired virtues: "The mediation of infused virtue is more properly said to (again, literally) trans-form the act of acquired virtue to make it meritorious. In some sense the acts of acquired virtue do persist, namely as acts with the same material object."[21]

The last sentence is important, because it indicates a key difference between Mattison's account and Goris's. Where Goris and others argue that it is the possessor of the virtue more than the virtues themselves that are transformed by grace, Mattison's claim is that the virtues possessed by the Christian are a different kind altogether. This is why he insists that if the convert does possess any natural virtues, they are either "replaced" or entirely "trans-formed." The only aspect of the acquired virtue that persists is its "material object." Since Mattison argues that it is only their "material object" and not the acquired virtues themselves that persist through grace's transformation, understanding that claim will be key to understanding his view. In his "Revisiting the Relationship," Mattison uses Aquinas's discussion of formed and unformed faith as a means of flushing out this proposal.

Aquinas explicitly considers how grace (and charity) alters a virtue, and he explicitly argues that the gift of grace does not introduce a new habit of faith but rather "forms" a habit that already exists. For anyone who wishes to argue that grace "forms" the acquired virtues, this text seems very promising. In order to consider whether and how Aquinas's description of faith's formation can shed light on the relationship between the natural and supernatural virtues, however, we will need to take a deeper look at Aquinas's claims and Mattison's interpretation of them.

Aquinas makes a number of claims about faith (which he defines as the habitual belief in true claims about God) that are relevant for present purposes. First, he distinguishes between "formed" and "unformed," or "living" and "dead," faith. Faith properly speaking is a habit that involves both the intellect, which assents to something as true, and the will, which moves the intellect to assent. In the act of faith properly speaking, the faith that is an infused theological virtue, the virtue of charity in the will prompts the intellect to assent to the truths of faith. But a will not formed by charity can still prompt the

Interpretive Options, Part II   137

intellect to assent to the truths of the faith, and this does not change *what is assented to*. It merely changes the manner in which one assents: the "mode" of acting. When charity is absent, Aquinas holds that the habit of assent to true claims about God persists in the intellect, and it remains *specifically the same* habit: it remains a disposition to affirm true things about God. The difference is that faith properly speaking is prompted or "formed" by charity.

Second, Aquinas claims that the habit of belief, *whether formed by charity or not*, is necessarily a gift from God. Faith, says Aquinas, requires both that something be proposed to us to believe and that our will assent. Both require God. Since "the things that belong to the faith" exceed human reason, they "cannot be included in man's contemplation unless God reveals them."[22] Moreover, once something is revealed, it must be assented to. And this too, Aquinas argues, must come from God: "Since, in assenting to what belongs to the Faith, a man is elevated above his nature [*elevetur supra naturam suam*], this assent must exist in him from a supernatural principle moving him interiorly, and this is God. And so as regards the assent, which is the principal act of faith, faith is from God moving the man interiorly through grace."[23] The description of faith given here refers to faith properly so called, namely, the faith that is a theological virtue. But Aquinas argues that even "dead," or "unformed," faith is necessarily still a gift from God.

Mattison argues that the continuity between dead and living faith offers a potential avenue of understanding the transformation that grace effects in existing acquired virtues. Both the acquired moral virtues and unformed faith are habits "that are not charity yet are informed by charity."[24] In both cases, Mattison argues, "the 'essence,' or material object, of the habit remains the same whether informed by charity or not."[25] What differs is the will that commands the habit: "Nonetheless they do indeed differ as to the object of the will as end, which is provided by charity. Thus their difference is not of essence, but in their form, or mode of acting, as imperfect to perfect."[26] Thus, Mattison concludes that the acquired virtues, like unformed faith, are "habits the same in the activity to which they directly pertain, their material object."[27]

It is important to be clear about what Mattison is and is not saying. Aquinas says that formed and unformed faith do not differ in species; indeed, Aquinas argues that formed and unformed faith are numerically the same habit. Mattison is well aware of this. He is equally well aware that Aquinas says that the infused and acquired virtues *do* differ in species. Mattison's claim is about what he calls the "material object" of the acquired virtues. It is the *material object* that he wants to argue "remains the same whether informed by charity or not." This is already a remove from what happens between formed and unformed faith, because it is the habit of faith itself, not its "material object," that Aquinas claims remains the same habit regardless of whether it is formed by faith or not.

In what follows, I want to reexamine Aquinas's remarks on the difference between formed and unformed faith, on the one hand, and infused and acquired virtue, on the other, with an eye toward attempting to understand Mattison's claim that the latter habits are "the same in the activity to which they directly pertain, their material object." An examination of these texts does not establish any substantive continuity between the infused and acquired virtues.

In *ST* II-II, q. 4, a. 4, Aquinas asks whether formed and unformed faith are "numerically the same habit." He replies that they are. Habits are diversified by what belongs to them per se. Faith is a perfection of the intellect, and so what belongs to faith per se belongs to the intellect. It is the presence of charity in the will that determines whether charity is formed or unformed. Unformed faith is imperfect, but its lack of perfection does not pertain to the nature of faith itself. When a thing's imperfection does not belong to the nature of the thing, then, says Aquinas, it is numerically the same thing that becomes perfect.

Aquinas's description of the difference between the infused and acquired virtues is rather different. In article 4 of question 63, Aquinas asks whether the infused and acquired virtues belong to different species of virtue, and he argues that they do. He argues that a specific difference can be caused either by the "specific and formal character of the object" or by what it is that the virtue is ordered to.[28] Aquinas argues that the infused and acquired virtues are specifically different in both respects, but it is the first respect that is directly relevant to our present purposes. The object of a virtue is "the good considered in some proper subject matter."[29] So the object of temperance, for instance, is "the good of what is pleasurable in sentient desires associated with touch."[30] Aquinas then further distinguishes what is formal and what is material in the object of temperance. What is formal in the object of temperance, says Aquinas, comes from reason, "which establishes a mean in the relevant desires."[31] The material "aspect" of the object of temperance, on the other hand, "is what comes from the sentient desires."[32] Since it is from reason, or more precisely the mean that reason establishes in the relevant desires, that the object of (acquired) temperance receives its formal character," and since "the mean imposed on these desires by human reason is different from the rule imposed by God's law," Aquinas concludes that the infused and acquired virtues necessarily differ in species.

There are a number of things that could be noted about these two different explanations, but let's focus on the question of what does and does not persist in each case. Aquinas clearly believes that formed and unformed faith are perfect and imperfect versions of the same habit. The habit in the intellect does the same thing regardless of the state of the will that commands it: it assents to true beliefs about God. The "form" that the will imposes is not on the *object* of faith, but on the manner in which what is believed is believed. Aquinas is clear, then, that in the case of faith, the habit itself persists.

Mattison is not proposing, of course, that what happens in the case of faith can directly explain what happens in the case of the (ostensible) transformation of the acquired virtues. He is not proposing that the habit of acquired virtue itself persists through the change—but that the "material object" persists through the change. Yet when we look again at Aquinas's explanation of why it is that the infused and acquired virtues differ in species, we find no reference to "material object."[33] Aquinas refers to the material *aspect* of the object, as he also refers to the formal aspect of the object. But what is the material aspect? It is clear that the "material aspect" of the object of an acquired moral virtue is simply the desire that is formed: "The formal character of this object comes from reason, which establishes a mean in the relevant sentient desires, whereas the material aspect of the object is what comes from the sentient desires."[34] In every act of temperance, desire is conformed to—brought under the rule of—reason. But it is not as if there are discrete "desires" waiting around for reason's formation. Indeed, it is not at all clear that one can separate actual "formal" and "material" components of the object of acquired virtue. This is why Aquinas speaks not of "formal object" and "material object" but rather of formal and material *aspects* of the object of acquired virtue.

Aquinas's remarks about the specific difference between the infused and acquired virtues highlight the important—and crucial—contrast with Aquinas's account of formed and unformed faith. In the latter case, Aquinas is clear that there is a *habit* that persists and is formed by charity. But what would be left of an acquired virtue if reason's formation were absent? The faculty of desire, certainly, perhaps a faculty that possessed certain prerational tendencies or inclinations, but it is not clear that there would be much else. If the claim is that in the case of acquired virtue, desires are formed by reason, and in the case of the infused virtues, desires are formed by the rule of divine law, then that is true, but it reveals nothing at all about the relationship between the infused and acquired virtues. It has not been established that there is something—beyond the faculty of desire itself and its prerational tendencies—that persists through the loss of acquired virtue and receives subsequent formation by the infused virtues. More importantly, it is not clear that anything that *did* persist would be specific to an acquired virtue. For instance, how, absent reason's formation, would the "material object" of an acquired virtue differ from the "material object" of an acquired vice? Consider, for instance, the difference between two career soldiers, one who possesses acquired courage and one who possesses a habit that is to external appearances very similar but is in fact motivated by pride. Now suppose both convert. Does the "material object" (whatever it is) persist in both cases? If not, why not?

Mattison's account has much to recommend it, but it attempts to do something unnecessary. His fundamental insight is twofold: the infused virtues are the only virtues that matter in the Christian moral life, and the infused virtues are not simply redirected acquired virtues. As will become clear in chapter 6, I fully agree with both of these insights. I simply believe that one can defend both claims without also

Interpretive Options, Part II   141

holding that any existing acquired virtues are transformed into infused virtues along with the gift of grace.

Two Contributors to a Single Act

Some scholars have argued that each of the Christian's morally good acts includes — or at least can include — contributions from both the infused and the acquired virtues. This is the position defended by George Klubertanz and Reneé Mirkes, who maintain that the infused and acquired virtues are related as "form to matter," and it is also the position more recently defended by David Decosimo.[35] Though the details differ, all three accounts have some common components. First, all three scholars emphasize that one virtue can make use of another virtue. Second, all three scholars focus on the difference in "rule" as a way of distinguishing the respective contributions of the infused and acquired virtues. Finally, all offer a similar way of accounting for situations where the infused virtues are present in the absence of the acquired virtues. Since Mirkes's position is mainly derived from Klubertanz's, I will be primarily concerned with unpacking the interpretation put forward by Klubertanz and Decosimo.[36]

Both Klubertanz and Decosimo heavily emphasize the fact that Aquinas believes one habit can make use of another. Klubertanz uses the example of the habit of science. Science is a habit of the intellect, but it must make use of something, namely, the imagination. This leads Klubertanz to assert that the habit of scientific knowledge is a "composite" habit: the habit in the intellect is "like the form," while the habit in the imagination that science makes use of is "like the matter."[37] Although the comparison between form and matter goes beyond anything that can be found in Aquinas, Klubertanz is certainly correct in his assertion that one habit can make use of another.

Decosimo does not speak of one habit "forming" another, but rather what he calls "subalternation," the meaning of which is not immediately clear. Decosimo uses "subalternation" as interchangeable with "virtual presence," but this does not help matters much because the term "virtual presence" is itself unclear.[38] "Virtual presence" is a

142 *Aquinas and the Infused Moral Virtues*

term that Aquinas uses to explain how it is that the elements are present in mixed bodies: how it is, for instance that—to use an anachronistic example—hydrogen and oxygen are present in water. Aquinas refuses to acknowledge (or would have, had he known of it) that the substantial forms of hydrogen and oxygen are present in the mixed body that is water. Water, in Aquinas's view, has a single substantial form.[39] The elements of which it is a mixture do not continue to exist, but nonetheless their "power" is preserved.[40] Aquinas's notion of virtual presence is not only difficult to understand in its own right, but also limited in scope: he clearly does not believe that "virtual presence" can be used to explain the way in which nonelemental components of other composites are present.[41] For this reason, I will assume Decosimo's reference to "virtual presence" is intended metaphorically. His examples are more revealing. Decosimo points out that a musician who is also a mathematician can make use of his habit of mathematics in the practice of music. He likewise points out that a captain of a ship who also has knowledge of subordinate skills can, as a captain, make use of those subordinate skills.[42] The point, then, seems to be more or less the same as that made by Klubertanz: one habit can make use of another.

As we have already seen, there is nothing particularly controversial about the claim that Aquinas believes one habit can make use of another. The more controversial and more complicated question lies in the details. Exactly *how* do the infused virtues make use of the acquired virtues, and vice versa? Both Klubertanz and Decosimo answer this question by appealing to Aquinas's assertion that the infused and acquired virtues each operate according to different "rules."

Klubertanz argues that the difference between the infused and acquired virtues should be understood in terms of the kinds of premises that are operative in our deliberations. When we reason from faith alone, our act is purely an act of infused virtue and does not cause an acquired habit. When we act from reason alone, on the other hand, our act is purely an act of acquired virtue. It causes an acquired virtue but does not involve or make use of infused virtue. But when we make use of *both* faith *and* human reason in our acts, then our act involves both an infused virtue (insofar as we are guided by faith) and an acquired virtue (insofar as we make use of reason). This is how acts of infused virtue can sometimes cause an acquired virtue: because in acting out of infused virtue we sometimes also make use of natural reason.[43] Insofar as we reason from what we know by faith, we are acting from a supernatural principle and hence operating out of infused virtue. Insofar as we rely on natural reason, we act from a natural principle and hence cultivate an acquired virtue.

Decosimo is similarly focused on the "rule" that guides the action. Like Klubertanz, he argues that infused and acquired virtue are distinguished by their relation to reason: "Acquired virtues dispose to action immediately in accord with right reason. Infused moral virtues generate action dictated immediately by New Law." For Decosimo, what the action is "immediately" concerned with is particularly important: "The 'immediately' here is vital. . . . To say that both are immediately concerned with this is to say that this exhausts their activity. They conduce to some act that exemplifies the application of their rule and their rule only."[44] Decosimo's claim that what the action is "immediately concerned with" is important, as is his claim that it "exhausts" the activity of the virtue in question. The idea seems to be that the infused and acquired virtues are distinct, and each governed by distinct rules, but that sometimes the virtue concerned with the higher rule recognizes that it needs to make use of the lower rule, and when it does, both infused and acquired virtue are operative. It is through infused virtue that one recognizes an act of acquired virtue is necessary, and through infused virtue that the act of acquired virtue is commanded, but it is acquired virtue that does the work. His examples indicate that this is indeed the interpretation he wishes to defend.

As examples of the relationship he has in mind, Decosimo points to instances where an individual uses one habit in the service of another. A captain of a ship can make use of habits that are not directly tied to being a captain, such as a habitual knowledge of sail rigging. A musician can make use of his habitual knowledge of mathematics. It is as captain that the use of the sail rigging habit is commanded, or as musician that the habitual knowledge of mathematics is employed, but it is the subordinate habit that actually does the work. The same, Decosimo argues, is true of the infused and acquired virtues, which "stand to their matter as distinct mathematical functions. A virtue conduces to *one formally specified act.* Infused virtue cannot apply right reason to some matter any more than acquired virtue can apply New Law or a cake baking habit can produce sweaters."[45]

Both Klubertanz and Decosimo, then, believe that the respective contributions of the infused and acquired virtues appear in the specific details of the virtuous act. Insofar as the virtuous act has to do with the new law, it will be an act of infused virtue. But insofar as the virtuous act has to do with right reason, it will be an act of acquired virtue. And insofar as one using the new law recognizes the need to make use of right reason, infused virtue will make use of acquired. For instance, sometimes it may be the case that the best way to fulfill the new law "may be to undertake an act in immediate accord with right reason, an act of acquired virtue. In such cases, infused virtue is also at work. Infused virtue determines that such an act best honors New Law. Additionally, it commands it."[46]

An interpretation like this can seem to solve a great many problems. It offers an account of the Christian moral life that accommodates both the infused and the acquired virtues, and it allows one to give an apparently seamless account of how one can move from possessing only acquired virtues to possessing both infused and acquired virtues and back again. It is also attentive to Aquinas's explicit remarks about the infused and acquired virtues, and especially to his assertion that each kind of virtue is governed by a different "rule." At the same time, however, I don't think this view is plausible, either in its own right or as an interpretation of Aquinas.

Both Decosimo and Klubertanz insist that the infused virtues "make use of" the acquired. But although both offer examples of how one habit might make use of another, neither offers examples of how an infused moral virtue makes use of an acquired moral virtue. This omission is significant, precisely because it is not clear how the examples that are offered could be translated to a situation where an infused moral virtue ostensibly makes use of an acquired. It is clear that a boat captain could make use of a previously cultivated habit, such as sail rigging, and it is likewise clear that his sail rigging habit, even while used in the service of his goals as a captain, would remain a separate habit. But the ability to rig sails, like the ability to pilot a boat, is a skill. Even if contemporary scholars have made much of the important similarities that exist between skills and virtues, they are still not the same. The most notable difference between them, of course, is that a skill can be put to the service of good and evil ends alike, but virtue cannot. It is unsurprising that a habit such as sail rigging can be put to the service of other aims and goals; it is precisely the sort of thing than can be used in that way. But if the analogy is to go through, it will have to be the case that infused courage can "make use of" acquired courage in the same way that the captain can "make use of" the skill of sail rigging.

Even if they do not offer specific examples, Decosimo and Klubertanz do imply an account of how it is that an infused virtue makes use of an acquired insofar as they emphasize the different "rules" of the infused and acquired virtues. If the agent makes use of natural reason, then the agent is making use of the "rule of reason." If the agent makes use of faith, then the agent is making use of the "rule of divine law." But this, as I argue in what follows, is not the right way to understand a difference in rule. Aquinas's distinction about the different "rules" of the infused and acquired virtues is at heart a distinction about the proportionality of one's acts, not the specific reasons one appeals to in acting. To fully address this point, we will need a reminder of some aspects of the discussion of the first part of this book.

We saw in earlier chapters that Aquinas does indeed consistently distinguish the infused and acquired virtues on the basis of their respective "rules." But in order to understand what the "rule" really is and how it really functions in guiding virtue, it is important to consider the context in which Aquinas introduces the notion of the "rule" of a virtue. Aquinas contrasts the "rule" of reason and the "rule" of divine law in order to distinguish the different standards against which virtue is measured. The discussion of the different "measures" or "rules" of virtue, in turn, is something that arises from Aquinas's insistence that virtues produce acts proportionate to their end. Thus in order to understand how the discussion of the "rule" of virtue operates in Aquinas's thought, we first have to return to his insistence that virtues produce acts proportionate to their end.

As we saw in earlier chapters, Aquinas locates the need for the infused virtues in the insufficiency of our natural principles. Our natural principles order us to the good proportionate to our nature in a very specific way: they give us an inchoate knowledge of our natural good, a knowledge that in turn generates a desire for that good. Acts of natural moral virtue occur when we reason from those natural principles to a correct conclusion about what ought to be done and act accordingly. Doing so repeatedly creates dispositions in the powers of the soul, making them appropriately responsive to reason. This is the sense in which reason is the "rule" of the natural virtues. Reason is the rule of the natural virtues because the person who possesses them has desires that are proportionate to or commensurate with reason's apprehension of the good.

It is on the basis of these same insights that Aquinas argues for the necessity of the infused virtues. The infused virtues are necessary because our natural principles—our natural, habitual knowledge of the first speculative and practical principles—are insufficient. Our natural principles produce acts proportionate to our natural good: they enable us to act in a manner commensurate with right reason. But they do not and cannot enable us to act in a manner proportionate to our supernatural good; they cannot enable us to act in a manner commensurate with supernatural beatitude. This is why, if we are to act in a manner befitting that higher good, we need the gift of higher principles. This is what Aquinas proposes that the theological virtues of faith, hope, and love do: they give us an inchoate knowledge of and desire for our supernatural fulfillment and thus do for our supernatural good what our natural principles do for our natural good.

THE GIFT OF THE THEOLOGICAL VIRTUES DOES NOT COMPLETELY solve the problem, however, because even this inchoate knowledge is not enough: the theological virtues order us to something more perfect than our natural principles do, but they are possessed less perfectly than our natural principles are. Reason cannot apply these supernatural principles in action without help; this is why Aquinas (at least in his mature writings) insists that it needs the additional help of the

Holy Spirit, something made possible by the gifts. More importantly, we cannot cause desires commensurate to this higher end in our appetites through our own repeated acts. A true ordering to supernatural beatitude means that this order is present even in our appetites, that our desires, too, are commensurate to supernatural beatitude. And we cannot cause such desires in ourselves. This is the sense in which the infused virtues are ordered to "a mean imposed by God's rule."[47] Through the infused virtues, we are capable of desiring and acting in a manner proportionate to supernatural beatitude rather than merely in a manner proportionate to our natural good, capable of acting according to a rule set by God rather than one set merely by reason.

In light of all this, it should be clear just how dramatically we miss the mark when we attempt to ascertain which kind of virtue we act in accord with by looking merely to the "kind" of reason we appeal to in acting. "Rule" refers to the *source* of my action and to the end that governs it, not to whether some specific premise can be known through the natural light of reason or only by revelation. The theological virtues shape our reason and will; they do not constitute some kind of separate sphere of action. When we reason in the light of faith, we still make use of truths unaided reason can grasp, and it is merely that we now, for the first time, see those truths in their fullness, in the light of faith. I can see that it is good to help someone in need through my own unaided natural reason, and if I have cultivated the relevant virtues in my appetitive powers, I will also experience desires commensurate with that recognition. I can see the same thing in the light of grace: grace does not eliminate that natural recognition but fulfills it. In the light of grace, I am all the more aware that I ought to help, because I see the needs of others not merely in the context of my natural good but in the light of charity and my supernatural good. But the desires commensurate to the first recognition are importantly *not*—not, at least, on Aquinas's account—the same as the desires commensurate to the second recognition. *This* is what the distinction in the "rules" that measure virtue is intended to capture.

All three versions of the unification view are motivated by important concerns. They all seek to offer a coherent picture of the Christian moral life, and they all seek to secure a genuine role for the infused moral virtues in that life. But each version also leaves important questions unanswered. In chapter 6, I propose a different way of understanding the relationship between the infused and acquired virtues.

CHAPTER 6

A Proposal for a Way Forward

*Trust in the Lord with all thine heart; and lean
not unto thine own understanding. In all thy ways
acknowledge him, and he shall direct thy paths.*

—Proverbs 3:5–6

Thus far we've seen that Aquinas's account of the infused virtues and acquired virtues is founded on both his Aristotelian understanding of nature and his Christian understanding of how grace transforms nature. For Aquinas, grace does not simply redirect nature and order it to a further end, but also it alters the very principles that order us to our end in the first place. I have argued that the different theories of the relationship between the infused and acquired virtues have to be evaluated in terms of how we understand that alteration. Does grace give us a new set of principles that exist alongside our natural principles? Or does grace transform the natural principles themselves? Insofar as both the "coexistence" and "unification" theories are problematic, it may seem that we have arrived at an impasse. In point of fact, however, both theories get something right. The coexistence view is right to draw a sharp distinction between the infused and acquired virtues and to insist that grace does not directly transform any existing acquired virtues into infused virtues. At the same time, however, those who argue that grace "transforms" existing acquired virtues into infused virtues are correct in

149

this much: the cultivation of the infused virtues is the only coherent goal of the Christian moral life. In this chapter, my goal is to contextualize and defend these two claims and to explore what their combined truth means for an account of the Christian moral life.

In the first three sections of this chapter, I propose an account of how we ought to understand the transformation brought about by grace and the activity of the virtues that are bestowed along with it. Specifically, I claim that (1) the transformation brought about by the theological virtues is incomplete, that (2) the actions made possible by the theological and infused virtues differ in essential ways from the acts ordered to our natural fulfillment, and that (3) it is entirely plausible to think that previously cultivated habits (virtuous or otherwise) persist as dispositions after the gift of grace. The life that grace makes possible *is* different from the life of acquired virtue, and although grace makes this life possible, it does not immediately make us proficient practitioners of it. The new life is something that we must struggle (with God's help) to cultivate.

In the final section of this chapter, I consider the relationship between the virtues bestowed through grace and one's previously possessed habits (virtuous or otherwise). It will seem to many that my claims that (1) the acquired and infused virtues are very different and that (2) previously cultivated habits persist in some form, if true, are themselves evidence that there *must* be a place for the cultivation of the acquired virtues in the Christian moral life. If the infused virtues are both so different and initially so weak, isn't this evidence that the cultivation of the acquired virtues will be a necessary component of moral progress? I will argue that this view is untenable. It is not only incompatible with Aquinas's remarks about moral growth, but implies that one should deliberately lower one's moral aspirations, that having been made capable of acts befitting an adopted child of God, we should nonetheless be content with a lesser kind of action. If my account is correct, it will of course be true that many—even most—of those who possess the supernatural virtues frequently fail to live up to them. Given *that* we fail, it will also be true that some failures are less serious than others. But this does not mean those less serious failures are a worthy goal in and of themselves.

I conclude by addressing the question of what all this means for our understanding of the Christian moral life.

NATURE'S TRANSFORMATION

Scholars often describe grace as something that changes everything all at once. One scholar, for instance, imagines a young man in an identical situation to the rich young man of the Gospels but who accepts Christ's call instead of going away sad. The hypothetical young man "is moved to sell everything and to follow Jesus. Thereafter he centers his life around his relationship with Jesus, whom he strives to emulate and to serve."[1] Making Christ the center of his life, this scholar proposes, "changes everything. For instance, the young man's previous and morally upright resolve to do the best he can at his job (say, investment banking) now becomes a resolve to do the best he can at his job out of love of God and of neighbor for the sake of God."[2] An account like this seems to be true in one respect but false in another.

In a very important sense it does indeed seem to be the case that the acceptance of Christ's call "changes everything" all at once. Those who tell stories of conversion often point to some particular moment when "everything" changed. John Newton, for instance, is famous for authoring the song "Amazing Grace" and equally famous for the conversion experience that inspired the song. After being impressed into the Royal Navy at eighteen, Newton had a checkered career at sea that eventually led to a job aboard a slave trader's ship. One day, out of sheer boredom, Newton picked up Thomas à Kempis's *The Imitation of Christ*. He soon put it down again, "afraid it might all be true," but that night the boat was rocked by a terrible storm. Newton found himself praying for the first time. His experience on the morning after that storm inspired "Amazing Grace."

So, it seems more or less accurate to talk about how "everything changes" in the moment of conversion. But in another respect, it doesn't seem accurate at all. Newton certainly seems to have had a powerful religious experience that forever changed his life. But visible changes in his behavior came slowly. Although he immediately began to study the

Bible, Newton continued to work in the slave trade for some time. Only gradually did he begin to give up his former way of life.

Newton's example is a dramatic one, because he gave up a life of sin. The rich young man of the Gospels, by contrast, has made every effort to live an upright life. In many respects, it seems like the rich young man, should he accept Christ's call, would have an *easier* time following through with his decision, since his previously cultivated habits at least point him toward a genuine good. The point of the Gospel story, of course, is rather different: it is that the rich young man wanted to accept Christ's call but could not.

This is not to take a stand on the respective ease or difficulty experienced by Newton and the rich young man, but rather to highlight the way in which the new life that grace begins is incomplete. Let's look at three points. First, Aquinas consistently compares the theological virtues to "first principles," but the analogy is imperfect. The theological virtues are habits that perfect our natural principles, and although they are more perfect, they are also less perfectly possessed. Second, even the previous possession of the natural virtues does not translate easily or readily to any degree of ease or expertise in the practice of supernatural virtue. Third, there is good reason to think that our previously cultivated habits, whether virtuous or vicious, persist as dispositions even in the life of grace. Together, these points indicate that our first steps in the life of grace are likely to be hesitant and uncertain.

Imperfectly Possessed Principles

Throughout this book I have resisted the idea that the new principles provided by faith operate independently of the natural practical principles known through synderesis. Faith is not contrary to reason, and action that arises out of faith is not somehow separate from or cut off from reason. Far to the contrary, faith helps us to see what reason knows in a new light. Because of this, it seems to me that the only plausible option is to maintain that the first principles known through faith, when they are operative in us, form and illuminate the first principles known through synderesis. That is to say, the Christian's morally good actions do not stem from supernatural principles of faith *instead of* natural ones, but from natural principles that are themselves formed and illumined by faith. At the same time, however, it would be overly hasty to maintain that grace simply effects, once and for all, a thorough and complete "transformation" of our natural principles. It would be hastier still to maintain that that transformation extends to any natural virtues we may have cultivated or have been in the process of cultivating prior to receiving the gift of habitual grace.

My goal in this section is to consider just what the notion that the theological virtues provide us with new first principles does and does not mean. I will argue that while grace does indeed give us, in the theological virtues, habits that perfect our natural principles, those habits are imperfectly possessed. Our imperfect possession of those habits means, among other things, that not everything that is true of our natural first principles will be true of them.

At the beginning of his *Introduction to Christianity*, Joseph Ratzinger cites a story often told by theologians as an analogy of how difficult it is to convey the Christian faith to a secular audience. In the story, a traveling circus catches fire just as it is preparing for its performance. The clown, already dressed for the night's show, runs into town seeking help. The townspeople, seeing the clown's comical attire, think he is merely advertising the performance. The more he pleads for help, the more amused the townspeople are, and the circus burns to the ground. Ratzinger thinks the story illuminates a false perception that the theologian needs to guard against.

The story of the clown can convey the false impression that the theologian who wants a hearing from a secular audience need only "take off" his clown suit, that is, find a way to convey what is already abundantly clear to him in a way his audience can understand. The problem with such an image, Ratzinger believes, is that it implies that "the theologian is a man possessed of full knowledge who arrives with a perfectly clear message" and that the villagers "have to be told something of which they are completely unaware."[3] Ratzinger argues that if the person of faith is honest with himself, he will recognize that his difficulty in conveying the truths of the faith stems not just from a difficulty in finding the right words but also from himself, from "the insecurity of his own faith, the oppressive power of unbelief in the midst of his own will to believe."[4] The person of faith must recognize "that his own situation is by no means so different from that of others as he may have thought at the start."[5]

Ratzinger argues that no one, not even the greatest saint, ever possesses faith so securely as to be immune from doubt. Even St. Thérèse of Lisieux, whose faith seems to have pervaded even the most minute details of her life, and for whom religion really did become "a self-evident presupposition of her daily existence," admitted being plagued by horrible doubts.[6] For Ratzinger, this is evidence that even in an "apparently flawlessly interlocking world someone here suddenly catches a glimpse of the abyss lurking—even for her—under the firm structure of the supporting conventions."[7]

The story of the clown and the example of St. Thérèse underscore the possibility of doubt: we never possess our faith so perfectly as to be immune from all doubt. But Ratzinger's words are also pertinent to the present discussion in two respects. First, his account points to a way in which new first principles given in grace will not and cannot simply take the place of or even completely transform our natural principles. Second, his example of St. Thérèse indicates that one's transformation will become more and more complete as the Christian moral life progresses.

Up to this point in the book, we have focused heavily on the central role of first principles in virtue, which give us both an inchoate knowledge of and desire for our end, and we have seen that any and all virtuous action ultimately stems from those principles. The moral virtues are necessary insofar as they help reason move from the inchoate knowledge and the desire those principles provide to a correct conclusion about what is to be done. It is clear that Aquinas believes that faith and the theological virtues provide the supernatural analogue of our natural knowledge of and desire for our natural fulfillment, and in this sense they are very much "first principles."

Ratzinger's remarks indicate, however, that not everything true of our natural first principles will be true of faith and the theological virtues. Our natural speculative and practical first principles necessarily frame our every interaction with the world: we cannot not presuppose them in every thought and action. We can attempt to deny the principle of noncontradiction, or that the whole is greater than the part, or that one should do good and avoid evil, but any such attempt will be belied by our actions. Those principles are so much a part of us that they are constitutive of our every interaction with the world. Ratzinger's point, however, seems precisely to be that faith is *not* so securely possessed as to be continually operative in us in this way, that even in the saints, for whom faith has *almost* become operative in this way, there is still some instability. Faith and the theological virtues *should* frame everything we do, but because we possess them incompletely, they frequently do not. Even the saint can still see the world through another lens than with the eyes of faith. If this is true of the saint, it is surely even truer for the rest of us.

Even if conversion comes in a moment, consistently living as befits the life of grace frequently does not: Newton converted in a moment, but only gradually gave up his old way of life. One way of explaining the gradual transition is to say that the gifts he received at conversion did not yet pervade his life, that faith and the theological virtues gave him an inchoate knowledge and desire, but that in much of his life he continued to persist in his previous ways of acting. Only as faith came to operate as a first principle in more and more of his life did his old ways of acting disappear. Such an account is consistent with Ratzinger's claim that for St. Thérèse faith had become "a self-evident presupposition of her daily existence." The new principles given in grace *should* invariably operate as self-evident presuppositions that form our natural principles and frame our every thought and act. For most of us, however, they frequently do not. Our imperfect possession of the theological virtues, in short, means that we not only remain capable of seeing the world in a light other than that of faith, but that we frequently act in accord with that lesser vision.

ENDS AND VIRTUES

Growth in the Christian moral life occurs insofar as the theological virtues come to operate more and more as first principles in us. John

Newton is an example of how the principles of faith might not yet frame our every action even after conversion. But by his own admission, Newton lived a vicious and dissolute life before his conversion. And many scholars argue that (1) any of Newton's residual deficiencies were be remedied by the cultivation of natural virtue and/or that (2) those who *had* previously cultivated acquired virtues would make a much more seamless transition into the Christian moral life. It is the contention of this chapter that both claims are false. The cultivation of the acquired virtues does dispose one to the initial gift of grace, but it is important to acknowledge just how far from the ideal of the Christian moral life the acquired virtues are. Without diminishing the importance of the acquired virtues, it is nonetheless the case that their cultivation can never be the Christian's goal. In order to appreciate this claim, it is important to understand just how and in what way acts of infused virtue differ from acts of their acquired counterpart.

In what follows, I will use the examples of infused and acquired courage to illustrate the difference between the acts of infused and acquired virtue, respectively. The essential difference between acts of infused and acquired virtue has to do with the difference in how the principles from which they stem are possessed. It is one thing for an appetite to be ordered to a good that reason can comprehend, and quite another for an appetite to be ordered to a good that reason *cannot* comprehend, and the extent to which one has achieved the former indicates nothing at all about the extent to which one has achieved the latter. In fact, it is conceivable that the achievement of the former might in some circumstances even detract from one's ability to pursue the latter.

In his general discussion of martyrdom, Aquinas says that a martyr is anyone who is killed for living his faith. Later in the same discussion, he elaborates on the good in which the martyr stands firm. The martyr is someone who bears witness to the Christian faith. Through faith, we "[hold] visible things of little account compared to the invisible."[8] Through his death, then, the martyr bears witness to an "invisible" good. In his discussion of faith, Aquinas explains what he has in mind when he distinguishes between visible and invisible goods. He tells us that "things that are said to be seen are those that by themselves move our intellect or sensory power to its cognition."[9] It is this—the difference in the kind of good that moves our intellect and senses in the virtuous act—that really gets to the heart of the difference between the infused and acquired virtues.

When Aquinas elaborates on "visible" goods, that is to say, the things that "by themselves" move the intellect to its cognition, he draws a distinction that is important for present purposes. When the intellect assents to something, says Aquinas, one of two things occurs. First, the intellect can be moved to assent "because it is moved to assent by the object itself."[10] Second, the intellect can be moved to assent "not because it is sufficiently moved by its own object, but because it is moved voluntarily by an act of choosing [*per quandam electionem voluntarie*] that inclines it toward the one part [of a contradiction] rather than the other part."[11]

When the intellect assents to something in the first way, that is, when it is moved to assent by the "object itself," Aquinas says, one of two things occurs. The first possibility is that the object of cognition is itself sufficient to compel consent. The (natural) first principles are among such objects, because to know them is to recognize their truth.[12] But even if the object is not itself sufficient to compel consent, it might be the case that its truth can be arrived at via things that are, such as the conclusions that one arrives at on the basis of first principles. Thus, Aquinas says, when the intellect is moved to assent "by means of something else that there is a cognition of," then this is also a case of the intellect being moved to assent by the object itself.[13] When the intellect is not sufficiently moved to its assent by the object of cognition—either in itself or because of a principle that generates a conclusion—then, says Aquinas, the intellect's assent is either opinion or faith.[14] Only something that is assented to in the first way is said to be "seen."

The distinction described above is vital for understanding Aquinas's claim that the martyr bears witness to an "invisible good." It points to an essential difference, not just between martyrdom and acts of acquired courage, but between any act of infused virtue and any act of acquired virtue. Our consistent theme throughout has been the different principles from which the infused and acquired virtues arise. The first practical principles, the principles through which we have an inchoate knowledge of and desire for our natural fulfillment, are the principles from which reason takes its departure in an act of acquired virtue. These principles are clearly the kind of principles described above, the principles that of themselves move the intellect to its assent. When an act of acquired virtue occurs, our reason moves from the naturally known principles of synderesis to a correct conclusion about what is to be done. In Aquinas's view, even when we receive assistance from others, that assistance merely ministers to our own reason: it is still our reason that moves from the principles to the conclusion. It follows, then, that every act of natural virtue is aimed at a good that reason (at least in principle) can fully grasp. To grow in natural virtue is to gain an ever-increasing comprehension of the good to which reason is ordered.

The principles of supernatural virtue, by contrast, arise from and are ordered to a good that reason cannot fully comprehend and that consequently does not "by itself" move the intellect to assent. The good to which faith is ordered is one that the intellect assents to without full comprehension. This difference has important consequences for how we understand the virtues that arise from each.

When Aquinas discusses whether non-Christians can cultivate the acquired moral virtues, he says that although someone outside the life of grace cannot act in accord with right reason all the time, nothing prevents him "from being able to acquire the habit of a virtue through which he might abstain from bad actions in most cases [*ut in pluribus*] and especially from actions that are strongly opposed to reason."[15] Some actions are more clearly contrary to reason than others. Aquinas's point is that even those outside the life of grace will be able to create habits that allow them to abstain from such actions. But even before one can create the habits that allow one to refrain from them, one has to recognize that the actions in question ought to be avoided. The implication is clear. The more contrary to reason an action is, the easier it will be to comprehend the evil of it. The truth of this claim becomes especially clear when we look at examples of ordinary human courage.

A Proposal for a Way Forward   159

Almost five hundred years before the birth of Christ, the Spartan king Leonidas and a small band of Greeks gave their lives to delay advance of the Persian hordes at Thermopylae. Most of us lack the courage to do what Leonidas and his men did at Thermopylae, but we can all recognize that they did a good and awe-inspiring thing. We are all moved by their sacrifice, and we would all like to be able to exhibit the courage they did.[16] The ancient Greeks erected a plaque to honor the sacrifice made at Thermopylae; even today we still celebrate the event with books and movies. We celebrate actions like these, not because we are particularly brave ourselves, but because the goodness of their act is so obvious. We can comprehend its value. That comprehension does not make such acts any easier; most of us would likely be unable to act as they did. The acquired virtues are ordered to a thoroughly comprehensible good, a good so comprehensible that even the nonvirtuous can understand the goodness of its most dramatic acts. The goodness of acts of infused virtue is far more difficult for us to grasp.

In the Acts of the Apostles, by contrast, we find the story of the death of Stephen, who is widely acknowledged to be the first Christian martyr—the first person to be killed for his defense of the Christian faith. We are told that he was selected as an apostle for his character: he was "deeply spiritual and prudent" and "filled with faith and the Holy Spirit."[17] Stephen was chosen as an apostle not to preach the gospel but to ensure that widows were adequately cared for. But he also preached the gospel and argued with unbelievers, and he did this so well that he made enemies. He was brought before the Sanhedrin on the false charge of blasphemy and asked to explain himself. Stephen, filled with the Holy Spirit, gave his testimony, a testimony that "stung" his hearers "to the heart."[18] At the end of his testimony, he saw a vision he described to his audience and so angered them that they stoned him to death. As he died, he was heard to pray, asking that God not hold his assailants' sins against them.[19]

I want to make three points about the difference between what Stephen did and what Leonidas did. First, I think it is no accident that there are so many books and movies about what happened at Thermopylae and so few about Stephen. We can comprehend the goodness of what the Greeks did at Thermopylae in a way that we cannot comprehend the goodness of the first martyr, and we cannot accurately depict what we cannot ourselves fully comprehend. It's not hard to imagine oneself saying and doing the things Leonidas is supposed to have said and done. Even those of us who would in fact run from the most minor danger *want* to be the kind of person who would face certain death in order to save his family and countrymen from slaughter. But it's hard for us even to imagine praying for our assailants, as Stephen did. Why is it so hard to imagine this? I think it's because these things take a more than human strength. We *can't* return evil with love all by ourselves. We *can't* peacefully endure something like starvation or stoning for the sake of our Christian faith all by ourselves. We need God's help even to find such actions appealing, let alone to do them.

Second, it is not at all obvious that a courageous pagan, were he to convert, would simply be able to put his previously acquired courage to the service of his newfound faith. The courageous pagan rightly comprehends that certain things are good, and he desires in a general way to defend those goods, even at the risk of his life. But an inclination to stand firm for the sake of a good one fully comprehends is not the same as an inclination to stand firm for the sake of something one only partially comprehends, in something one believes by faith. The martyr is true to his faith in the same way the person of Aristotelian courage is true to his reason. I am not implying, of course, that faith and reason are in any way opposed to each other. The light of faith puts what we see by reason in its proper context; it allows us to see it in its proper place. The visible goods the warrior dies for are not irrelevant to the martyr, but the martyr may well see those goods differently than the warrior does, because he sees them in their proper context, in the light of faith. This is why Aquinas says that what is extreme—and hence not virtuous—when evaluated by the standards of our own reason is sometimes moderate by God's standards, and why he gives martyrdom as an example of something that fits the bill.

Third, Stephen very clearly needed and received the guidance of the Holy Spirit in order to act as he did. He was very clearly filled with faith, and he very clearly desired to stand firm in and defend what he believed by faith. But neither Stephen's faith nor his desire to defend it was sufficient to guide his actions. The biblical account is very clear: Stephen was guided in his actions by the Holy Spirit, not just occasionally, but continuously. Acts of acquired virtue, by contrast, need no such further guidance. Our initial order to our natural good is so firmly rooted that we need only our first natural principles, reason, and rightly ordered appetites. All three of these differences are vital to understanding the difference between the infused and acquired moral virtues.

When we examined Aquinas's account of acquired virtue in chapter 1, we saw that he believes the moral virtues do more than merely cause our appetites to be obedient to whatever it is that reason happens to decide. Our natural habitual knowledge of the first practical and speculative principles gives us an inchoate knowledge of and desire for the fulfillment proportionate to our created human nature. But although we can in principle reason from that inchoate knowledge to a correct conclusion about what needs to be done and act accordingly, we cannot do so readily, easily, or consistently without the moral virtues. As we also saw in chapter 1, Aquinas says that the first practical and speculative principles make us rightly ordered to the universal principles of action, but that in order for reason to move from those principles to a correct conclusion, we need to be rightly ordered not just to the universal principles of action, but also to what Aquinas calls the "particular principles" of action. Only when our appetites are rightly ordered to those particular principles, which include (but are not limited to) the ends of the various moral virtues, are we able to reason and act correctly. Finally, we saw that our appetites are rightly ordered to those particular principles when obedience to their directives seems connatural to us, when we "feel in our heart" the rightness of those principles. Someone who "feels in his heart" the goodness of the virtue of truthfulness or chastity or justice will have a constant, abiding, general desire to tell the truth, or be faithful to his spouse, or to stand up for what is right. That connaturality serves as a help and guide for our reason, because it keeps us focused on the goal and makes us alert to what detracts from it.

If the acquired moral virtues give us a connaturality for "particular principles" and thus help us move from the universal principles of synderesis to a correct conclusion about what acts are in accord with reason in a particular instance, it follows that the infused moral virtues should do something similar at the supernatural level. In this book, the discussion of the difference between the infused and acquired moral virtues has been anchored in the fact that each type of virtue originates from different principles: the acquired from synderesis and the infused from faith (and, indirectly, from the other theological virtues).

If the universal principles from which the infused and acquired moral virtues arise differ, it should come as no surprise that their particular principles also differ: it is one thing to render the universal knowledge of synderesis specific in action and quite another to render the order given by faith specific in action. Acquired courage, says Aquinas, seeks to "establish man's spirit in human justice," while infused courage seeks to "establish man's spirit in divine justice." Acquired temperance makes us desire to eat and drink the amount conducive to bodily health, but infused temperance seeks to "castigate the body and bring it into subjection."[20] Aquinas does not explicitly contrast the ends of all the other infused and acquired moral virtues in this way, but the indications that he believes such a contrast exists are clear. Indeed, on Aquinas's account this *should* be the case. Particular principles are further specifications of universal principles. If the universal principles differ, it only stands to reason that the relevant particular principles would differ.

But now consider all of this in light of the argument that an important function of acquired moral virtue is to give us a connatural inclination to the ends of the acquired moral virtues. On the same account, an important function of infused moral virtue should be to give us a connatural inclination to the ends of the infused moral virtues. To possess infused courage should mean possessing a connatural inclination in our appetites to stand firm in the good of divine justice, just as to possess acquired courage means possessing a connatural appetitive inclination to stand firm for human justice. Understanding infused virtue as including a connatural appetitive inclination of this kind is helpful in illuminating how the courage of someone like St. Stephen differs from the kind of acquired courage a pagan might possess.

If the parallel holds, it should follow that infused courage causes a connatural appetitive inclination to stand firm in what Aquinas refers to in his discussion of martyrdom as an "invisible good": infused courage should give one an appetitive inclination to defend one's faith. On this account, the person with infused courage will want, at an instinctive level, to stand firm in and give witness to his faith, no matter what the obstacles; he will feel "in his heart" the good of being steadfast in his faith. This inclination will be *general*, which means it will be felt prior to any particular act of infused courage and prior to any particular activity of infused prudence, prior, indeed, to any direct assistance one receives from the Holy Spirit.

Understanding the difference between infused and acquired courage in this way can illuminate the flaw in the claim that the person of acquired courage already possesses "most" of what infused courage requires, that he has the requisite "strength" and only needs a bit of redirecting. Moral virtues do not confer a sort of portable mental firmness that can be applied at will to any end whatever. Moral virtues make us feel in our hearts that a given end is a good end to have, and in so doing they help to keep the deliberations of prudence on track. The person of acquired courage can't simply take his "strength" and apply it to a new goal; the strength his acquired courage confers is *tied up in* the goals of acquired courage. Infused courage, of course, will not provide one with an ordering to the particular principles that is sufficient for reason to arrive at a correct conclusion: we will still need the prompting of the Holy Spirit. But the infused virtues, importantly, will order us to the ends of the infused moral virtues in the same way that the acquired virtues order us to the ends of the acquired moral virtues.

Since Aquinas is clear that (1) not everyone receives the same degree of infused virtue and that (2) the infused virtues can increase, it is also clear that not everyone who receives infused courage will experience the same instinctual inclination to defend or be steadfast in his faith; not everyone who possesses infused courage will "feel in his heart" that defending the faith is good with the same intensity. The infused virtues increase, says Aquinas, when they become more deeply "rooted" in us. It is reasonable to assume that as the infused virtues become more deeply rooted, we will experience a greater appetitive connaturality for the ends of the infused moral virtues.

When we think of infused virtue and acquired virtue, in general, and infused courage and acquired courage, in particular, in terms of the difference in the goods to which they are ordered and in terms of the different connatural appetitive inclinations that correspond to them, it becomes clear that the possession of a high degree of the one implies nothing at all about the degree to which one possesses the other. To possess acquired courage (or any other acquired virtue) is to possess an appetitive inclination toward a fully comprehensible good, a good that by itself is sufficient to move our intellect to assent to it. Those appetitive inclinations are caused by our own repeated assent to those goods. But to possess infused courage is to possess an appetitive inclination to a good that we do not and cannot fully comprehend; it is to possess an appetitive inclination that we cannot cause in ourselves, no matter how hard we try. This difference is important.

Someone in whom the theological and infused moral virtues are weak will not only have weak faith, he will also have less deeply rooted instinctual appetitive inclinations to defend and be steadfast in it. But it is entirely plausible to think that someone with a great deal of acquired courage—someone in whom the general, instinctual appetitive inclination to stand up for the clear and comprehensible goods of human justice is very strong—might also have weak faith. One can feel very strongly the goodness of giving one's life to save one's family and country and still feel lukewarm about giving one's life for one's faith. And there is no obvious contradiction in possessing a strong appetitive inclination to defend the goods of human justice while also possessing only the weakest of appetitive inclinations to be steadfast in and defend one's faith. Far to the contrary, such examples are likely quite common. Thus, though one certainly might agree that the cultivation of acquired courage disposes one to receive the initial gift of infused courage, there is no reason to think that the former simply becomes the latter. At the same time, it also seems plausible that the former inclinations persist after the initial gift of grace.

Understanding the infused and acquired virtues in terms of the goods they are ordered to helps to illustrate how the latter, even while disposing to the initial gift of grace, might still in some circumstances also pose an obstacle in their own right. Practicing the infused virtues requires at a minimum that we recognize the insufficiency of human reason, that we allow ourselves to be guided by a good that we do not fully comprehend. Faith orders us to that good. The infused virtues give us corresponding appetitive inclinations, but even with the inchoate knowledge of faith and the inclinations of the infused moral virtues, we still need the constant and continual guidance of the Holy Spirit. This can only happen if we open ourselves to that guidance, primarily through prayer. The uncertainty of faith stands in sharp contrast to the security of reason. The believer will always face the temptation to retreat to the apparent bedrock of what he can fully know and grasp and comprehend.

RESIDUAL DISPOSITIONS

Two points have been made. First, the habits of the theological virtues, although more perfect than the habitual knowledge of our natural principles, are also imperfectly possessed. They *should* function as first principles that necessarily frame our every action, but our imperfect possession of them means, among other things, they frequently do not. Second, actions consistent with those more perfect principles differ in dramatic ways from acts of acquired virtues. Together, these points raise a still further question: What happens to habits cultivated prior to the gift of grace? Specifically, what happens to acquired *virtues* cultivated prior to the gift of grace? In the preceding chapters, I have examined some different answers to this question and argued that they all fall short. The view (which may well have been Aquinas's) that acquired virtues continue to produce acts proportionate to man's natural good but receive a further, "exterior" direction from grace that renders those acts meritorious makes sense only under the assumption of a compartmentalized moral life. The claim that the infused virtues just *are* acquired virtues that have received a "further" direction is even less appealing, because it seems to reduce infused virtue to "redirected" acquired virtue. Finally, the claim that the acquired virtues are completely transformed, so that *all* the Christian's virtues are infused virtues, cannot give a clear account of how anything at all persists through the transformation.

In this section, I propose a different option: namely, that previously acquired habits, whether virtuous or vicious, persist as inclinations but not as distinct virtues or vices after the infusion of grace. I will argue that this interpretation is most consistent with both common sense and with Aquinas's broader account. In what follows, I will first look at two texts where Aquinas discusses the effect of grace on vicious dispositions. I will argue that if one rejects the coexistence account (as I believe we should) then the reasoning that underpins Aquinas's account of how grace alters vice leads to a similar conclusion about how grace alters acquired virtue. On the basis of this, I will offer a proposal about why it would be inappropriate for a Christian to deliberately cultivate the acquired moral virtues.

In both article 10 of the *Disputed Questions on the Virtues in General (DQVG)* and in article 2 of the *Disputed Questions on the Cardinal Virtues (DQVC)*, Aquinas addresses the question of how grace affects existing vices. Article 10 of *DQVG* asks whether virtues are infused by God. Objection 16 argues that they are not. Many of those who repent and receive grace, the objector argues, possess vicious habits as a result of previous sinful acts.[21] Since a single act cannot erase an acquired habit, a virtue infused along with grace would have to coexist with its opposing vice, which is impossible.[22] Article 2 of the *DQVC*, which asks whether the virtues are interconnected, raises a similar objection. Some people who possess charity nonetheless find it difficult to do good acts because of a previously cultivated vicious habit. Since a vicious habit cannot coexist with its opposing virtue, the virtue in question must therefore be absent.[23]

In the *DQVG* text, Aquinas responds by agreeing with the major premise: a single act cannot erase a previously acquired habit.[24] But, says Aquinas, the act of repentance does destroy the vicious *habit* qua habit. The vicious habit remains, but as a disposition, not a "full-blown" habit.[25] But there is no contradiction in possessing a virtue together with a *disposition* to contrary acts. Thus, Aquinas concludes, there is no contradiction in maintaining that all the moral virtues are infused along with grace.[26]

How do the dispositions that remain after the infusion of grace affect action? Aquinas says that grace causes it to be the case that we are no longer *controlled* by our vicious desires, even though we may well continue to feel them.[27] Habits enable us to act "readily and with pleasure," unless some other obstacle gets in the way.[28] If we are sleepy or inebriated, for instance, we are less able to use a habit of knowledge.[29] Similarly, although everyone who possesses charity also possesses the infused virtues, when those virtues exist alongside previously cultivated vicious dispositions, those dispositions can make it more difficult for us to practice the infused virtues.[30]

In the remarks examined above from *DQVG*, Aquinas is explicitly focused on the question of how grace affects *vicious* habits. Some scholars argue that Aquinas's remarks apply only to vicious dispositions, and that they would not and do not apply to previously cultivated acquired virtues.[31] The accuracy of this claim will of course depend on one's view of the relationship between the infused and acquired virtues. If one ascribes to the kind of coexistence view of virtue described in chapter 4 and consequently believes that the Christian should continue to cultivate (meritorious) acquired virtues in some areas of the moral life, then it is plausible to conclude that previously cultivated virtues remain more or less unchanged: grace would simply allow us to cultivate them more perfectly, and it would give them an "external" direction to supernatural beatitude. But if one rejects the notion that the Christian moral life is compartmentalized in this way, if one thinks that the Christian should seek to perform acts proportionate to supernatural beatitude in all of his actions, then it is worth asking whether—given this assumption—Aquinas's account of how grace affects vicious habits might apply in a similar way to previously cultivated acquired virtues.

Two aspects of Aquinas's account of grace's effect on previously cultivated vicious habits are especially noteworthy. First, whatever qualifications he later offers, Aquinas nonetheless accepts the claim that a single act does not destroy an acquired habit. Second, he claims that previously cultivated vicious habits remain, but do not remain as habits. Both points are worth unpacking.

Aquinas agrees that a single act does not (at least in the typical case) abolish a tendency caused by repeated actions. He also maintains, however, that after repentance, vices do not remain qua vices. Aquinas does not elaborate on this point, but an obvious reason suggests itself. In someone who has a vice, the evil object functions as end: the vicious person orders all his acts to some evil end. The greedy person's desire for money drives all his choices. His desire for money "rules" him in the sense that it commands all of his other actions. The same can be said of other vices. This is why there is no such thing as the "unity" of the vices: one's decisions will always be subject to one's dominant disordered desire.[32] The vicious person is in an important sense unable to act in any other way: his desire for money (or power and so on) will always win out over any better impulses that might emerge. Given all of this, it is clear that if morally good action is to be possible, sin's dominion must be broken.

The above indicates an explanation of why Aquinas says that in the person who has received grace, vicious habits persist, but that they do not "rule" him, and of why he says that vicious tendencies persist as dispositions rather than as "full-blown" habits. The possession of grace and the infused virtues is in principle compatible with inordinate desires. An inordinate desire for wealth or power will of course put obstacles between us and the practice of our supernatural virtues: such desires will make the practice of supernatural virtue difficult in the way that fatigue or hunger makes it difficult to exercise the habit of knowledge. But although obstacles make right action more difficult, they do not render it impossible. A "full-blown" vice, on the other hand, *rules* us. To say that someone possesses a vice means that when acting in a manner appropriate to supernatural beatitude conflicts with the pursuit of that vice, the vice will invariably win. To put the same point differently, unless the vice is corrupted qua vice, unless it ceases to be a "full-blown" habit and instead becomes a "mere" disposition, we cannot truly be said to be ordered to the end of eternal life.

The intimate relationship between virtues (and vices) and the ends to which they are ordered helps to explain why one cannot simultaneously possess both vices and the virtues ordered to supernatural (or even to natural) beatitude: we cannot simultaneously be governed in all of our acts by two different and incompatible ends. Only one end can "rule" our actions. But to concede this point is to see that it has implications for the persistence of natural virtues qua virtues.

The "coexistence" view described in chapter 4 maintains that the Christian's acquired virtues continue to produce acts proportionate to natural human flourishing, but that those acts also receive a further "extrinsic" direction to supernatural beatitude. If we maintain that the Christian practices (meritorious) natural virtues in some areas of life and supernatural virtues in others, we have a picture that—however unappealing it may be—is at least coherent. On such a picture, the Christian still only has one end. What is unappealing about it is the view that it is only sometimes appropriate for the Christian to act in a manner proportionate to his one true end. But if we reject the coexistence view on the grounds that it divides the Christian moral life, what consequences follow for the persistence of acquired *virtues*?

A virtue is a stable disposition to perform acts proportionate to a given end. To possess an acquired virtue is to be ordered in a stable way to the good proportionate to created human nature, so much so that one regularly and consistently produces acts ordered to that good. If we possess the acquired virtues, our natural fulfillment will be the rule and measure of our acts. But this seems to pose a version of the same problem addressed earlier in this section. One cannot simultaneously have two ultimate ends. There can only be one "rule" in our lives, that is, one end that guides and directs all our actions. If we are ruled in all our acts by considerations of our natural fulfillment, we cannot be ruled by considerations of our supernatural fulfillment, and vice versa. Can we, although ordered to supernatural fulfillment, although "ruled" in our acts by that good, nonetheless still be *disposed* to pursue our natural, as opposed to our supernatural, fulfillment? Surely. But it will not make sense to call those dispositions *virtues* in any robust sense.

If we accept Aquinas's general account and reject the coexistence view's claim that the infused virtues only have to do with a limited sphere of the Christian moral life, then it makes most sense to conclude that the acquired virtues remain, but as dispositions rather than as "full-blown" virtues.

This conclusion is consistent not only with Aquinas's account but with common sense. Scholars—rightly—tend to make much of the fact that an account of the moral life needs to accommodate our intuitions about continuity. In support of this, they typically point out that vicious people who repent don't lose their old desires all at once. But surely something similar would have to be true of someone who had previously cultivated the acquired virtues. An excellent example of such an individual can be found in the rich young man of the Gospels, who has conscientiously lived an upright life and who wants to accept Christ's call. He goes away sad, because Christ asks more than he wants to give, most likely more than he *can* give without divine help. But suppose that the rich young man had accepted Christ's call. What then? It would not then suddenly be the case that our young man would easily and joyously give up his possessions or that he would not ever feel the pull of his former life. Accepting Christ's call, living the life of grace, is not something that one does once. It is a choice that needs to be made again and again. And if we agree that it demands a great deal more of us than the life of Aristotelian acquired virtue does, then it stands to reason that everyone will at first find it difficult. This is perfectly consistent, of course, with the view that the person who possesses the acquired virtues will find it a great deal *less* difficult than those who turn from a life of vice.

Acquired Virtue, Infused Virtue, and Venial Sin

We've seen that the only coherent goal for the Christian is living the life of grace, that is, cultivating and practicing the infused virtues. But this claim can also seem bleak. For if it is correct, then the majority of those who receive the gifts of grace will (at least at first) have only weak infused virtues and a great many competing dispositions. The result will be that those who possess the gifts of grace very frequently fail to live up to them. This raises two related questions. First, how should we understand those failures? Second, are those failures a problem for the picture I am proposing?

It is important to be clear about the different ways in which one can fail to live up to the goal of the Christian moral life. Even if the infused virtues are bestowed and increased by God, it is still far from true that the cultivation and exercise of them is entirely outside our control. We can make use of the gifts of grace or we can neglect them, and it is almost certainly the case that most of us neglect them. I have argued throughout this book that acting in a manner proportionate to the new order given by the theological virtues requires the continual guidance and prompting of the Holy Spirit. When it comes to the order given by grace, reason, even reason aided by the affective inclinations of the infused moral virtues, is an insufficient guide. If we are fully cognizant of those limitations, and if we genuinely wish to act in a manner commensurate with an order to supernatural beatitude, then it follows that we should pray constantly for the guidance of the Holy Spirit, that we should practice the kinds of spiritual disciplines that would help to open our hearts to that guidance. Insofar as we fail to seek out divine guidance and are content to rely on our own reason, we will fall short of living the life made possible by grace. Second, even those who do make that concerted effort have no gauge of how successful they have been. The most one can do, having prayed sincerely for guidance, is to act in the manner one's conscience dictates. It is entirely plausible to think that even those who *do* make a concerted effort to live up to the goal of the Christian moral life might still fall short of the ideal.

In what follows I will argue that some aspects of Aquinas's discussion of venial sin offer a way of understanding how we might understand these failures. My goal is not to argue that such acts *would be* considered venial sins by Aquinas — it is abundantly clear that he would not — but simply to argue that his account of venial sin offers a good way for us to understand what occurs when our actions fall short of the goal of the Christian moral life.

Aquinas offers the distinction between venial sin and mortal sin as a way of distinguishing those sins that destroy our order to supernatural beatitude from those that do not. A sin is mortal, says Aquinas, in the same way a disease is mortal, namely, when "it causes an irreparable defect through the loss of some principle."[33] Our order "toward the ultimate end" is the principle of the spiritual life, because it is that order that makes "life in accord with virtue" possible.[34] It follows that any sin that destroys our order to the spiritual life will be mortal, since "it cannot be repaired by any intrinsic principle," but only by God's grace.[35] This, says Aquinas, is because such errors are akin to errors about first principles. Someone who is in error about first principles cannot be corrected except through replacing the erroneous first principles with correct ones.

Some sins destroy our order to the spiritual life altogether and are akin to possessing erroneous first principles, but other sins are more akin to the errors that arise when we possess correct first principles but apply them incorrectly. These sins are reparable, since they have to do with the means to the end, and "disorders with respect to the means to the end are repaired by the end, in the way that an error with respect to the conclusions is corrected by the truth of the principles."[36] These sins are called "venial," because they do not result from an incorrect order, but rather from a failure to conform in the right way to the order that one has.

When Aquinas explains what venial sin involves, he makes a further distinction that is particularly relevant to our present purposes. In response to the objection that any act outside the law is a mortal sin, he says that the person who commits a venial sin neither does what the law prohibits nor fails to do what the law obliges. Rather, the person who commits a venial sin "does not observe the mode of reason the law intends."[37]

On Aquinas's account, then, one commits a venial sin when one's act fails to conform appropriately to one's "first principles." Moreover, one way in which our acts fail to conform to those principles is when they, though not obviously contrary to the law, nonetheless fail to "observe the mode of reason the law intends." Aquinas is speaking here, of course, of eternal law. But if we consider instead the new law, we can give an analogous account of what happens when our acts fall short of the life made possible by grace.

If grace both orders us to the end of supernatural beatitude and transforms our natural principles, then the Christian who attempts to live rightly must be seen as attempting to act in a manner proportionate to the end of supernatural beatitude. What, then, are we to say of someone who, though ordered toward supernatural beatitude, attempts to pursue the good he desires by means of his natural abilities alone? If the choice is deliberate—if he either rejects the end itself or rejects the idea that he needs help in achieving it—then this would seem to be an error with respect to the principles themselves and hence to constitute a deliberate rejection of the gifts of grace. But if it is not deliberate—if our acts fall short of the standard because of some other cause—then we will fall short of the goal, but not in a way that destroys our order to supernatural beatitude. This latter kind of falling short can, it seems to me, occur in one of two ways. First, we might simply neglect the call of grace. Without rejecting the supernatural order, we might nonetheless be content to rely on our own understanding and neglect our spiritual lives, or otherwise fail to open ourselves to the motion of the Holy Spirit and the working of grace in our lives. Second, we might, even while sincerely attempting to grow in the life of grace and to listen to the Holy Spirit's prompting, still fall short of the actions that would be most consistent with our order to supernatural beatitude. I think the latter kind of action, while still falling short of perfection, would dispose toward growth in the Christian moral life in a way the former would not. In the latter case, we would still be acting to the best of our ability, while in the former case we would not. I will address this distinction at greater length in what follows.

AN OBJECTION

One might raise an objection at this point. The infused virtues are very different from the acquired virtues and we do not readily or easily practice them. We are never self-sufficient in our practice of them: part of cultivating the infused virtues will mean attempting to open ourselves to the guidance of the Holy Spirit. But, one might object, if the infused virtues are so hard and so different, isn't this precisely *why* the Christian would *also* need to cultivate the acquired moral virtues?[38] The acquired virtues might order us to a good that falls short of Christian perfection, but they order us to a real good nonetheless. And surely it is better to possess habits ordered to a genuine good than to possess evil habits, even if the genuine good is not the best good.

Very many scholars will find an objection like this intuitively appealing, and such intuitions are likely at the heart of many attempts to achieve some kind of reconciliation between the infused and acquired virtues. It is thus important to give this objection careful consideration. In what follows, I will first strengthen it by considering a text from Aquinas's discussion of charity in *ST* II-II that might appear to support it. Aquinas argues that the first work of the beginner in charity is to resist sin. One might therefore argue that a very good way to "resist sin" is to cultivate acquired virtue and hence that this—the cultivation of acquired virtue—ought to be the primary goal of the beginner in charity. Although the goal of the beginner in charity must undoubtedly be to "resist sin," this is not identical to the cultivation of the acquired virtues. Far to the contrary, in the Christian the concerted effort to cultivate acquired virtues would constitute a deliberate falling short.

In *ST* II-II, q. 24, a. 9, Aquinas describes three "stages" of charity: "beginning" charity, "proficient" charity, and "perfect" charity.[39] Aquinas says that the different stages of charity are distinguished by the "different endeavors to which man is led by an increase of charity."[40] As charity grows in us, that is to say, our goals change. Different aims are appropriate to different levels of charity. For those who have only recently received charity, "the principal endeavor that falls to a man is to withdraw from sin and to resist those desires of his that move him in a direction contrary to charity."[41] This is because "charity must be nourished or kept warm in order not to be corrupted." As one advances in charity, it becomes appropriate to turn one's attention to other things, such as making progress in the good (the aim of those proficient in charity) and to be united to God (the aim of the perfect).[42]

Aquinas's response here highlights his claim that the first aim of those who newly possess charity must be to "resist those desires that move him in a direction contrary to charity." It is abundantly clear that vicious desires move us in a direction that is more directly contrary to charity than do the desires of the acquired virtues. Even if the acquired virtues do not order us to the one good that truly fulfills us, they do nonetheless order us to the good proportionate to our created human nature. Given all this, it might well seem that an important first step in resisting sinful desires would be the cultivation of the acquired moral virtues. For example, suppose that a glutton converts and receives the gifts of grace. On Aquinas's account, the glutton's inordinate desires will remain, but they will no longer "rule" him: grace will give him the strength to resist them. Aquinas also holds that the first aim of our repentant glutton must be to resist the desires that used to rule him. Given all this, shouldn't we then conclude that the first task of our repentant glutton will be to cultivate acquired temperance? Such a conclusion would not only be incorrect but would also misunderstand the distinction between infused and acquired virtue.

Aquinas does indeed say that the first aim of the beginner in charity must be to resist sin. It is equally important to note, however, that he describes the resisting of sin as itself being *an act of charity*. This point is worth thinking about. Aquinas holds that charity destroys sin's dominion over us: it does not take away our vicious dispositions, but it does cause it to be the case that they no longer control us. To put the same point more prosaically, the gifts of grace enable us to do out of love for God what we would be incapable of doing for ourselves. When the repentant sinner resists a vicious disposition, he does so not out of any desire for the flourishing proportionate to his created human nature, but out of love for God and with God's help and guidance. If he continually resists the pull of his previous life, it is not through any cultivation of acquired virtue, but through the new strength given in grace. Given this, it is not at all clear how the resisting of sin would amount to the cultivation of *acquired* rather than infused virtue. It is merely the case that the practice of infused virtue looks different in one who has newly received charity than it does in one who has practiced charity for a great deal of time.

There is a second and equally important point. In his remarks about the increase of charity and even in his remarks about the increase of virtue more generally, Aquinas makes it clear that we do not prepare ourselves for moral growth by aiming at less than we are capable of.[43] In *ST* II-II, q. 24, a. 6, Aquinas asks whether charity increases with every act of charity. The body of his reply focuses on the idea that acts of charity do not immediately produce an increase in charity, but rather prepare one for it in the way that water hollows out a stone. But in the *sed contra*, he also seems to argue that growth in charity parallels the intensity with which one exercises it: "An effect does not exceed the power of its cause. But sometimes an act of charity is done with lukewarmness [*tepor*] or lack of intensity [*remissio*]. Therefore, it does not lead to a more excellent charity, but instead disposes one toward a lesser charity."[44] If it is inappropriate even to act with less charity than one is capable of, then surely it would be even more inappropriate to eschew the infused virtues altogether in favor of the acquired virtues?

The appeal of the idea that Christians need to cultivate "acquired" virtues may well stem from the intuition that Christians need moral training as much as anyone else: that we must gradually work to build up habits over time and so on. I do not dispute this. But the mere fact that a habit is developed gradually and that its growth corresponds to our own efforts in cultivating it does not itself make that habit an acquired virtue. Acquired virtues are "acquired" because they are ordered to an end proportionate to our created human nature and because our nature is itself sufficient to cause them. The facts that God is the source and cause of the infused virtues and that they are ordered to an end that exceeds the capacity of our nature do not entail that the infused virtues are not in need of development or that their growth will not in the typical case parallel our own efforts. It merely means that (1) when they do grow, it will be God, not we, who is responsible for that growth, and that (2) we need God's help not merely to receive and increase them, but even in the very practice of them.

Those who insist that the Christian needs to cultivate acquired virtues sometimes raise the problem of mortal sin. If someone has cultivated infused virtues over a long period of time and then sins mortally, mustn't we suppose that they have some acquired habits to fall back on? Surely we can't suppose that they are suddenly without any habits at all? With respect to this objection, it is important to be clear. On the account I am proposing, those who receive grace do not immediately lose their previous habits; they remain as dispositions. It is merely the case that the only appropriate goal of the life of grace is growth in that life: attempting to cultivate the infused moral virtues, to be attentive to the promptings of the Holy Spirit, and so on. Given that most of us will fail and fail frequently in this endeavor, and that like acts cause like dispositions, we will hardly lack for dispositions. One can always tweak the situation a bit, however, and ask about the saint. What would happen if a saint—someone who for a long time had exclusively practiced the infused virtues — were to fall into mortal sin?

With respect to this last question, it is important to distinguish habits and even dispositions from what Aquinas calls "natural inclinations" — inclinations to act in certain ways that lack the guidance of reason. What would happen if St. Thérèse, say, had given into the doubts that plagued her and rejected God? No one can deny that many ways of acting that she regularly engaged in, ways of acting that we typically refer to as "habits," would remain. If St. Thérèse had woken up to pray at 5 a.m. for a decade, she would surely still continue to wake up at 5 a.m. for a time, even if she no longer prayed. If she had spent a similar amount of time practicing infused temperance, she would most likely continue to be inclined to eat and drink the same amount. But to agree to all of this — as we should — is not to say anything at all about the end to which those habit-like actions are ordered. It is clear that actions, even actions ordered to supernatural beatitude, leave a mark: regardless of the intention with which we do it, if we do the same action enough times, a tendency toward that action will arise, and that tendency will remain even when we reject the end toward which that action was ordered. What I am not willing to do is to automatically call that residual tendency a virtue, to say that that residual tendency is necessarily ordered toward our natural flourishing or indeed to any end at all. More work needs to be done on the question of these residual tendencies, and I cannot do that work here.[45] My point is merely that one can agree that something persists through the loss of infused virtue without positing the whole unwieldy apparatus of the acquired moral virtues. It would make much more sense to suppose that what would persist would be akin to those inclinations that we possess as a result of our bodily constitution, or what Aquinas calls "natural inclinations."

THE CHRISTIAN MORAL LIFE

In this book, I have attempted to tackle Aquinas's thorny notion of an "infused" moral virtue. We can best understand such virtues by focusing on the different sources from which they stem. Our natural habitual knowledge of the first principles of practical reason, or synderesis, gives us an inchoate knowledge of the good proportionate to our created human nature, and that knowledge in turn gives rise to a desire for that good. Through cultivating the acquired moral virtues, we become able to act in a manner proportionate to that good. The theological virtues given in grace, by contrast, give us an inchoate knowledge of and desire for an infinitely higher good: participation in the divine life. The infused moral virtues enable us to act in a manner proportionate to that good. But the theological and infused virtues, though more perfect, are also less perfectly possessed: even those who possess them still need the help and prompting of the Holy Spirit in order to practice them.

I have argued that the sole task of the Christian is to attempt to cultivate the infused moral virtues and to grow in the life of grace. The acquired virtues are ordered to genuine goods, and the pagan who cultivates them does indeed become disposed to receive the gift of grace. But it would be entirely inappropriate for a Christian to set his sights on Aristotelian acquired virtues. For the Christian, anything less than the cultivation of the infused moral virtues will always be a falling short.

I want to emphasize two points implicit in the preceding. First, the account of infused virtue that I have defended in this book and especially in this chapter highlights our insufficiency and dependence in the face of the only goal that truly matters for the Christian. Christianity calls us to a good that exceeds our nature, a goal that no human effort can achieve. Answering that call requires divine assistance—not just at the outset, but at every stage of the way. Alfred Freddoso, describing the difference between the infused and acquired virtues, writes that the infused virtues will of course differ from the acquired, because "the Holy Spirit is always urging us forward, beyond what we think (and know) we are capable of on our own. The whole point is that we are not on our own and that we must be humble enough to realize this and welcome it."[46] The Aristotelian ethic of acquired virtue is an ethic centered around the notions of self-perfection and self-sufficiency. An ethic of infused virtue is an ethic of humility and dependence. To grow in infused virtue is to become more in tune with the divine and hence more dependent on divine help rather than less.

Will the practice of the infused virtues, to all external appearances, look very much like the practice of the acquired virtues? In many respects, of course they will. Someone attempting to cultivate the infused virtues will still reason about the right thing to do, and he will still attempt to cultivate habits. But someone who is really attempting to live the life of infused virtue will realize that his own reason is imperfect and inadequate; he will realize that he needs to seek the help and guidance of the Holy Spirit through prayer and other spiritual disciplines. He will likewise recognize that whatever moral progress he does make results not from his own effort but from God's free gift.

It is also important to emphasize that, on the picture I have been presenting, the gifts of grace and infused virtue do not represent some kind of completion or culmination of the Christian moral life. Far to the contrary, they represent its *beginning*. Someone who receives grace, the infused moral virtues, and the gifts of the Holy Spirit must still learn how to act in a manner befitting the light of faith. This is no easy task. It is one that must be chosen again and again and will involve many false starts and failures.

The picture of the Christian moral life offered in this book is not one Aquinas explicitly defends. It is the account that I believe makes the most sense, given Aquinas's most fundamental claims and commitments, and given a commitment to offering a coherent and unified picture of the Christian moral life. But it is in many ways a very far cry from the ethics that Aristotle presents in his *Nicomachean Ethics*. Is this Aquinas irreconcilable with Aristotle? In some ways yes, and in some ways no. It has been my contention throughout that Aquinas takes from Aristotle what is conceptual and foundational. Aristotle's understanding of nature and of the way our natural capacities point us toward the fulfillment of it gives Aquinas the framework on which he builds an account of how grace perfects nature and of how the virtues given in grace order us to our supernatural fulfillment. The virtues that matter for Aquinas are very different from Aristotelian virtue, but this is to be expected, not least because the only end that truly matters is very different.

NOTES

INTRODUCTION

1. Jean Porter, "The Subversion of Virtue: Acquired and Infused Virtues in the *Summa theologiae*," *The Annual of the Society of Christian Ethics* 12 (1992): 19–41; and Thomas F. O'Meara, "Virtues in the Theology of Thomas Aquinas," *Theological Studies* 58, no. 2 (1997): 254–85.

2. Robert Florent Coerver, *The Quality of Facility in the Moral Virtues* (Whitefish, MT: Kessinger, 2007).

3. See, for instance, Anthony Falanga, *Charity the Form of the Virtues according to Saint Thomas Aquinas* (Washington, DC: Catholic University of America Press, 1948); John Harvey, "The Nature of the Infused Moral Virtues," *Proceedings of the Ninth Annual Convention of the Catholic Theological Society of America* (1954): 172–221; and Louis Billot, *De virtutibus infusis: Commentarius in secundam partem S. Thomae* (Rome: Ex Typographia Polyglotta, 1905).

4. For fuller discussions of the various sides of this debate, see Lawrence Feingold, *The Natural Desire to See God according to St. Thomas Aquinas and His Interpreters*, 2nd ed. (Ave Maria, FL: Sapientia Press of Ave Maria University, 2010); Henri de Lubac, *The Mystery of the Supernatural*, trans. Rosemary Sheed (New York: Crossroad, 1998); and Jorge Laporta, *La Destinée de la nature humaine selon Thomas d'Aquin* (Paris: J. Vrin, 1965). For helpful overviews, see Nicholas Healy, "Henri de Lubac on Nature and Grace: A Note on Some Recent Contributions to the Debate," *Communio* 35, no. 4 (2008): 540; and Thomas Joseph White, "Imperfect Happiness and the Final End of Man: Thomas Aquinas and the Paradigm of Nature–Grace Orthodoxy," *The Thomist: A Speculative Quarterly Review* 78, no. 2 (2014): 247–89.

CHAPTER I

1. Some even describe Aquinas's contribution in these terms. See Philippa Foot, "Virtues and Vices," in *Virtue Ethics*, ed. Roger Crisp and Michael Slote (Oxford: Oxford University Press, 1997), 163–77.

182 Notes to Pages 12–14

2. In making this claim I am primarily referring to claims made in general overviews and sweeping summaries of Aquinas's moral theory. In Fr. Austin Fagothey's much reprinted ethics textbook, *Right and Reason*, for instance, he says that Aquinas "follows Aristotle, omitting some points, developing others more thoroughly, and adding the theological virtues"; see Fagothey, *Right and Reason: Ethics Based on the Teachings of Aristotle and St. Thomas Aquinas*, 4th ed. (St. Louis: The C.V. Mosby Company, 1967), 195. Even the *Catechism of the Catholic Church* (*CCC*), which is heavily informed by the writings of Aquinas, omits reference to the infused moral virtues, implying that the virtues relevant to the moral life are the acquired moral virtues and the theological virtues of faith, hope, and love (see *CCC*, nos. 1810–13, http://www.vatican.va/archive/ccc_css/archive/catechism/p3s1c1a7.htm). Moral theologians such as Louis Billot, Anthony Falanga, and John Harvey certainly *did* recognize Aquinas's notion of infused moral virtues. See, for instance, Falanga, *Charity the Form of the Virtues according to St. Thomas Aquinas* (Washington, DC: Catholic University of America Press, 1948).

3. See Servais Pinckaers, *The Sources of Christian Ethics*, trans. Sr. Mary Noble (Washington, DC: Catholic University of America Press, 1995).

4. See Porter, "The Subversion of Virtue."

5. For recent scholarly work on this topic, see Harm J. M. J. Goris and Henk J. M. Schoot, eds., *The Virtuous Life: Thomas Aquinas on the Theological Nature of Moral Virtues* (Leuven: Peeters, 2017).

6. This is particularly reflected in the discussion of such virtues by non-Thomist Christians, some of whom maintain that the very idea of divinely given virtue is incoherent. See, for instance, Linda Zagzebski, *Virtues of the Mind* (Cambridge: Cambridge University Press, 1996).

7. See, for instance, Andrew J. Dell'Olio, *Foundations of Moral Selfhood: Aquinas on Divine Goodness and the Connection of the Virtues* (New York: Peter Lang, 2003).

8. See Michael S. Sherwin, "Infused Virtue and the Effects of Acquired Vice: A Test Case for the Thomistic Theory of Infused Cardinal Virtues," *The Thomist: A Speculative Quarterly Review* 73, no. 1 (2009): 30.

9. See Bonnie Kent, "Augustine's *On the Good of Marriage* and Infused Virtue in the Twelfth Century," *Journal of Religious Ethics* 41, no. 1 (2013): 112–36; and István P. Bejczy, "The Problem of Natural Virtue," in *Virtue and Ethics in the Twelfth Century*, ed. István P. Bejczy and Richard G. Newhauser (Leiden: Brill, 2005), 131–54.

10. See Bejczy, "The Problem of Natural Virtue," 131.

11. Ibid.

12. See ibid., 134; and William C. Mattison III, "Thomas's Categorizations of Virtue: Historical Background and Contemporary Significance," *The Thomist: A Speculative Quarterly Review* 74, no. 2 (2010): 198.

13. The importance of the qualifier "a kind" cannot be overemphasized; it would be Pelagian to maintain that pagans can cultivate virtues ordered to the one good that truly matters, namely, participation in the divine life.

14. See Mattison, "Thomas's Categorizations of Virtue"; and Odon Lottin, *Psychologie et morale aux XIIe et XIIIe siècles*, vol. 3, pt. 2 (Louvain: Abbaye du Mont César, 1946).

Notes to Pages 15–19   183

15.   See Pinckaers, *Sources of Christian Ethics*, 286; and Alasdair MacIntyre, *A Short History of Ethics: A History of Moral Philosophy from the Homeric Age to the Twentieth Century*, 2nd ed. (Notre Dame, IN: University of Notre Dame Press, 1998), 122. For a list of similar statements, see Sebastian Rehnman, "Virtue and Grace," *Studies in Christian Ethics* 25, no. 4 (2012): 472–93. Pinckaers tells us that Protestantism "created a deep gulf between faith and ethics, so deep that it could not be crossed . . . isolating faith and rejecting as useless if not dangerous all its teachings on virtues and all else that might fall under ethics or morality" (*Sources of Christian Ethics*, 286). This rejection, Pinckaers claims, extended not merely to Aristotelian natural virtues, but even to the notion of supernatural virtue. Pinckaers does not offer any footnotes, either for this or his earlier claim, so it is difficult to know what evidence he would offer for this assertion. But given his frequent references to Luther in the surrounding text, it is possible that he takes Luther to be representative of the reformed view more broadly. MacIntyre and others make similar claims.

16.   See Rehnman, "Virtue and Grace"; and Luca Baschera, "Ethics in Reformed Orthodoxy," in *A Companion to Reformed Orthodoxy*, edited by Herman Selderhuis (Leiden: Brill, 2013), 40:519–52.

17.   Dante Alighieri, *Inferno*, trans. Stanley Lombardo (Indianapolis: Hackett, 2009), 4.42.

18.   See Kent, "Augustine's *On the Good of Marriage* and Infused Virtue."

19.   I refer here only to the "hypothetical necessity" of a state of pure nature. I have no intention of implying that before sanctifying grace human nature is ordered to a purely natural end.

20.   The point here, again, is merely that God *could have* created man for a purely natural perfection. It is no contradiction to maintain that although God could have created man in that way, he did not.

21.   For a good explanation of this, see Reinhard Hütter, "'Palaeothomism?'—The Continuing Debate over the Natural Desire for the Vision of God," and Hütter, "'Thomist Ressourcement'—A Rereading of Thomas on the Natural Desire for the Vision of God," in *Dust Bound for Heaven: Explorations in the Theology of Thomas Aquinas* (Grand Rapids, MI: Eerdmans, 2012), 129–183 and 184–246.

22.   See Healy, "Henri de Lubac on Nature and Grace."

23.   Whether and to what extent this is possible is the subject of the debate over "pagan" virtue, about which I will have more to say later in this chapter.

24.   See Thomas Aquinas, *On Virtues and Gifts: Texts from the "Commentary on the Sentences of Peter Lombard"* (*CS* III), trans. Joseph Bowlin (unpublished translation, December 6, 2008), d. 33, q. 1, a. 2, qa. 1; Thomas Aquinas, *Summa theologiae* (*ST*) I-II, q. 51, a. 1, and q. 63, a. 1, trans. Alfred J. Freddoso, https://www3.nd.edu/~afreddos/summa-translation/TOC.htm; and Aquinas, *Disputed Questions on the Virtues* (*DQVG*), ed. E. M. Atkins and Thomas Williams (Cambridge: Cambridge University Press, 2005), q. 1, a. 8. Unless otherwise indicated, citations from these texts will be from the aforesaid editions.

25.   See Renée Mirkes, "Aquinas's Doctrine of Moral Virtue and Its Significance for Theories of Facility," *The Thomist: A Speculative Quarterly Review* 61, no. 2 (1997): 195.

26. Thomas Aquinas, *Quaestiones disputatae de veritate* (*DV*) q. 14, a. 2, c., trans. Fred Freddoso, https://www3.nd.edu/~afreddos/translat/aquinas5.htm. Unless otherwise indicated, citations from this text will be from the aforesaid edition.

27. Ibid.

28. In the early *CS* III text, Aquinas uses "seed" to refer indiscriminately to *all* components of man's natural aptitude for virtue. In later texts, however, he consistently reserves the term "seed" for our natural habitual knowledge of the principles of the natural law. See, for instance, *ST* I-II, q. 63, a. 1, c.; *ST* I, q. 79, a. 12, arg. 3; *DV* q. 16, a. 1, c.; and *DQVG* q. 1, a. 8, ad 10.

29. Aquinas, *DV* q. 11, a. 1, c.

30. See *ST* I-II, q. 63, a. 1, c.; and *DQVG* q. 1, a. 8, c. The E. M. Atkins translation of *De virtutibus in communi* translates *aptitudo* as "suitability" rather than "aptitude."

31. *DQVG* q. 1, a. 8, c.

32. Ibid.

33. Ibid.

34. *DV* q. 14, a. 2, c.

35. For an interesting and thorough discussion of Aristotle's view, see Anselm Winfried Müller, "Aristotle's Conception of Ethical and Natural Virtue," in *Was ist das für den Menschen Gute?*, ed. Jan Szaif and Matthias Lutz-Bachmann (Berlin: Walter de Gruyter, 2004), 18–53. If Müller is correct, then Aristotle's position differs substantially from Aquinas's.

36. *ST* I-II, q. 58, a. 4, ad 3.

37. *DQVG* q. 1, a. 8, ad 10.

38. Ibid.

39. Ibid.

40. Ibid.

41. *ST* I-II, q. 49, a. 2.

42. *ST* I-II, q. 49, a. 2, ad 3.

43. See ibid.

44. Andrew Whitmore attributes a rather extreme version of this position to me on the basis of my article "Aquinas and the Pagan Virtues." My view is in fact most similar to the position David Decosimo defends; see Whitmore, "Dispositions and Habits in the Work of St. Thomas Aquinas" (Washington, DC: Catholic University of America, 2018), 90–130; Decosimo, *Ethics as a Work of Charity* (Stanford, CA: Stanford University Press, 2016), 91; and Angela Knobel, "Aquinas and the Pagan Virtues," *International Philosophical Quarterly* 51, no. 3 (2011): 331–54.

45. See Giuseppe Butera, "On Reason's Control of the Passions in Aquinas's Theory of Temperance," *Mediaeval Studies* 68, no. 1 (2006): 133–60; Richard K. Mansfield, "Antecedent Passion and the Moral Quality of Human Acts according to St. Thomas," *Proceedings of the American Catholic Philosophical Association* 71 (1997): 221–31; Nicholas E. Lombardo, *The Logic of Desire: Aquinas on Emotion* (Washington, DC: Catholic University of America Press, 2012); Steven J. Jensen, "Virtuous Deliberation and the Passions," *The Thomist: A Speculative Quarterly Review* 77, no. 2 (2013): 193–227; and Nicholas Kahm, "Thomas Aquinas on the Sense Appetite as Participating in Reason" (Ph.D. diss., Catholic University of America, 2014).

46. *ST* I, q. 81, a. 1.

Notes to Pages 30–50   185

47. *ST* I, q. 81, a. 2.

48. Ibid.

49. Jean Porter, *The Perfection of Desire* (Milwaukee: Marquette University Press, 2018), 19.

50. *ST* I, q. 81 a. 3.

51. For a thorough discussion of these texts, see Butera, "On Reason's Control of the Passions in Aquinas's Theory of Temperance," and Jensen, "Virtuous Deliberation and the Passions."

52. *ST* I-II, q. 58, a. 4.

53. Aquinas, *Disputed Questions on the Cardinal Virtues* (*DQVC*), a. 2, ad 4; *ST* II-II, q. 124, a. 2 ad 1; *ST* II-II, q. 109, a. 2; and *ST* II-II, q. 58, a. 1.

54. *ST* I-II, q. 63, a. 4.

55. Nicholas Kahm, *Aquinas on the Emotions' Participation in Reason* (Washington, DC: Catholic University of America Press, 2019), 260. A similar account is offered by Tobias Hoffmann, "Prudence and Practical Principles," in *Aquinas and the "Nicomachean Ethics,"* ed. Tobias Hoffmann, Jorn Muller, and Mattias Perkams (Cambridge: Cambridge University Press, 2013), 165–83.

56. See Hoffmann, "Prudence and Practical Principles."

57. See, for instance, Bonnie Kent, "Moral Provincialism," *Religious Studies* 30, no. 3 (1994): 269–85; Thomas Osborne, "The Augustinianism of Thomas Aquinas' Moral Theory," *The Thomist: A Speculative Quarterly Review* 67, no. 2 (2003): 279–305; David Gallagher, "The Role of God in the Philosophical Ethics of Thomas Aquinas," in *Miscellania Medievialia*, ed. Jan A. Aertsen and Andreas Speer (Berlin: Walter de Gruyter, 1998), 26:1024–33; Brian J. Shanley, "Aquinas on Pagan Virtue," *The Thomist: A Speculative Quarterly Review* 63, no. 4 (1999): 553–77; and Angela McKay, "Prudence and Acquired Moral Virtue," *The Thomist: A Speculative Quarterly Review* 69, no. 4 (2005): 535–55.

58. A much fuller discussion of this text and of my proposed solution can be found in Angela Knobel, "Ends and Virtues," *Journal of Moral Theology* 3, no. 1 (2014): 105–17.

59. *ST* I-II, q. 81, a. 2, c.

60. *ST* I-II, q. 85, a. 3, c.

61. *ST* I-II, q. 63, a. 2, ad 2.

62. *ST* I-II, q. 109, a. 3.

63. Ibid.

64. Ibid.

65. *ST* I-II, q. 109, a. 8, ad 1. This remark occurs in a reply to an objection, but Aquinas makes it clear ("as we have said") that he is summarizing the reply he has just given in the body of the article.

66. *ST* I-II, q. 109, a. 8.

Chapter 2

1. *ST* I-II, q. 110, a. 1.

2. Ibid.

3. Ibid. Parentheses and brackets in the original.

186 Notes to Pages 50–58

4. Ibid.

5. *CS* III, d. 23, q. 1, a. 4, qa. 3.

6. *DV* q. 14, a. 2, c.

7. See *ST* I-II, q. 62, a. 2, c.; and *DQVG* q. 1, a. 10, c.

8. *ST* I-II, q. 62, a. 1, c.

9. See *CS* III, d. 23, q. 1, a. 4, qa. 3: "Man does not have a sufficient inclination to that end from his natural endowments alone, and so something additional must be added to man, by which he may have an inclination to that end, as by his natural endowments he has an inclination to the end connatural to him. These things added over and above his natural endowments are called theological virtues."

10. See *DV* q. 14, a. 2, c.

11. See *DQVG* q. 1, a. 10, c.: "Each thing is ordered to its end by what it does, and the things that contribute to the end ought to correspond in some way to that end. Consequently, it is necessary for there to be some sorts of completeness in us that exceed the abilities of the principles natural to us and that order us to our supernatural end. This could only be the case if God infused in human beings certain *supernatural* principles of activity on top of [*supra quorum*] the natural ones."

12. *DV* q. 14, a. 2, c.

13. *DQVG* q. 1, a. 10, c.

14. *DV* q. 14, a. 2, c.

15. See *ST* I-II, q. 68, a. 2, c.

16. *DQVG* q. 1, a. 10, c. (emphasis original). See also *CS* III, d. 33, q. 1, a. 2, qa. 3: "It should be said that as was said, the seeds of virtues that are in us are the ordering of will and reason to the good connatural to us. Now since man is ordered by the divine liberality to a certain supernatural good, namely eternal glory, virtues proportionate to this end cannot be caused by the aforesaid seeds of virtue. Hence virtues that order our life to that end must be caused by him who puts the inclination to that end in us. But God's grace does this. Hence we must have some infused moral virtues"; and *ST* I-II, q. 63, a. 3, c.: "In place of these natural principles God confers on us the theological virtues, by which, as was explained above (q. 62, a. 1), we are ordered toward our supernatural end. Hence, corresponding proportionately to these theological virtues there have to be other habits which are caused in us by God and which are related to the theological virtues in the same way that the moral and intellectual virtues are related to the natural principles of the virtues."

17. *ST* I-II, q. 54, a. 2.

18. *ST* I-II, q. 54, a. 2, c.

19. Ibid.

20. *CS* III, d. 33, q. 1, a. 2, qa. 4, c.

21. Ibid.

22. Ibid. Two different aspects of Aquinas's treatment here also might be taken to indicate a thesis about how he envisions the relationship between the virtues. I will address these aspects of the text in chapter 3.

23. *ST* I-II, q. 63, a. 4.

24. Ibid.

25. Ibid.

26. See ibid.

Notes to Pages 58–65   187

27. For a fuller discussion of the term "mode," see Edwin O'Connor, "The Evolution of St. Thomas's Thought," appendix 4 of "The Gifts of the Holy Spirit" (1a 2ae. 68–70), in *Summa Theologiae*, edited by Edwin O'Connor, 24:110–30 (London: Blackfriars, 1974).

28. Ibid.

29. Ibid.

30. *DQVG* q. 1, a. 10, ad 10.

31. *ST* I-II q. 63, a. 4.

32. *CS* III, d. 33, q. 1, a. 2, qa. 4. Aquinas does not in this earlier text assert that the infused virtues belong to a different mode. He appears to believe that the difference in mean asserted here is a direct consequence of the different ends to which they are ordered.

33. *CS* III, d. 33, q. 1, a. 2, qa. 4, ad 2.

34 Ibid. See also *DQVG* q. 1, a. 10, ad 8; and, to a lesser extent, *ST* I-II, q. 63, a. 4.

35. Both John Inglis and Romanus Cessario, for instance, seem to take Aquinas to mean that *what is done* is identical in each case, but that the end to which what is done differs. See Inglis, "Aquinas's Replication of the Acquired Moral Virtues," *Journal of Religious Ethics* 27, no. 1 (1999): 12 and 21; and Romanus Cessario, "How to Distinguish Infused from Acquired Virtues," *The Moral Virtues and Theological Ethics*, 2nd ed. (Notre Dame, IN: University of Notre Dame Press, 2015). Others take a more minimalist interpretation, namely, that the infused and acquired virtues may sometimes but do not always produce outwardly identical acts. I agree with the more minimal interpretation.

36. *DQVG* q. 1, a. 10, obj. 8.

37. Ibid.

38. *DQVG* q. 1, a. 10, ad 8.

39. Ibid.

40. See *CS* III, d. 33, q. 1, a. 2, qa. 4, ad 2.

41. *CS* III, d. 33, q. 1, a. 2, qa. 4, obj. 2.

42. See ibid.

43. See *CS* III, d. 33, q. 1, a. 2, qa. 4, ad 2.

44. Ibid.

45. *ST* II-II, q. 124, a. 3, ad 1.

46. *ST* II-II, q. 24, a. 3.

47. Ibid.

48. Ibid. Aquinas is quoting Ephesians 4:7.

49. *ST* II-II, q. 24, a. 3, ad 1.

50. See *DQVG* q. 1, a. 10, ad 14.

51. Ibid.

52. Ibid.

53. *DQVG* q. 1, a. 10, ad 15.

54. See, for instance, Sherwin, "Infused Virtue and the Effects of Acquired Vice," 29–52.

55. *DQVG* q. 1, a. 11.

56. Ibid.

57. *ST* II-II, q. 24, a. 6.

58. Ibid.

59. Ibid.

60. Ibid.

61. *ST* I-II, q. 52, a. 3.

62. Ibid.

63. Ibid.

64. *ST* I-II q. 68 a. 2, c.

65. Ibid.

66. Ibid.

67. Ibid.

68. Ibid.

69. *ST* I-II, q. 68, a. 2, obj. 2.

70. See ibid. I find it interesting that Aquinas does *not* say that acting well in human matters is made possible by the natural principles of virtue, but by the moral virtues themselves. I think this means that connection between the gifts and the infused moral virtues is much closer than is commonly assumed.

71. *ST* I-II, q. 68, a. 2, ad 2 (emphasis mine). Given the objection Aquinas is replying to, it seems reasonable to assume that the "moral virtues" referenced in the reply are the natural moral virtues, not the supernatural moral virtues.

72. *ST* I-II, q. 68, a. 1.

73. Ibid.

74. Ibid.

75. *ST* I-II, q. 68, a. 1, c.; Isaiah 11:2–3.

76. Ibid.

77. Some scholars are critical of the use of "instinct" as a translation of *instinctus*. See, for instance, Andrew Pinsent, *The Second-Person Perspective in Aquinas's Ethics: Virtues and Gifts* (New York: Routledge, 2012).

78. Servais Pinckaers, "Morality and the Movement of the Holy Spirit: Aquinas's Doctrine of Instinctus," in *The Pinckaers Reader: Renewing Thomistic Moral Theology*, ed. John Berkman and Craig Steven Titus (Washington, DC: Catholic University of America Press, 2005), 389.

79. Ibid.

80. Réginald Garrigou-Lagrange, *The Three Ages of the Interior Life: Prelude of Eternal Life*, trans. Sr. M. Timothea Doyle (St. Louis: Herder, 1947), 2:72–74. I focus here on Garrigou-Lagrange, but his treatment is consistent with the account given by many other Thomist commentators. For a fuller discussion of his view, see John Meinert, *The Love of God Poured Out: Grace and the Gifts of the Holy Spirit in St. Thomas Aquinas* (Steubenville, OH: Emmaus Academic, 2018).

81. See Garrigou-Lagrange, *Three Ages of the Interior Life*, 2:73.

82. See ibid., 2:81.

83. For a nice overview of the literature on this, see O'Connor, "The Evolution of St. Thomas's Thought," 24:110–30.

84. *CS* III, d. 34, q. 1, a. 1, c.

85. Ibid.

86. Ibid.

Notes to Pages 76–84   189

87. *CS* III, d. 34, q. 1, a. 2, c.
88. See ibid.
89. *CS* III, d. 33, q. 1, a. 1, qa. 3, c.
90. Ibid.

CHAPTER 3

1. In subsequent chapters, I address different ways in which these views might be held. Those distinctions are not pertinent to the present discussion.

2. See Thomas Aquinas, *Disputed Questions in General* (*DQVG*) q. 1, a. 10: "Hoc autem esse non posset, nisi supra principia naturalia aliqua supernaturalia operationum principia homini infundantur a Deo"; see *Sancti Thomae de Aquino Quaestiones disputatae de virtutibus*, trans. Robert Busa, S.J. (1953), http://www.corpusthomisticum.org/qdw103.html. See also Thomas Aquinas, *Scriptum Super Libros Sententiarum Magistri Petri Lombardi Episcopi Parisiensis*, vol. 3, ed. R. P. Mandonnet, O.P. (Paris: Sumptibus P. Lethielleux, 1933), d. 23, q. 1, a. 4, qa. 3, sol. 3: "Unde per naturalia tantum homo non habet sufficienter inclinationem in finem illum; et ideo oportet quod superaddatur homini aliquid per quod habeat inclinationem in finem illum, sicut per naturalia habet inclinationem ad finem sibi connaturalem."

3. See *ST* I-II, q. 62, a. 1: "Unde oportet quod superaddantur homini divinitus aliqua principia, per quae ita ordinetur ad beatitudinem supernaturalem, sicut per principia naturalia ordinatur ad finem connaturalem, non tamen absque adiutorio divino."

4. I address each of these claims in considerably more detail in Angela Knobel, "Relating Aquinas's Infused and Acquired Virtues: Some Problematic Texts for a Common Interpretation," *Nova et Vetera* 9, no. 2 (2011): 411–31. As will become clear in the next section, however, the account I give in that article is also somewhat different. I now believe that the sources of the claim that charity "forms" the virtues are some remarks Aquinas makes in *CS*, and I also now believe that those remarks are indicative of his early view of the relationship (or lack thereof) between the two.

5. See, for instance, Inglis, "Aquinas's Replication of the Acquired Moral Virtues," 18; Étienne Gilson, *The Christian Philosophy of St. Thomas Aquinas* (Notre Dame, IN: University of Notre Dame Press, 1994), 343; and Reneé Mirkes, "Moral Virtues and Theories of Facility," *The Thomist: A Speculative Quarterly Review* 61, no. 2 (1997): 189–218. Other references can be found in Robert Florent Coerver, *The Quality of Facility in the Moral Virtues* (Whitefish, MT: Kessinger, 2007), 46–54. Not all scholars who make this claim cite the text I refer to in what follows in its defense. Terrence Irwin, who likewise claims that Aquinas believes the infused virtues perfect the acquired virtues, cites *ST* I-II, q. 69, a. 3. In that text, however, Aquinas is describing not the differences between the infused and acquired virtues but the differences between the virtues and the gifts of the Holy Spirit; see Irwin, *The Development of Ethics* (Oxford:

Oxford University Press, 2007), 1:647. Still other scholars have made this claim without citing a specific text in defense of it. See, for instance, Réginald Garrigou-Lagrange, *The Three Ages of the Interior Life: Prelude of Eternal Life*, trans. Sr. Timothea Doyle (St. Louis: Herder, 1947), 1:64. Some other scholars, such as Anthony Falanga and Andrew Dell'Olio, cite Aquinas's numerous statements that charity is the "form" of the virtues in defense of this claim; see Falanga, *Charity the Form of the Virtues according to Saint Thomas Aquinas* (Washington, DC: Catholic University of America Press, 1948); and Dell'Olio, *Foundations of Moral Selfhood* (New York: Peter Lang, 2003), 129–30. An adequate defense of this latter position would need to show that Aquinas intends this claim to apply equally to infused and acquired virtue, and neither Falanga nor Dell'Olio establishes that this is the case.

6.   Inglis, "Aquinas's Replication of the Acquired Moral Virtues," 19.

7.   Gilson, *The Christian Philosophy of St. Thomas Aquinas*, 343.

8.   *ST* I-II, q. 51, a. 4.

9.   See *ST* I-II, q. 51, a. 4, arg. 3.

10.   See *DQVG* q. 1, a. 10, arg. 19.

11.   *ST* I-II, q. 51, a. 4, ad 3.

12.   *DQVG* q. 1, a. 10, ad 19.

13.   This interpretation does not commit Aquinas to the claim that we increase virtues through our own power because, as we saw in our previous account of how the infused virtues increase, repeated acts of infused virtue may make us more likely to perform the act but do not cause their increase. I have also addressed this question in Knobel, "Relating the Virtues."

14.   Dell'Olio, *Foundations of Moral Selfhood*, 137; Inglis, "Aquinas's Replication of the Acquired Moral Virtues," 21; Herdt, *Putting on Virtue*, 87; and Mirkes, "Aquinas's Doctrine of Moral Virtue and Its Significance for Theories of Facility," 191. Garrigou-Lagrange makes this assertion without citing a text (see Garrigou-Lagrange, *The Three Ages of the Interior Life*, 63). Irwin reads this text in the opposite way, claiming that the acquired virtues make it more difficult to practice the infused (see Irwin, *Development of Ethics*, 647).

15.   Dell'Olio, *Foundations of Moral Selfhood*, 138.

16.   We have already examined these texts with respect to the general question of the kind of "facility" conferred by the infused virtues, but not with respect to the specific claim that the requisite facility is provided by the cultivation of the acquired virtues.

17.   The *ST* I-II text is more specifically concerned with whether all the moral virtues are infused along with *charity*, but that difference is irrelevant to the present discussion.

18.   See *ST* I-II, q. 65, a. 3, ad 2: "If an individual has the habit of a virtue, then it is easy for him to do what belongs to the virtue and pleases him in its own right; hence, as *Ethics* 2 says, 'A sign of a habit is the pleasure that is effected in its work.' But there are many who have charity, existing without mortal sin, and who nonetheless experience difficulty with the works of the virtues and take pleasure in them not in their own right but only insofar as they are referred back to charity. Therefore, there are many individuals who have charity but do not have the other virtues." See also *DQVG* q. 1, a. 10, arg. 14: "If the virtues are infused, they should

all be infused at the same time as grace. Grace, though, is infused into someone who is in a state of sin by an act of repentance; the dispositions of the moral virtues are not, however, infused in him at that same time. For even after repenting, we are still troubled by the emotions; this is the experience of someone who is self-controlled, but not of someone who is virtuous."

19. See *ST* I-II, q. 65, a. 3, ad 2.
20. Ibid.
21. Ibid.
22. *DQVG* q. 1, a. 10, ad 14.
23. Ibid.
24. Ibid.
25. Ibid.
26. Scholars who make this claim include Pieper, *Prudence*, 30; Dell'Olio, *Foundations of Moral Selfhood*, 136; Herdt, *Putting on Virtue*, 87–88; Bonnie Dorrick Kent, "Habits and Virtues," in *The Ethics of Aquinas*, ed. Stephen Pope (Washington, DC: Georgetown University Press, 2002): 124–25; and Sherwin, "Infused Virtue and the Effects of Acquired Vice."
27. Pieper, *Prudence*, 30–31.
28. *ST* II-II, q. 47, a. 14, ad 1.
29. Ibid.
30. Ibid.
31. See *ST* I-II, q. 78, a. 4, *sed contra.*
32. See *ST* II-II, q. 168, a. 1, ad 2.
33. *ST* I-II, q. 58, a. 4.
34. Ibid.
35. Ibid.
36. I do not see the scriptural references Aquinas uses in his reply as evidence against this, since he often cites pagan philosophers in his account of supernatural virtues and scripture in his account of natural virtues.
37. *CS* III, d. 33, q. 1, a. 2, qa. 4.
38. *CS* III, d. 33, q. 1, a. 2, qa. 4, arg. 3.
39. *CS* III d. 33, q. 1, a. 2, qa. 4, ad 3.
40. See *CS* III, d. 33, q. 1, a. 2, qa. 4, ad 4.
41. Ibid.
42. *ST* I-II, q. 61, a. 5.
43. Ibid.
44. Ibid.
45. Ibid.
46. Ibid.
47. I discuss this text at length in Angela McKay Knobel, "Aquinas's *Commentary on the Sentences* and the Relation between Infused and Acquired Virtue," *Proceedings of the Society for Medieval Logic and Metaphysics* (forthcoming).
48. It's noteworthy that "matter" here seems to have the same meaning I proposed earlier.
49. See *CS* III, d. 33, q. 1, a. 4.
50. See ibid.
51. *CS* III, d. 33, q. 1, a. 4, ad 2.

52. Ibid.

53. Any number of accounts of just *how* this occurs, of course, could be given. Even if one thinks that progress in the moral life means that more and more of one's acts will be acts of infused virtue, that need not commit one to the view that grace turns existing acquired virtues into infused virtues. One could conceivably hold that the Christian can perform acts of both types of virtue, but that as he grows in the moral life, he will perform fewer acts of acquired virtue and more acts of infused virtue.

54. *DQVG* q. 1, a. 10.

55. *DQVG* q. 1, a. 10, arg. 4.

56. Ibid.

57. *DQVG* q. 1, a. 10, ad 4.

58. See, for instance, the contrasting interpretations of William C. Mattison III, "Can Christians Possess the Acquired Cardinal Virtues?," *Theological Studies* 72, no. 3 (2011): 558–85; and Sherwin, "Infused Virtues and the Effects of Acquired Vice."

59. Aristotle, *Politics*, bk. 3.

60. See *ST* II-II, q. 47, a. 11: "Diversi autem fines sunt bonum proprium unius, et bonum familiae, et bonum civitatis et regni. Unde necesse est quod et prudentiae differant specie secundum differentiam horum finium."

61. See ibid.: "alia autem oeconomica, quae ordinatur ad bonum commune domus vel familiae; et tertia politica, quae ordinatur ad bonum commune civitatis vel regni."

62. See *ST* II-II, q. 47, a. 12: "Respondeo dicendum quod prudentia in ratione est. Regere autem et gubernare proprie rationis est. Et ideo unusquisque inquantum participat de regimine et gubernatione, intantum convenit sibi habere rationem et prudentiam. Manifestum est autem quod subditi inquantum est subditus, et servi inquantum est servus, non est regere et gubernare, sed magis regi et gubernari."

63. Ibid.: "Et ad hoc pertinet species prudentiae quae politica vocatur."

64. See ibid.: "Et similiter, licet bonum unius ordinetur ad bonum multitudinis, tamen hoc non impedit quin talis diversitas faciat habitus differre specie. Sed ex hoc sequitur quod habitus qui ordinatur ad finem ultimum sit principalior, et imperet aliis habitibus."

65. See ibid.: "Secundo quia, cum homo sit pars domus et civitatis, oportet quod homo consideret quid sit sibi bonum ex hoc quod est prudens circa bonum multitudinis, bona enim dispositio partis accipitur secundum habitudinem ad totum; quia ut Augustinus dicit, in libro Confess., turpis est omnis pars suo toti non congruens."

CHAPTER 4

1. It seems likely that this is what Osborne has in mind with his discussion of perfect and imperfect virtue (see Thomas Osborne, "Perfect and Imperfect

Virtue," *The Thomist* 71, no.1 [2007] : 39–64). It is unclear whether defenders of this view believe that previously cultivated, imperfect, acquired virtues immediately *become* perfect at the moment of grace, or whether they merely believe that the acquired virtues can now be more perfectly cultivated because the nature of the one who possesses them has been healed.

2. I know of no interpreter of Aquinas who denies this.

3. John R. Bowlin, "Elevating and Healing: Reflections on *Summa Theologiae* I-II, q. 109, a. 2," *Journal of Moral Theology* 3, no. 1 (2014): 39–53.

4. *CS* III, d. 33, q. 1, a. 4; and Aquinas, *Disputed Questions on the Cardinal Virtues* (*DQVC*), in *Sancti Thomae de Aquino Quaestiones disputatae de virtutibus*, trans. Robert Busa, S.J. (1953), a. 4, http://www.corpusthomisticum.org/qdw5 .html. Unless otherwise indicated, citations from this text will be from this edition.

5. Bonnie Kent, "Habits and Virtues," in *The Ethics of Aquinas*, ed. Stephen Pope (Washington, DC: Georgetown University Press, 2002), 125.

6. Ibid., 125.

7. Ibid., 125–26 (original emphasis).

8. Pieper, *Prudence*, 30.

9. Sherwin, "Infused Virtue and the Effects of Acquired Vice," 42.

10. Ibid.

11. See, for instance, Andrew Dell'Olio, *Foundations of Moral Selfhood* (New York: Peter Lang, 2003), 136: "While it is true, for Aquinas, that every Christian receives supernatural, infused prudence in baptism, this prudence extends only to what is necessary for eternal salvation." See also Jennifer Herdt, *Putting on Virtue* (Chicago: University of Chicago Press, 2008), 87, and Reneé Mirkes "Aquinas's Doctrine of Moral Virtue and Its Significance for Theories of Facility," *The Thomist: A Speculative Quarterly Review* 61, no. 2 (1997): 205.

12. In the text cited by Kent, Aquinas is concerned with the ability to take counsel.

13. For a different kind of response, see Jean Porter, "Virtue and Sin: The Case of the Connection of the Virtues and the Flawed Saint," *The Journal of Religion* 75, no. 4 (1995): 521–53. I am not prepared to go as far as Porter goes.

14. Sherwin, "Infused Virtue and the Effects of Acquired Vice," 42.

15. Ibid.

16. Kent, "Habits and Virtues," 126.

CHAPTER 5

1. I will focus primarily on the view put forward in Decosimo in "More to Love." However, Decosimo defends a similar view in his *Ethics as a Work of Charity*. See David Decosimo, "More to Love: Ends, Ordering and the Compatibility of Acquired and Infused Virtues," in *The Virtuous Life: Thomas Aquinas on the Theological Nature of Moral Virtues*, ed. Harm J. M. J. Goris and Henk J. M. Schoot (Leuven: Peeters, 2017), and Decosimo, *Ethics as a Work of Charity* (Stanford, CA: Stanford University Press, 2016).

194   Notes to Pages 129–135

2.   See http://www.vatican.va/archive/ccc_css/archive/catechism/p3s1c1a7 .htm, nos. 1810–13. For a thorough discussion of the *Catechism*'s omission and an attempt to reconcile it with Aquinas's notion of infused virtue, see Bill Mattison, "Thomas's Categorizations of Virtue: Historical Background and Contemporary Significance," *The Thomist: A Speculative Quarterly Review* 74, no. 2 (2010): 189–235.

3.   Foot, "Virtues and Vices," 163–64.

4.   Ibid.

5.   For an example of such an attribution, see Kent, *Virtues of the Will*, 42.

6.   Étienne Gilson, *The Christian Philosophy of St. Thomas Aquinas* (Notre Dame, IN: University of Notre Dame Press, 1994), 347 and 339.

7.   Harm Goris, "Moral Virtues in Wounded Nature," in Goris and Schoot, eds., *The Virtuous Life*, 21–46. Bill Mattison has also noted the ambiguity of Gilson's position. See Mattison, "Thomas's Categorizations of Virtue."

8.   Goris, "Moral Virtues in Wounded Nature," 23.

9.   Ibid.

10.   Ibid.

11.   Ibid.

12.   Ibid., 24. Several other scholars have also used the language of "virtual presence" in an attempt to explain the relationship between the infused and acquired virtues. See, for instance, Scott Cleveland and Brandon Dahm, "The Virtual Presence of the Acquired Virtues in the Christian," *American Catholic Philosophical Quarterly* 93, no. 1 (2019): 75–100. In my view this analogy is unlikely to be helpful, because the notion of virtual presence is itself insufficiently developed by Aquinas. An idea that is itself used in an unclear and confusing way is unlikely to be helpful in explaining another, equally confusing idea.

13.   Although neither describes their view in these terms, the accounts of John Inglis and Romanus Cessario seem to me to be similar in important respects. See Inglis, "Aquinas's Replication of the Acquired Moral Virtues," *Journal of Religious Ethics* 27, no. 1 (1999): 3–27, and Cessario, *The Moral Virtues and Theological Ethics*, 2nd ed. (Notre Dame, IN: University of Notre Dame Press, 2015).

14.   This, as is well known, is Scotus's view. It is significant, of course, that Scotus offers a very different account of charity and of the transformation effected by grace than Aquinas does. See John Duns Scotus, *Opus oxoniense* III, dist. 36, n. 28, in *Duns Scotus on the Will and Morality*, trans. William Wolter, ed. William Frank (Washington, DC: Catholic University of America Press, 1986), 414–16.

15.   William C. Mattison III, "Aquinas, Custom, and the Coexistence of Infused and Acquired Virtue," *Journal of Moral Theology* 8, no. 2 (2019): 1–24.

16.   A defender of the coexistence view, or of the view that I will propose in chapter 6, could also ascribe to such an account.

17.   William C. Mattison III, "Can Christians Possess the Acquired Cardinal Virtues?," *Theological Studies* 72, no. 3 (2011): 558–85, and Mattison, "Revisiting the Relationship between Infused and Acquired Cardinal Virtues: Lessons from Thomas Aquinas on Dead Faith," in *Proceedings of the Society for Medieval Logic and Metaphysics* (forthcoming).

Notes to Pages 135–142   195

18. Mattison, "Can Christians Possess the Acquired Cardinal Virtues?," 567.

19. Since I have already addressed this text at length in an earlier chapter, I will not here address Mattison's argument in detail. It is worth noting, however, that if the infused and acquired virtues belong to distinct realms of the Christian moral life, as Aquinas may well have believed they do, then it is not at all clear that Mattison's criticism would go through.

20. Mattison, "Can Christians Possess the Acquired Cardinal Virtues?," 568. As noted in the previous footnote, even though I do not think the coexistence theory is a good account of the Christian moral life, I think the coexistence theorist has a way around this particular argument.

21. Ibid.

22. *ST* II-II, q. 6, a. 1.

23. Ibid.

24. Mattison, "Revisiting the Relationship," 12.

25. Ibid.

26. Ibid.

27. Ibid., 14.

28. *ST* I-II, q. 63, a. 4.

29. Ibid.

30. Ibid.

31. Ibid.

32. Ibid.

33. This is unsurprising, since "material object" is Suarez's innovation. See Duarte Sousa-Lara, "Aquinas on the Object of the Human Act: A Reading in Light of the Texts and Commentators," *Josephinum Journal of Theology* 15, no. 2 (2008): 243–76.

34. *ST* I-II, q. 63. a. 4.

35. George Klubertanz, "Une theorie sur les virtues morales 'naturelles' et 'surnaturelles,'" *Revue Thomiste* 59 (1959): 565–75; Reneé Mirkes, "Aquinas's Doctrine of Moral Virtue and Its Significance for Theories of Facility," *The Thomist* 61, no. 2 (1997): 189–218; David Decosimo, "More to Love: Thomas Aquinas on the Relationship between the Infused and Acquired Virtues," in Goris and Schoot, eds., *The Virtuous Life*, 47–72.

36. In articulating and defending the position defended by Klubertanz, Mirkes also makes some errors that in my view detract from the main claim Klubertanz wishes to put forward. She claims, for instance, that prudence is the "form" of the moral virtues, and that the natural dispositions are the "seeds" of the acquired virtues. Aquinas directly denies the first of these claims, and it should be clear from our discussion in chapter 1 that the second is also incorrect.

37. Klubertanz, "Une theorie sur les virtues morales 'naturelles' et 'surnaturelles,'" 570–71.

38. Decosimo, "More to Love," 56.

39. For more on Aquinas's view, see John Wippel, *The Metaphysical Thought of Thomas Aquinas* (Washington, DC: Catholic University of America Press, 2000), 350, and Christopher Decaen, "Elemental Virtual Presence in St. Thomas," *The Thomist* 64 (2000), 271–300.

40. Decaen, "Elemental Virtual Presence," 282. Decaen argues that "power" cannot be understood as potential presence, but that what is present is akin to a "flavor"—one can perceive aspects of the element in the composite.

41. Decaen, "Elemental Virtual Presence," 288.

42. Decosimo, "More to Love," 56, 57.

43. Ibid.

44. Decosimo, "More to Love," 55.

45. Ibid.

46. Decosimo, "More to Love," 57.

47. *ST* I-II, q. 63, a. 4.

CHAPTER 6

1. Fred Freddoso, "St. Thomas on Prudence and the Moral Virtues," appendix 1, https://www3.nd.edu/~afreddos/papers/prudence%20and%20the%20moral%20virtues.pdf.

2. Ibid.

3. Joseph Ratzinger, *Introduction to Christianity*, 2nd ed. (San Francisco: Ignatius Press), Kindle ed., location 371 of 4795.

4. Ibid.

5. Ibid.

6. Ibid., loc. 414 of 4795.

7. Ibid., loc. 420 of 4795.

8. *ST* II-II, q. 124, a. 4.

9. *ST* II-II, q. 1, a. 4.

10. Ibid.

11. Ibid.

12. Ibid.

13. Ibid.

14. Ibid.

15. *ST* I-II, q. 63, a. 2, ad 2.

16. For the purposes of the present discussion, we need not assume that Leonidas and the Spartans possessed the fullness of the virtue of courage.

17. Acts 6.

18. Ibid.

19. Ibid.

20. *ST* I-II, q. 63, a. 4.

21. *DQVG* a. 10, obj. 16. Although this translation translates *habitus* as "disposition" and *dispositio* as "tendency," I follow the more common usage and translate the words as "habit" and "disposition," respectively.

22. Ibid.

23. *DQVC* a. 2, obj. 2.

24. *DQVG* a.10, ad 16; *DQVC* a. 2, ad 2.

25. *DQVG* a. 10, ad 16.

26. Ibid.
27. *DQVG* a. 10, ad 14.
28. *DQVC* a. 2, ad 2.
29. Ibid.
30. Ibid.
31. Sherwin, "Infused Virtue and the Effects of Acquired Vice," 40.
32. For a fuller discussion of this point, see Angela Knobel, "Aquinas and the Pagan Virtues," *International Philosophical Quarterly* 51, no. 3 (2011): 339–54.
33. *ST* I-II, q. 88, a. 1.
34. Ibid.
35. Ibid.
36. Ibid.
37. Ibid.
38. My thanks to an anonymous referee for posing this objection.
39. *ST* II-II, q. 24, a. 9.
40. Ibid.
41. Ibid.
42. Ibid.
43. *ST* I-II, q. 52, a. 3; II-II, q. 24, a. 6.
44. *ST* II-II, q. 24, a. 6.
45. See Bill Mattison, "Aquinas, Custom, and the Coexistence of Infused and Acquired Virtue," *Journal of Moral Theology* 8, no. 2 (2019): 1–24.
46. Freddoso, "St. Thomas on Prudence and the Moral Virtues," appendix 1, 10.

Bibliography

Alighieri, Dante. *Inferno*. Translated by Stanley Lombardo. Indianapolis: Hackett, 2009.

Aquinas, Thomas. *Disputed Questions on the Cardinal Virtues (DQVC)*. In *Sancti Thomae de Aquino Quaestiones disputatae de virtutibus*, translated by Robert Busa, S.J., 1953. http://www.corpusthomisticum.org/qdw103.html.

———. *Disputed Questions on the Virtues*. Edited by E. M. Atkins and Thomas Williams. Cambridge: Cambridge University Press, 2005.

———. *Disputed Questions on the Virtues in General (DQVG)*. In *Sancti Thomae de Aquino Quaestiones disputatae de virtutibus*, translated by Robert Busa, S.J., 1953. http://www.corpusthomisticum.org/qdw5.html.

———. *On Virtues and Gifts: Texts from the Commentary on the Sentences of Peter Lombard*. Translated by Joseph Bowlin. Unpublished translation, December 6, 2008.

———. *Quaestiones disputatae de veritate (DV)* q. 14 ("On Faith"). Translated by Fred Freddoso. https://www3.nd.edu/~afreddos/translat/aquinas5.htm.

———. *Scriptum Super Libros Sententiarum Magistri Petri Lombardi Episcopi Parisiensis*. Vol. 3. Edited by R. P. Mandonnet, O.P. Paris: Sumptibus P. Lethielleux, 1933.

———. *Summa Theologiae*. Translated by Alfred J. Freddoso. https://www3.nd.edu/~afreddos/summa-translation/TOC.htm.

———. *Truth: Questions X–XX*. Vol. 2. Translated by James V. McGlynn, S.J. Chicago: Henry Regnery Company, 1953.

Aristotle. *Nicomachean Ethics*. 2nd ed. Translated by Terrence Irwin. Indianapolis: Hackett, 1999.

Austin, Nicholas. *Aquinas and the Virtues*. Washington, DC: Georgetown University Press, 2018.

Baschera, Luca. "Ethics in Reformed Orthodoxy." In *A Companion to Reformed Orthodoxy*, vol. 40, edited by Herman Selderhuis, 519–52. Brill's Companions to the Christian Tradition. Leiden: Brill, 2013.

Bejczy, István P. "The Problem of Natural Virtue." In *Virtue and Ethics in the Twelfth Century*, edited by István P. Bejczy and Richard G. Newhauser, 131–54. Leiden: Brill, 2005.

Billot, Louis. *De virtutibus infusis: Commentarius in secundam partem S. Thomae.* Rome: Ex Typographia Polyglotta, 1905.

Bowlin, John R. "Elevating and Healing: Reflections on *Summa Theologiae* I-II q. 109, a. 2." *Journal of Moral Theology* 3, no. 1 (2014): 39–53.

Butera, Giuseppe. "On Reason's Control of the Passions in Aquinas's Theory of Temperance." *Mediaeval Studies* 68, no. 1 (2006): 133–60.

Cessario, Romanus. *The Moral Virtues and Theological Ethics.* 2nd ed. Notre Dame, IN: University of Notre Dame Press, 2015.

Chiasson, Charles C. "The Herodotean Solon." *Greek, Roman, and Byzantine Studies* 27, no. 3 (1986): 249–62.

Cleveland, Scott, and Brandon Dahm. "The Virtual Presence of the Acquired Virtues in the Christian." *American Catholic Philosophical Quarterly* 93, no. 1 (2019): 75–100.

Coerver, Robert Florent. *The Quality of Facility in the Moral Virtues.* Whitefish, MT: Kessinger, 2007.

Decosimo, David. *Ethics as a Work of Charity.* Stanford, CA: Stanford University Press, 2016.

———. "More to Love: Ends, Ordering and the Compatibility of Acquired and Infused Virtues." In *The Virtuous Life: Thomas Aquinas on the Theological Nature of Moral Virtues,* edited by Harm J. M. J. Goris and Henk J. M. Schoot, 47–72. Leuven: Peeters, 2017.

Dell'Olio, Andrew. *Foundations of Moral Selfhood.* New York: Peter Lang, 2003.

de Lubac, Henri. *The Mystery of the Supernatural.* Translated by Rosemary Sheed. New York: Crossroad, 1998.

De Young, Rebecca Konydyck. "Power Made Perfect in Weakness: Aquinas's Transformation of the Virtue of Courage." *Medieval Theology and Philosophy* 11, no. 2 (2003): 147–80.

Fagothy, Austin. *Right and Reason: Ethics Based on the Teachings of Aristotle and St. Thomas Aquinas.* 4th ed. St. Louis: The C. V. Mosby Company, 1967.

Falanga, Anthony. *Charity the Form of the Virtues according to Saint Thomas Aquinas.* Washington, DC: Catholic University of America Press, 1948.

Feingold, Lawrence. *The Natural Desire to See God according to St. Thomas Aquinas and His Interpreters.* 2nd ed. Ave Maria, FL: Sapientia Press of Ave Maria University, 2010.

Feingold, Lawrence, and John Milbank. "Recent Interventions in the Debate over the Natural Desire to See God." *Nova et Vetera* 5, no. 1 (2007): 81–132.

Foot, Philippa. "Virtues and Vices." In *Virtue Ethics,* edited by Roger Crisp and Michael Slote, 163–77. Oxford: Oxford University Press, 1997.

Freddoso, Alfred. "St. Thomas on Prudence and the Moral Virtues." Appendix 1. https://www3.nd.edu/~afreddos/papers/prudence%20and%20the%20moral%20virtues.pdf.

Gallagher, David. "The Role of God in the Philosophical Ethics of Thomas Aquinas." In *Was ist Philosophie im Mittelalter?,* edited by Jan A. Aertsen et al., Miscellanea Mediaevalia 26:1024–33. Berlin: Walter de Gruyter, 1998.

Garrigou-Lagrange, Réginald. *The Three Ages of the Interior Life: Prelude of Eternal Life*. Vols. 1–2. Translated by Sr. M. Timothea Doyle. St. Louis, MO: Herder Book Company, 1947–1948.

Gilson, Étienne. *The Christian Philosophy of St. Thomas Aquinas*. Notre Dame, IN: University of Notre Dame Press, 1994.

Goris, Harm J. M. J. "Moral Virtues in Wounded Nature." In *The Virtuous Life*, edited by Harm J. M. J. Goris and Henck J. M. Schoot, 21–46. Leuven: Peeters, 2017.

Healy, Nicholas. "Henri de Lubac on Nature and Grace: A Note on Some Recent Contributions to the Debate." *Communio* 35, no. 4 (2008): 535–64.

Herdt, Jennifer. *Putting on Virtue*. Chicago: University of Chicago Press, 2008.

Hoffmann, Tobias. "Prudence and Practical Principles." In *Aquinas and the "Nicomachean Ethics,"* edited by Tobias Hoffmann, Jorn Muller, and Mattias Perkams. Cambridge: Cambridge University Press, 2013.

Hütter, Reinhard. "'Palaeothomism?' — The Continuing Debate over the Natural Desire for the Vision of God," and "'Thomist Ressourcement' — A Rereading of Thomas on the Natural Desire for the Vision of God." In *Dust Bound for Heaven: Explorations in the Theology of Thomas Aquinas*, 129–246. Grand Rapids, MI: Eerdmans, 2012.

Inglis, John. "Aquinas's Replication of the Acquired Moral Virtues." *Journal of Religious Ethics* 27, no. 1 (1999): 3–27.

Irwin, Terence H. *The Development of Ethics*. Vol. 1. Oxford: Oxford University Press, 2007.

———. "Permanent Happiness: Aristotle and Solon." *Oxford Studies in Ancient Philosophy* 3 (1985): 89–124.

Jensen, Steven J. "Virtuous Deliberation and the Passions." *The Thomist: A Speculative Quarterly Review* 77, no. 2 (2013): 193–227.

Kahm, Nicholas. *Aquinas on the Emotions' Participation in Reason*. Washington, DC: Catholic University of America Press, 2019.

———. "Thomas Aquinas on the Sense Appetite as Participating in Reason." Ph.D. diss., Catholic University of America, 2014.

Kent, Bonnie Dorrick. "Augustine's *On the Good of Marriage* and Infused Virtue in the Twelfth Century." *Journal of Religious Ethics* 41, no. 1 (2013): 112–36.

———. "Habits and Virtues." In *The Ethics of Aquinas*, edited by Stephen Pope, 116–30. Washington, DC: Georgetown University Press, 2002.

———. "Moral Provincialism." *Religious Studies* 30, no. 3 (1994): 269–85.

———. *Virtues of the Will: The Transformation of Ethics in the Late Thirteenth Century*. Washington, DC: Catholic University Press, 1995.

Knobel, Angela. "Aquinas and the Pagan Virtues." *International Philosophical Quarterly* 51, no. 3 (2011): 331–54.

———. "Aquinas's *Commentary on the Sentences* and the Relation between Infused and Acquired Virtue." *Proceedings of the Society for Medieval Logic and Metaphysics* 16. Forthcoming.

———. "A Confusing Comparison." In *The Virtuous Life*, edited by Harm J. M. J. Goris and Henck J. M. Schoot, 97–116. Leuven: Peeters, 2017.

———. "Ends and Virtues." *Journal of Moral Theology* 3, no. 1 (2014): 105–17.

———. "Relating Aquinas's Infused and Acquired Virtues: Some Problematic Texts for a Common Interpretation." *Nova et Vetera* 9, no. 2 (2011): 411–31.

Laporta, Jorge. *La Destinée de la nature humaine selon Thomas d'Aquin.* Paris: J. Vrin, 1965.

Lombardo, Nicholas E. *The Logic of Desire: Aquinas on Emotion.* Washington, DC: Catholic University of America Press, 2012.

Lottin, Odon. *Psychologie et morale aux XIIe et XIIIe siècles.* 8 vols. Louvain: Abbaye du Mont César, 1946.

MacIntyre, Alasdair. *A Short History of Ethics: A History of Moral Philosophy from the Homeric Age to the Twentieth Century.* 2nd ed. Notre Dame, IN: University of Notre Dame Press, 1998.

Mansfield, Richard K. "Antecedent Passion and the Moral Quality of Human Acts according to St. Thomas." *Proceedings of the American Catholic Philosophical Association* 71 (1997): 221–31.

Mattison, William C., III. "Aquinas, Custom, and the Coexistence of Infused and Acquired Virtue." *Journal of Moral Theology* 8, no. 2 (2019): 1–24.

———. "Can Christians Possess the Acquired Cardinal Virtues?" *Theological Studies* 72, no. 3 (2011): 558–85.

———. "Revisiting the Relationship between Infused and Acquired Cardinal Virtues: Lessons from Thomas Aquinas on Dead Faith." In *Proceedings of the Society for Medieval Logic and Metaphysics.* Forthcoming.

———. "Thomas's Categorizations of Virtue: Historical Background and Contemporary Significance." *The Thomist: A Speculative Quarterly Review* 74, no. 2 (2010): 189–235.

McKay, Angela. "Prudence and Acquired Moral Virtue." *The Thomist: A Speculative Quarterly Review* 69, no. 4 (2005): 535–55.

Meinert, John. *The Love of God Poured Out: Grace and the Gifts of the Holy Spirit in St. Thomas Aquinas.* Steubenville, OH: Emmaus Academic, 2018.

Mirkes, Renée. "Aquinas's Doctrine of Moral Virtue and Its Significance for Theories of Facility." *The Thomist: A Speculative Quarterly Review* 61, no. 2 (1997): 189–218.

Müller, Anselm Winfried. "Aristotle's Conception of Ethical and Natural Virtue." In *Was ist das für den Menschen Gute?*, edited by Jan Szaif and Matthias Lutz-Bachmann, 18–53. Berlin: Walter de Gruyter, 2004.

O'Connor, Edwin. "The Evolution of St. Thomas's Thought," appendix 4 of "The Gifts of the Holy Spirit" (1a 2ae. 68–70). In *Summa Theologiae*, vol. 24, edited by Edwin O'Connor, 110–30. London: Blackfriars, 1974.

O'Meara, Thomas F. "Virtues in the Theology of Thomas Aquinas." *Theological Studies* 58, no. 2 (1997): 254–85.

Osborne, Thomas. "The Augustinianism of Thomas Aquinas' Moral Theory." *The Thomist: A Speculative Quarterly Review* 67, no. 2 (2003): 279–305.

———. "Perfect and Imperfect Virtue." *The Thomist: A Speculative Quarterly Review* 71, no. 1 (2007): 39–64.

Pinckaers, Servais. "Morality and the Movement of the Holy Spirit: Aquinas's Doctrine of Instinctus." In *The Pinckaers Reader: Renewing Thomistic*

Moral Theology, edited by John Berkman and Craig Steven Titus, 385–96. Washington, DC: Catholic University of America Press, 2005.

———. *The Sources of Christian Ethics*. Translated by Sr. Mary Thomas Noble. Washington, DC: Catholic University of America Press, 1995.

Pinsent, Andrew. *The Second-Person Perspective in Aquinas's Ethics: Virtues and Gifts*. New York: Routledge, 2012.

Porter, Jean. *The Perfection of Desire*. Milwaukee: Marquette University Press, 2018.

———. *The Recovery of Virtue: The Relevance of Aquinas for Christian Ethics*. Louisville, KY: John Knox, 1990.

———. "The Subversion of Virtue: Acquired and Infused Virtues in the *Summa theologiae*." *The Annual of the Society of Christian Ethics* 12 (1992): 19–41.

———. "Virtue and Sin: The Case of the Connection of the Virtues and the Flawed Saint." *Journal of Religion* 75, no. 4 (1995): 521–39.

Ratzinger, Joseph. *Introduction to Christianity*. 2nd ed. San Francisco: Ignatius. Kindle ed.

Rehnman, Sebastian. "Virtue and Grace." *Studies in Christian Ethics* 25, no. 4 (2012): 472–93.

Scotus, John Duns. *Duns Scotus on the Will and Morality*. Translated by Allan B. Wolter. Edited by William Frank. Washington, DC: Catholic University of America Press, 1986.

Shanley, Brian J. "Aquinas on Pagan Virtue." *The Thomist: A Speculative Quarterly Review* 63, no. 4 (1999): 553–77.

Sherwin, Michael S. "Infused Virtue and the Effects of Acquired Vice: A Test Case for the Thomistic Theory of Infused Cardinal Virtues." *The Thomist: A Speculative Quarterly Review* 73, no. 1 (2009): 29–52.

Sousa-Lara, Duarte. "Aquinas on the Object of the Human Act: A Reading in Light of the Texts and Commentators." *Josephinum Journal of Theology* 15, no. 2 (2008): 243–76.

White, Thomas Joseph. "Imperfect Happiness and the Final End of Man: Thomas Aquinas and the Paradigm of Nature–Grace Orthodoxy." *The Thomist: A Speculative Quarterly Review* 78, no. 2 (2014): 247–89.

Whitmore, Andrew. "Dispositions and Habits in the Work of St. Thomas Aquinas." Ph.D. diss., Catholic University of America, 2018.

Wippel, John. *The Metaphysical Thought of Thomas Aquinas*. Washington, DC: Catholic University of America Press, 2000.

Zagzebski, Linda. *Virtues of the Mind*. Cambridge: Cambridge University Press, 1996.

Index

Abelard, Peter, on virtue in non-Christians, 13

acquired/natural virtues
aptitude for, 18–24, 26, 40, 41, 184n.30
Aristotle on, 2, 8, 11, 13, 14–15, 24–25, 29, 54, 64, 78–79, 178
as completing infused virtues, 84, 88–92
courage as acquired vs. infused, 59, 61–62, 132–33, 145, 156–60, 162–64
cultivation of, 27–28, 44–45, 47, 55, 68
as differing in species from infused virtues, 56–58, 61, 86, 92–95, 138–39
as extrinsically ordered to supernatural beatitude, 93, 94–96, 100–101, 105, 106, 108, 109–10, 115–17, 124, 137, 138, 146, 169, 189nn.4–5
vs. infused moral virtues, 1–3, 4, 5, 8, 9, 12–13, 15–18, 27, 34–35, 38–39, 44, 47, 49–50, 51, 52–54, 55–62, 63–64, 65–66, 67, 69–70, 77–79, 81–82, 84–96, 100–104, 107, 114, 116, 118, 119, 122–23, 132–33, 135, 138–39, 145, 156–64, 165, 173–79, 182n.2,

183n.15, 186n.22, 187n.35, 189n.5, 190n.14
as ordered to fulfillment of created human nature, 2–3, 16–18, 19, 43, 51, 52, 54, 55, 57–58, 68, 70, 77, 82–84, 93, 94, 95, 105, 106, 108, 109, 110, 115–17, 119, 124, 125–26, 130–31, 135, 145–46, 149, 150, 154, 156, 159, 161–62, 163–64, 165, 168–69, 173, 174, 176, 177–78, 179, 183n.19, 186n.16
as ordering other natural virtues, 100–106, 110–16
of pagans, 13–14, 15–16, 17–18, 38–44
prudence as acquired vs. infused, 88–91, 101–4, 114, 116, 118, 119, 122–23, 163
reason as rule of, 32, 58, 59, 60, 76–77, 131, 139–40, 141–42, 143, 144, 145, 146, 147
relationship to charity, 94, 95, 100–101, 105, 110, 137, 138, 189nn.4–5
relationship to conversion, 82, 140, 151–52, 155–56
relationship to grace, 14, 39, 42–43, 109, 128, 129, 134, 135, 147, 149–50, 156, 165–67, 174–75, 176, 178, 192n.53, 192n.1 (chap. 4)

acquired/natural virtues *(cont.)*
  relationship to happiness, 118–19
  relationship to natural inclina-
    tions, 18, 25, 36–38, 40, 41, 162
  relationship to supernatural beati-
    tude, 6–7, 93, 94–96, 100–101,
    105–6, 107, 108, 109–10, 115–
    17, 124, 130, 137, 138, 146, 167,
    169, 177, 189nn.4–5
  role in Christian moral life, 79, 81,
    82, 83, 92, 105, 108, 114, 116–
    26, 127–28, 129–30, 135, 141,
    144, 150, 156, 158, 165, 166,
    167, 168–69, 176, 177–79,
    182n.2, 192n.53, 195n.19
  semina of, 18–22, 23, 24, 25, 27,
    38–39, 41, 184n.28, 186n.16,
    195n.36
  as strengthened by infused vir-
    tues, 84–86
  structure of, 1, 2, 8, 11–45, 49,
    77–79, 81, 107, 124, 125
  as supporting/facilitating infused
    virtues, 84, 87–88
  temperance as acquired vs.
    infused, 34–35, 58, 59, 60, 61,
    62, 65, 135, 162, 175, 177
  See also coexistence view of
    acquired and infused virtues;
    unification view of acquired
    and infused virtues
Allan of Lille, 14
appetitive inclinations, general, 54,
  62, 66, 67, 82, 162–65
  vs. passions, 32
  relationship to reason, 32–36,
    47–48, 55–56, 68, 72, 133–34
Aquinas, Thomas
  on active vs. passive capacity for
    virtue, 22–24
  on active vs. passive potency,
    27–28
  on aptitude for virtue, 18–24, 26,
    40, 41, 184n.30
  vs. Aristotle, 1, 2, 3, 7, 8, 11–14,
    16, 24–25, 28, 33, 44, 54, 64,

    78–79, 81, 101, 111, 129, 149,
      160, 170, 178, 179, 182n.2,
      184n.35
  vs. Augustine, 3, 43
  on baptism, 82, 89, 91, 93, 119,
    193n.11
  commentatorial tradition regard-
    ing, 5–6, 9
  on concupiscible power vs. iras-
    cible power, 30, 31
  on cultivation of acquired virtues,
    27–28, 44–45, 47, 55, 68
  on diligence *(industria)*, 89–92, 120
  on dispositions, 25–26, 166–67,
    168, 169
  on end for human life, 3, 5, 6–8
  on ends of individual virtues,
    34–35
  on faith, 19, 136–38, 139, 140, 146,
    154, 156–57
  on grace, 9, 12, 14, 16–17, 42–44,
    48–50, 51, 54, 55, 62–63, 65,
    66–67, 74, 81–82, 83–84, 85, 87,
    89, 90, 125, 126, 130–31, 136,
    137, 149, 158, 166–67, 168, 171,
    190n.18, 194n.14
  on habits, 12, 14, 23–24, 25–26,
    28–29, 33–34, 35–36, 41, 42, 47,
    49–50, 51, 53, 54, 56–58, 61, 62,
    64, 65, 72–73, 78, 82, 85–86,
    87–88, 125, 136–38, 139, 140,
    141, 142–45, 158, 161, 166–68,
    186n.16, 190n.18
  on happiness, 118–19, 129
  on human nature, 6–8, 11–12, 14,
    16–18
  on inception/inchoate knowledge
    of an end/the good, 19–20,
    21–22, 24, 26, 32, 41, 44, 47, 49,
    50, 51–54, 125, 146, 154, 157–
    58, 161, 164–65, 177–78
  on intellectual vs. moral virtue, 91
  interpretation of theory of virtue,
    3–6, 8, 9
  on love for God, 42–43
  vs. Macrobius, 96–97, 98, 99, 100

on martyrdom, 156–57, 160,
162–63
on moderation/the mean, 56,
58–59, 60, 61, 65, 76–77, 93,
135, 139, 147, 160, 187n.32
on moral progress, 96–98, 99, 100,
105–6, 127, 150, 174–76,
192n.53
on moral virtues and ends, 29,
31–36
on mortal sin, 171–72
on natural capacity for virtue, 14
on natural desire for God, 6–7
on natural inclinations, 18, 19,
23–26, 30, 32, 36–38, 40, 41, 50,
177, 186n.9
on nature of the species vs. nature
of the individual, 22, 23, 24–26
on original justice, 40, 41
on original sin, 8, 18, 19, 40–42,
43, 83
on original vs. actual ends, 95, 100
on particular principles of action,
33–36, 161, 162
on passions, 29, 32, 41, 58, 64–65,
76–77, 90
on perfect virtues, 97–98
on principles of nature, 40, 41
on reason, 14, 18, 19–22, 23–27,
28, 29, 30–33, 35–36, 38, 40, 41,
42, 43, 44, 47–48, 53–54, 76–77,
91, 139, 140, 156–58, 177
on repentance, 82, 130, 166, 167–
68, 175, 190n.18
on salvation, 69, 71–72, 74, 75,
89–90, 119–20, 193n.11
on *semina* of acquired virtues,
18–22, 23, 24, 25, 27, 38–39, 41,
184n.28, 186n.16, 195n.36
on sentient appetites, 29–31,
47–48, 55, 139–40, 161
on specific difference between
acquired and infused virtues,
56–58, 61, 86, 92–95, 138–39
on unity of the virtues, 23, 25
on venial sin, 171, 172

on virtual presence, 141–42,
194n.12
on virtue as fulfillment of a
capacity, 114–16
on visible vs. invisible goods, 156–
57, 163
on the will, 23–24, 31, 47, 52, 53,
136–37, 138, 139
See also acquired/natural virtues;
gifts of the Holy Spirit; infused
moral virtues; supernatural virtues; theological virtues
Aristotle
on acquired/natural virtues, 2, 8,
11, 13, 14–15, 24–25, 29, 54, 64,
78–79, 178
vs. Aquinas, 1, 2, 3, 7, 8, 11–14,
16, 24–25, 28, 33, 44, 54, 64,
78–79, 81, 101, 111, 129, 149,
160, 170, 178, 179, 182n.2,
184n.35
on courage, 101
on habits, 11, 14–15
on happiness, 119
on human flourishing, 11
on human good, 11
on moral virtues and ends, 29
on natural desire and capacity, 7
Nicomachean Ethics, 13, 33, 179
on reason, 11, 15, 24–25
Augustine, St.
vs. Aquinas, 3, 43
on faith and sin, 43

baptism, 81–82, 89, 91, 93, 119,
193n.11
Bejczy, István, 13
Billot, Louis, 182n.2
Bowlin, John, 110, 112–13

Calvin, John, on virtues, 15
cardinal virtues, 65, 97
See also courage; justice; pru-
dence; temperance
Catechism of the Catholic Church
(*CCC*), 129, 182n.2

Cessario, Romanus, 187n.35, 194n.13

charity, 83, 119, 130, 132, 133, 147, 166, 167

Aquinas on, 52, 53, 59, 63, 65, 66–67, 85, 94, 95, 100–101, 119, 129, 136–37, 138, 140, 146, 174–76, 190nn.17–18, 194n.14

as extrinsically forming acquired virtues, 94, 95, 100–101, 105, 106, 108, 109, 110, 189n.4

growth in, 65, 66–67, 85

love for God, 42–43, 66, 119, 123, 175

relationship to the will, 52, 53, 136–37

as theological virtue, 5, 12, 48, 50, 51, 125, 129, 146, 162, 182n.2

chastity, 36, 161

Christian moral life

role of acquired virtues in, 9, 79, 81, 82, 83, 92, 105, 108, 114, 116–26, 127–28, 129–30, 135, 141, 144, 150, 156, 158, 165, 166, 167, 168–69, 176, 177–79, 182n.2, 192n.53, 195n.19

role of gifts of the Holy Spirit in, 165, 171, 173, 176, 178, 179

role of grace in, 7, 12–13, 14, 15–16, 39, 57, 67–68, 78, 83, 124, 130, 134, 150, 154, 155, 156, 160, 164, 172–73, 178

role of infused moral virtues in, 9, 67–68, 81, 92, 102, 105, 108, 114, 116–26, 127–28, 129–30, 140–41, 144, 147–48, 149–51, 155–56, 165, 169, 170–71, 172, 177–79, 182n.2, 192n.53, 195n.19

role of prayer in, 165, 171, 179

Coerver, Robert: *The Quality of Facility in the Moral Virtues*, 5

coexistence view of acquired and infused virtues, 105–6, 107–26, 166, 167, 169, 194n.16, 195n.20

vs. unification view, 9, 83–84, 135, 149

Commentary on the Sentences (CS), 50, 51, 56–57, 59, 60, 61, 69, 75–76, 92, 106, 107, 127, 184n.28, 189n.4

CS III, d. 23, q. 1, a. 4, qa. 3, 186n.9

CS III, d. 33, q. 1, a. 2, qa. 4, 92–96, 100, 105, 187n.32

CS III, d. 33, q. 1, a. 4, 98–99

conversion and acquired virtues, 82, 140, 151–52, 155–56

1 Corinthians 9:27, 59

courage, 25, 34, 36, 37, 47–48, 54, 55, 73, 78, 101–2, 140

infused vs. acquired, 59, 61–62, 132–33, 145, 156–60, 162–64

of Spartans at Thermopylae, 158–60, 196n.16

of St. Stephen, 159–60, 162

Dante's *Inferno*, pagans in, 15–16

Decosimo, David, 128, 141–42, 143, 144, 145, 184n.44

Dell'Olio, Andrew, 87, 189n.5, 193n.11

Disputed Questions on Faith, 51

Disputed Questions on the Cardinal Virtues (DQVC), 88

DQVC a. 2, ad 2, 166, 167

DQVC a. 2, ad 3, 91

Disputed Questions on the Virtues in General (DQVG), 22, 27, 51, 52, 59, 65, 85–86, 87, 92, 100–106, 107, 127

DQVG a. 10, ad 4, 92, 99–106, 110, 135–36

DQVG a. 10, ad 16, 166

DQVG a. 10, obj. 16, 196n.21

DQVG q. 1, a. 10, arg. 14, 190n.18

DQVG q. 1, a. 10, c., 186n.11

Edwards, Jonathan, on virtues, 15

Ephesians 2:19, 58

Fagothey, Fr. Austin: *Right and Reason*, 182n.2
faith
Aquinas on, 19, 43, 48, 51–53, 83, 136–38, 139, 140, 146, 154, 156–57, 162–63
Augustine on, 43
conversion, 82, 140, 151–52, 155–56
doubt and, 153–54
formed vs. unformed, 136–38, 139, 140
knowledge of supernatural good provided by, 51–53
of martyrs, 132, 134, 156–57, 159–60, 162–63, 164
Ratzinger on, 153–55
vs. reason, 74–75, 122, 142–43, 145, 147, 152–53, 156–60, 164–65
as theological virtue, 5, 12, 48, 50, 51, 52, 125, 129, 146, 162, 182n.2
Falanga, Anthony, 182n.2, 189n.5
fear, 73
fidelity, 36
Foot, Philippa, on Aquinas vs. Aristotle, 129
Freddoso, Alfred, 178

Garrigou-Lagrange, Réginald, 190n.14
on gifts of the Holy Spirit and infused moral virtues, 74–75, 188n.80
gifts of the Holy Spirit
Aquinas on, 48–49, 54, 56, 57, 58, 59, 75–76, 163, 188n.70, 189n.5
as habits, 12, 72–73
vs. infused moral virtues, 74–75, 188n.80
instinctus of Holy Spirit and, 72, 73–74, 75, 188n.77
"mode" of action made possible by, 58, 75–77

relationship to appetitive powers, 73, 82
relationship to free will, 73–74
relationship to prayer, 165, 171, 179
relationship to salvation, 69, 71–72, 74, 75
relationship to supernatural beatitude, 12, 68–77, 78, 146–47, 171
role in Christian moral life, 165, 171, 173, 176, 178, 179
St. Stephen and, 159, 160–61
Gilson, Étienne, 85, 129–30, 131–32
Goris, Harm
on acquired vs. infused virtues, 130–32, 133
on Christian moral life and state of grace, 130, 134
vs. Mattison, 134, 136
"Moral Virtues in Wounded Nature," 130–32
grace
Aquinas on, 9, 12, 14, 16–17, 42–44, 48–50, 51, 54, 55, 62–63, 65, 66–67, 75, 81–82, 83–84, 85, 87, 89, 90, 125, 126, 130–31, 136, 137, 149, 158, 166–67, 168, 171, 190n.18, 194n.14
as gift, 2, 12, 13, 14, 16–17, 47, 49, 50, 62–63, 65–66, 67–68, 124, 125, 130–31, 132, 136, 137, 153, 164, 170–71, 179, 183n.20, 183n.23
impact on vices, 166, 167–68
loss of, 62–63, 82, 83, 128, 130, 134
and original justice, 40
original sin as healed by, 17, 39, 83, 95, 109
as perfecting human nature, 14, 125, 126, 130, 179, 183n.19
relationship to acquired virtues, 14, 39, 42–43, 95–96, 109, 128, 129, 130, 147, 149–50, 156, 165–67, 174–75, 176, 178, 192n.53, 192n.1 (chap. 4)

grace *(cont.)*
    relationship to avoiding sin, 42–44
    relationship to infused moral vir-
        tues, 2–3, 11–13, 27, 48–49, 62,
        119, 125, 127, 130–31, 132, 134,
        176, 178–79, 182n.6, 186n.16,
        190n.18
    relationship to nature in general,
        49, 109, 149–50
    relationship to supernatural beati-
        tude, 12, 93, 94, 95, 109, 124,
        126, 172–73
    role in Christian moral life, 7,
        12–13, 14, 15–16, 39, 57, 67–68,
        78, 83, 124, 130, 134, 150, 154,
        155, 156, 160, 164, 172–73, 178
    theological virtues given in, 83–84,
        93, 154, 155, 178, 179
    as transformative, 2, 9, 14, 17, 82,
        83–84, 89, 125, 126, 130–31,
        134, 135, 136–37, 141, 149–50,
        151–55, 165–67, 179

habits
    Aquinas on, 12, 14, 23–24, 25–26,
        28–29, 33–34, 35–36, 41, 42, 47,
        49–50, 51, 53, 54, 56–58, 61, 62,
        64, 65, 72–73, 78, 82, 85–86,
        87–88, 125, 136–38, 139, 140,
        141, 142–45, 158, 161, 166–68,
        186n.16, 190n.18
    Aristotle on, 11, 14–15
    vs. dispositions, 2, 25–26, 56,
        64–65, 150, 152, 165–77,
        196n.21
    gifts of the Holy Spirit as, 12,
        72–73
    habitual knowledge of first prin-
        ciples, 14, 18, 21–22, 26, 28, 34,
        41, 44, 47, 49, 51, 52–53, 55, 77,
        82–83, 93, 125, 146, 161, 165,
        177–78, 184n.28
    as making use of other habits, 142–44
    moral virtues as appetitive habits,
        28–31, 35, 36, 47–48, 55, 115–
        16, 132–33

vs. natural inclinations, 177
theological virtues as, 12, 51, 152,
    153, 165
vicious vs. virtuous habits, 166–
    68, 169–70
Harvey, John, 182n.2
Healy, Nicholas, 16
honesty, 34, 36, 54, 55, 161
hope, 52, 53, 83
    as theological virtue, 5, 12, 48, 50,
        51, 125, 129, 146, 162, 182n.2
human beings
    as adopted children of God, 12
    Aquinas on end for human life, 3,
        5, 6–8
    Aquinas on human nature, 6–8,
        11–12, 14, 16–18
    human nature as gift, 16–17, 23
human flourishing, 11, 122, 123, 125,
    131–32, 169

infused moral virtues
    vs. acquired virtues, 1–3, 4, 5, 8, 9,
        12–13, 15–18, 27, 34–35, 38–39,
        44, 47, 49–50, 51, 52, 55–62,
        63–64, 65–66, 67, 69–70, 77–79,
        81–82, 84–96, 101–4, 107, 114,
        116, 118, 119, 122–23, 132–33,
        135, 145, 156–64, 165, 173–79,
        182n.2, 183n.15, 186n.22,
        187n.35, 189n.5, 190n.14
    commentatorial tradition regard-
        ing, 5–6, 12–13
    as completed by acquired virtues,
        84, 88–92
    courage as infused vs. acquired,
        59, 61–62, 132–33, 145, 156–60,
        162–64
    as differing in species from
        acquired virtues, 56–58, 61, 86,
        92–95, 138–39
    failure in, 123, 124, 150, 170
    vs. gifts of the Holy Spirit, 74–75,
        188n.80
    growth of, 48, 56, 62–68, 123–24,
        163, 190n.13

as imperfectly possessed, 48, 163, 173, 178

as infused all at once in baptism, 62, 81–82, 87

prudence as infused vs. acquired, 88–91, 101–4, 114, 116, 118, 119, 122–23, 163

relationship to grace, 2–3, 11–13, 27, 48–49, 62, 119, 125, 127, 130–31, 132, 134, 176, 178–79, 182n.6, 186n.16, 190n.18

as remaining in heaven, 97–98

role in Christian moral life, 9, 67–68, 81, 92, 102, 105, 108, 114, 116–26, 127–28, 129–30, 140–41, 144, 147–48, 149–51, 155–56, 165, 169, 170–71, 172, 177–79, 182n.2, 192n.53, 195n.19

as strengthening acquired virtues, 84–86

structure of, 54–68, 77–79

as supported/facilitated by acquired virtues, 84, 87–88

temperance as infused vs. acquired, 34–35, 58, 59, 60, 61, 62, 65, 135, 162, 175, 177

vs. theological virtues, 48, 54–55, 63, 74, 81–82, 93, 182n.2, 186n.16

See also coexistence view of acquired and infused virtues; unification view of acquired and infused virtues

Inglis, John, 84–85, 187n.35, 194n.13

Irwin, Terrence, 189n.5, 190n.14

Jesus Christ
call to rich young man, 151, 152, 170
on Holy Spirit, 74

John Paul II, St., 121

Junipero Serra, St., 121

justice, 34, 76, 112–14, 161, 164
original justice, 40, 41

Kahm, Nicholas, 35

Kent, Bonnie, 118–19, 120, 122, 123

Klubertanz, George, 128, 141, 142, 144, 145, 195n.36

Leonidas, at Thermopylae, 158–60, 196n.16

liberality, 76

Louis IX, St., 121, 122–23

Luther, Martin, 183n.15

MacIntyre, Alasdair, 183n.15

Macrobius, 96–97, 98, 99, 100

magnificence, 76

martyrdom and faith, 132, 134, 156–57, 159–60, 162–63, 164

Mattison, Bill, 14, 134–41
"Can Christians Possess the Acquired Cardinal Virtues?," 135
vs. Goris, 134, 136
on grace, 134, 135
on infused vs. acquired virtues, 135–36, 195n.19
"Revisiting the Relationship between Infused and Acquired Cardinal Virtues," 135, 136

Mirkes, Reneé, 141, 195n.36

moderation/the mean, infused vs. acquired virtues regarding, 56, 58–59, 60, 61, 65, 76–77, 93, 135, 139, 147, 160, 187n.32

More, St. Thomas, 121, 123

mortal sin, 42, 62–63, 130, 171–72, 176–77

Newton, John, conversion of, 151–52, 155–56

obedience, 37

O'Meara, Thomas, on "Virtues in the Theology of Thomas Aquinas," 5

original justice, 40, 41

original sin
Aquinas on, 8, 17, 18, 19, 40–42, 43, 83

original sin *(cont.)*
  as healed by grace, 17, 39, 83, 95, 109
Osborne, Thomas, on perfect and imperfect virtue, 192n.1

pagan vs. Christian virtue, 4, 13–14, 15–16, 18, 38–44, 109, 182n.14, 183n.23
Pelagianism, 7, 182n.13
penance, 63
Pieper, Josef, 88–89, 119, 120
piety, 73, 75
Pinckaers, Servais
  on gifts of the Holy Spirit and free will, 73–74
  Les sources de la morale chrétienne, 12
  on Protestantism, 183n.15
Porter, Jean, 30, 193n.13
  "The Subversion of Virtue," 5, 12–13
Protestantism
  faith and ethics in, 183n.15
  virtue in, 15
Proverbs 3:5–6, 149
prudence, 33, 55, 97, 101–6, 193n.11, 195n.36
  household prudence, 102, 104, 111, 112, 113, 114, 116, 118
  infused vs. acquired, 88–91, 101–4, 114, 116, 118, 119, 122–23, 163
  political prudence, 102–4, 110–12, 113, 116, 118
  prudence *simpliciter*, 102–4, 110–12, 113, 116, 118

Quaestiones disputatae de veritate (*DV*), 19, 50, 51–52

Ratzinger, Joseph
  on faith, 153–55
  Introduction to Christianity, 153–55
reason
  Aquinas on, 14, 18, 19–22, 23–27, 28, 29, 30–33, 35–36, 38, 40, 41,

42, 43, 44, 47–48, 53–54, 76–77, 91, 139, 140, 156–58, 177
  Aristotle on, 11, 15, 24–25
  vs. faith, 74–75, 122, 142–43, 145, 147, 152–53, 156–60, 164–65
  first principles of practical reason (*synderesis*), 8–9, 14, 17–18, 19–22, 23, 24, 26–27, 28, 33, 34, 35, 41–42, 44–45, 47, 49, 51, 52–53, 55, 68, 69, 70, 77, 83, 93, 125, 146, 152–53, 154–55, 157–58, 177–78
  first principles of speculative reason, 21, 26–27, 28, 83, 93, 125, 146, 154–55, 161
  vs. God's rule, 58–59, 60, 77, 131, 139, 140, 142–44, 145–46, 147, 171, 172
  as insufficient guide, 78, 122, 164, 171, 179
  moral virtues as help and guide for, 28–36, 47–48, 55–56, 68, 72, 133–34
  particular principles of action, 33–36, 161, 162
  relationship to general appetitive inclinations, 32–36, 47–48, 55–56, 68, 72, 133–34
  relationship to gifts of the Holy Spirit, 71–72
  relationship to supernatural beatitude, 78
  as rule of acquired virtues, 32, 58, 59, 60, 76–77, 131, 139–40, 141–42, 143, 144, 145, 146, 147
repentance, 82, 130, 166, 167–68, 175, 190n.18

saints, 120–21, 122–23, 159–60, 162, 176–77
salvation
  actions necessary for, 69, 71–72, 75, 89–90, 118, 119–22, 123, 193n.11
  Aquinas on, 69, 71–72, 74, 75, 89–90, 119–20, 193n.11

relationship to gifts of Holy
Spirit, 69, 71–72, 74, 75
and sainthood, 120–21, 122–23
Scotus, John Duns, 194n.14
Sherwin, Michael, 119–20, 122
Simon of Tournai, 14
Stephen, St., martyrdom of, 159–60,
162
Suárez, Francisco, 195n.33
Summa theologiae (ST)
ST I-II, q. 51, a. 4, ad 3, 84–86,
135
ST I-II, q. 52, 66–67
ST I-II, q. 54, a. 1, 57
ST I-II, q. 58, a. 4, 33–34
ST I-II, q. 58, a. 4, ad 3, 91
ST I-II, q. 61, a. 5, 96–99, 107,
127–28
ST I-II, q. 63, a. 3, c., 186n.16
ST I-II, q. 63, a. 4, 138
ST I-II, q. 65, a. 1, 92, 105–6
ST I-II, q. 65, a. 3, ad 2, 87–88,
190nn.17–18
ST I-II, q. 68, a. 2, 69–74
ST I-II, q. 69, a. 3, 189n.5
ST I-II, q. 109, 42–44
ST II-II, q. 4, a. 4, 138
ST II-II, q. 24, a. 3, 63
ST II-II, q. 24, a. 6, 175
ST II-II, q. 24, a. 9, 174–75
ST II-II, q. 47, a. 14, ad 1, 88–92
ST II-II, q. 47, a. 14, obj. 3, 120
supernatural beatitude
acquired virtues extrinsically
ordered to, 93, 94–96, 100–101,
105, 106, 108, 109–10, 115–17,
124, 137, 138, 146, 169,
189nn.4–5
Aquinas on, 6–7, 11–12, 49–50, 56,
57, 65–66, 82, 109
inception of, 49–54, 55, 56
relationship to acquired virtues,
6–7, 93, 94–96, 100–101, 105–6,
107, 108, 109–10, 115–17, 124,
130, 137, 138, 146, 167, 169,
177, 189nn.4–5

relationship to gifts of the Holy
Spirit, 12, 68–77, 78, 146–47, 171
relationship to grace, 12, 74, 93,
94, 95, 109, 124, 126, 172–73
relationship to theological virtues,
51–53, 68–69, 70–71, 73, 74, 77,
82, 93, 110, 125, 162
supernatural virtues
as ordered to fulfillment of graced
human nature, 1, 2–3, 11–12,
16–17, 19, 48, 49, 51, 55, 57,
68–69, 74, 77, 82–84, 105, 106,
108, 109, 110, 115–17, 124, 125–
26, 130–31, 135, 145–46, 149, 154,
156, 158, 161–62, 163–64, 168,
171–73, 174, 177, 178, 179,
182n.13, 186n.16
relationship to happiness, 118–19
structure of, 1, 2, 8, 38, 47–79, 81,
107, 124, 125
See also gifts of the Holy Spirit;
grace; infused moral virtues;
supernatural beatitude; theological virtues

temperance, 22, 47, 78, 131–32,
139–40
infused vs. acquired, 34–35, 58, 59,
60, 61, 62, 65, 135, 162, 175, 177
Teresa, Mother, 121, 123
theological virtues
Aquinas on, 5, 12, 48–55, 56,
65–66, 68–70, 81–82, 125, 129,
136–37, 146, 152, 154, 186n.9,
186n.11
as given in grace, 83–84, 93, 154,
155, 178, 179
as habits, 12, 51, 152, 153, 165
as imperfectly possessed, 48, 68,
69–71, 74, 77–78, 146, 150, 152,
153–55, 164, 178
as infused all at once in baptism,
81–82
vs. infused moral virtues, 48,
54–55, 63, 74, 81–82, 93, 182n.2,
186n.16

theological virtues *(cont.)*
  as new first principles, 51–52, 53, 54, 55, 56, 68, 69, 70, 82, 83, 93, 126, 152–55
  relationship to gifts of the Holy Spirit, 68–69, 171
  relationship to reason and will, 147
  relationship to supernatural beatitude, 51–53, 68–69, 70–71, 73, 74, 77, 82, 93, 110, 125, 162
  See also charity; faith; hope
Thérèse of Lisieux, St., 154, 155, 177
Thomas à Kempis: *The Imitation of Christ*, 151

unification view of acquired and infused virtues, 127–48
  acquired-and-infused-virtues-distinct version, 128, 141–46
  acquired-virtues-transformed version, 128, 134–41
  vs. coexistence view, 9, 83–84, 135, 149
  same-virtues-different-agents version, 128, 129–34

venial sin, 171, 172–73
Vermigli, Peter, on virtues, 15
virtual presence, 141–42, 194n.12

Whitmore, Andrew, 184n.44
William of Auxerre, 14
Wisdom 8:1, 50

ANGELA McKAY KNOBEL
is associate professor of philosophy at the University of Dallas.
She is co-editor of *Character: New Directions from Philosophy,
Psychology, and Theology.*

Milton Keynes UK
Ingram Content Group UK Ltd.
UKHW021234190224
437936UK00020B/247